# EXEMPLUM ET SIMILITUDO

# MEDIAEVALIA GRONINGANA

edenda curant

L.J. Engels, A.G. Jongkees,
W. Noomen, N. van der Wal

*Fasciculus VIII*

MCMLXXXVIII
Egbert Forsten
Groningae

# Exemplum et Similitudo

*Alexander the Great
and other heroes
as points of reference
in medieval literature*

*edited by*

**W. J. Aerts and M. Gosman**

Egbert Forsten
Groningen 1988

Cover design: Françoise Berserik

Published with financial support by the Faculty of Arts, Groningen

CIP-GEGEVENS KONINKLIJKE BIBLIOTHEEK, DEN HAAG

Exemplum

Exemplum et similitudo : Alexander the Great and other heroes as points of reference in medieval literature /
ed. by W.J. Aerts and M. Gosman. - Groningen : Forsten. - (Mediaevalia Groningana ; 8)
Met lit. opg.
ISBN 90-6980-018-7
SISO 825.2 UDC 82(4)"04/14":937/938
Trefw.: Europese letterkunde ; geschiedenis ; Middeleeuwen.

ISBN 90 6980 018 7

# Contents

The study *L'Exemplum*, (written by Claude Bremond, Jacques le Goff and Jean-Claude Schmitt, published in the series *Typologie des sources du moyen-âge occidental* (Turnhout 1982), provided the impetus for the Groningen Work Group on Alexander the Great in the Middle Ages to organize a symposium on 'Exemplum et Similitudo', which took place May 14-16, 1986, at the University of Groningen. The motive was clear: not only in the classical context had Alexander the Great served as an exemplary figure, no matter whether in a positive sense (as e.g. in Plutarch) or in a negative one (as from a stoic viewpoint and in Orosius), but also in the middle ages, both eastern and western, had Alexander played an important role (alongside other kings and heroes), either as a shining example or as warning sign. It seemed to us interesting and useful to investigate this exemplary function in the light of the theory developed in the study of Bremond et al. In particular, the definition formulated on p. 37/38: The exemplum is 'un récit bref donné comme véridique et destiné à être inséré dans un discours (en général un sermon) pour convaincre un auditoire par une leçon salutaire', was used by the participants of the symposium as a rubbing-post. The results of the different reflections on the subject have been set down in the present book. On the one hand these reflections are of a more theoretical character, such as the articles of Knapp and Von Moos; on the other hand one will meet with rather testing approaches, such as is the case in the articles of Berlioz, Bunt, Mulder-Bakker and Gosman. The study of Engels takes an intermediate position, whereas Aerts scrutinizes by contrast the exemplary function of Alexander in the Byzantine world.

The editorial board is very sorry that, in spite of the favourable prospects in 1986 for a speedy publication, it encountered circumstances which delayed the production of the book considerably. Two main factors can be held responsible: 1° the negligence of some authors in respect of the deadline; 2° the technical problems of reproducing the Greek alphabet on the computer. This meant that the texts had to be proofread more often than normal. If someone must be blamed for the delay in production, it certainly is not the secretaries of the French and the Classical Institutes, Mrs A. Huizenga and W. Buurma, who were always ready to make either corrections or new proof pages. We also thank Ms M. Lens for her assitance with the proofreading. And we have, of course, to thank also the publisher Egbert Forsten, for the final reproduction of the book. This publication of the Groningen Alexander Work Group was preceded by three others, which met with an encouraging amount of approval. We hope that this fourth will not too unfavourably contrast with the preceding ones.

Groningen, November 1988
M. Gosman, W.J. Aerts

W.J. Aerts

# Alexander the Great in 'Exempla' and 'Similitudines' in Byzantine Literature

The first glance at the bibliography of the study *L"Exemplum'* produced by Claude Bremond, Jacques Le Goff and Jean-Claude Schmitt already shows an impressive amount of activity by many scholars in the field of the use of *exempla* in Western medieval literature. Seven titles are given concerning the use of *exempla* in Antiquity (1982:20). It may be a striking point that almost all titles mention the word *exemplum* or its vernacular equivalents, whereas only one title focusses on the use of 'similitudo'. The difference between *exemplum* and *similitudo* is perhaps more stylistic than factual, if one takes these concepts close to their common meanings. But also in their extended applications they have some features in common: just as e.g. the so-called Homeric similes offer the opportunity to dress up the simile proper bij adding digressions, broader descriptions etc. so can, e.g. in sermons, the examples take the shape of a little story, as often happened in Western medieval literature; and as such they have been the object of frequent investigation into the genre.

In Byzantine literature one may observe that, as far as sermons are concerned, a development similar to that in Western Europe did not occur, probably due to a different conception of the role of sermons within the liturgy in general on the one side, and on the other to the fact that sermonlike sections found themselves at an early stage of liturgical development transformed into poetical forms as e.g. *kontakion* or *kanon* (Beck 1959: 264, 425).

It will, of course, be clear that this liturgical poetry is full of references to biblical *exempla*, be it persons or events,[1] but it offers little or no room for 'spontaneous' exemplary narratives. And the presentation of the biblical *exempla* themselves may vary from a full repetition of paraphrase of the (well-known) story to a simple reference, such as *Noah's Ark* or *Job*, indications which for the true believers will evoke the whole setting of the stories and their implications.[2]

The same holds good, theoretically speaking, when a well-known historical figure or event has been chosen as a point of reference. One may assume that the indication ἐν τούτῳ νίκα was a sufficient reference for the average inhabitant of the Byzantine Empire to recall Constantine's transfer to Christianity, just as either the egg of Columbus or the Gordian knot needs no further explanation, unless for schoolchildren who may expect the stories in colourful tones told by the teacher.

As has clearly been shown in the very useful study *Das Alexanderbild der Byzantiner* (Gleixner 1961) Alexander the Great remained during the full period of existence of the Byzantine Empire one of the great heroes of the past, one who served many emperors as an example for imitation, many clerics as a creature who demonstrated (in a positive or negative way) the hand of God in ruling His creation, many historians as a king who changed the face of the οἰκουμένη and became the source of innumerable stories of amazing exploits and wondrous events in unknown parts of the world.[3]

For my investigation I made use of both the material gathered by Gleixner and of a full collection of texts on Alexander brought together some years ago in a Dutch workshop,[4] who read through all the volumes of the (Latin and) Greek Migne on passages concerning Alexander, Philip, the Macedonians, the Diadochs etc. Of this latter collection I took all the texts into account which occur in the volumes PG 70 (Cyrillus of Alexandria) up to the next to last one, PG 161 (Bessarion, Theodorus of Gaza), inclusive. In order to obtain a workable classification for the objective intended, I ordered them under twenty headings, such as e.g. Alexander in connection with the Daniel apocalypse and the four world empires, Alexander and the harem of Darius, (the foundation of) Alexandria, Alexander and the High Priest of Jerusalem, Alexander and the unclean nations, Alexander as a promotor of art and science, etc. In a number of cases a passage had to be mentioned under two or even three headings, but the number of doublets or triplets was restricted. To give an impression of the proportions of the most important headings: in a total of about 350 entries,[5] approximately 93 refer to Alexander as an example or to his exemplary behaviour; 38 times he is mentioned in the context of his place in history; 36 times in connection with Daniel; 34 times as a point of comparison with other emperors, such as Alexander, son of Mamaea, Julian the Apostate, Basil I and II but also western princes like Aldwin of Sicily; 25 times in critical views on his person or his empire. It struck me that in a number of cases the references differ from period to period. Thus those to the prophecies of Daniel and the four world empires seem to be bound to the early and middle Byzantine period: after Zonaras (12th C.) they are almost completely absent. The same picture is offered in the heading Alexander and the High Priest of Jerusalem. On the other hand one sees increasing references to other emperors like Caesar, August, Trajan, Hadrian, etc. in the later Byzantine period.

It will be clear that a discussion of all the more or less relevant passages would go far beyond the framework of this paper. Therefore I present a number of passages which are, in my opinion, representative for the question under discussion.

To begin with, I shall neglect a (possible) difference in stilistic appearance between an *exemplum* or a *similitudo*, taking both of them as expressions which intend to make an exemplary reference.[6] In a number of cases both elements are present in the same passage.

In the material, which I considered, I found only one *exemplum* modelled on the shape of a little story. It is told by Nicephorus Gregoras (*Byz. Hist.* Liber 10,8.2), who in so many words announces his story: 'For I wish also to add a short story from the days of yore to my history, that very well suits this subject: it is said that Alexander, the famous Macedonian, after his long expedition and his great victories, embarked on a trireme to have some leisure and joy, and made a sightseeing trip on the river Euphrates. But in about the middle of the river his royal headgear slipped, by one cause or another, from his head. A sailor jumped into the water and grabbed it quickly. Unable, however, to hold it in his hand and to swim at the same time, he put it on his head, swam to the ship and brought it to the king. And he, the king, endowed him with a talent, because he had saved his royal headgear; but due to the fact that he had it unworthly put on his own head, Alexander had the man beheaded'.[7]

The reason that Gregoras explicitly tells this story may be derived from the fact that this episode had became rather unknown, and is, in any case, absent from e.g. the Alexander romance.[8] Gregoras apparently felt some obligation to give the full adstruction to this Solomon-like specimen of Alexander's justice.

But most of the references to Alexander obviously start from the supposition that the episode mentioned is well-known enough to need no ample repetition of the story.[9] This is clear in those cases where Alexander is referred to as an example of self-control. The basis of this explanation is mostly provided by the story of Alexander's reserve and obligingness towards Darius' mother, wife and daughters, who were taken prisoners after the battle at Granicus, as told by Plutarch (*Alex.* 21). The evaluations show, however, different patterns. One of these evaluations uses the theme 'conquerors of men should not be conquered by women'. Thus e.g. Andrew the Cretan (PG 97, 1122 D - 1123 A): 'Did not you hear about the royal indignation of Alexander, Philip's son, when the daughters of Darius were brought to him for sexual intercourse, and his impressive exclamation, full of temperance: 'a shame if after a victory over men we should be the victim of women'?'[10] The same reference occurs in Isidorus Pelusiota (PG 78, 775 BC), Maximus Confessor (PG 91, 741 BC), Cedrenus (PG 121, 397 C), Nicephorus Blemmyda, *Oratio de regis officiis* 2 (PG 142, 616 C), Mich. Glykas, *Annales* 2 (PG 158, 276 C - 277 C). The key word is σωφροσύνη. Georgius Monachus (I,19 = PG 110, 75 A-C) 'widens the gap' between men and women by adding the qualification 'and these, brave' to the men.

All these passages have in common that they left out the philosophical 'setting', in which Plutarch presents Alexander's consideration: 'Alexander,' says he, 'meant, as it seems, that having control of himself was more up to royal standard than defeating enemies, and touched no one of them (the daughters of Darius, sc.), and he knew altogether no woman before marriage, with the exception of Barsina. She, a widow after Memnon's death, had been captured near

Damascus ... etc.' We meet this philosophical consideration again in Photios'
*Bibliotheca*, in the passage (*Bibl.* 245 PG 103 1443 A - 1446 B) where an abstract is given from Plutarch's *Vita Alexandri*. The moral side of Alexander's
behaviour receives a stronger accent in some other passages. One of these is to
be found in a letter of the same Photios (*Epistolarum Liber* 1,8,96 = PG 102,
688 B-C); he takes the passage of Plutarch, quoted above, as a starting point of
a moral generalization: 'Having conquered Asia (Minor) by force, Alexander the
Macedon used to say that the Persian women were projectiles to the eyes. But
a truly wise man, who keeps the Lord's commands, will not only avoid and turn
away from Persian women, but from the glance of every woman, sharp and
deadly weapon as it is. Etc'.[11]

The figure of the deadly dart (of passion) which penetrates the soul by way of
the eyes is as old as Aeschylus *Agamemnon* 742 where Helen is called a μαλθα-
κὸν ὀμμάτων βέλος, a smooth dart which hits the eyes of men. Achilles
Tatius I 4,4 uses it in full clearness: 'beauty wounds deeper than any arrow
and strikes down through the eyes into the soul; the eye is the passage for
love's wound'.[12] This text returns in the sayings gathered by Antonios Melissa
(PG 136, I 61) under the heading περὶ κάλλους 'on beauty'. Antiochus Monachos (PG 89, 1480 B) remarks: 'For a woman's glance is a poisoned arrow. It
wounds the soul and leaves the poison and the longer it lasts, the more it
causes decay. But he, who takes care of himself, will not fall under her spell
and will not be wounded by her arrows'.[13] Equally, John of Damascus takes the
same Alexander story as a starting point for his exegesis of Math. 5,28[14]:
comparing this passage with the Alexander story he says: 'this (word of the
gospel) is related to the same thing: he who looks on a woman to lust after
her, does not commit real fornication, but admitting the lust into his heart
already makes him guilty'.[15] Returning to Photios' letter cited above, we can
observe that Photios sharpened the expression for the danger caused by the
women's glances by changing Plutarch's ἀλγηδόνας ὀμμάτων ('which hurts
the eyes') into βολίδας ὀμμάτων ('javelins that hit the eyes'). But this
expediency for Photios' purpose eliminated an element of importance in Plutarch's text. Plutarch, to be precise, is suggesting that Alexander with his
ἀλγηδόναςὀμμάτων reacts to a story which obviously belonged to a tradition
which lived on at the Macedonian court. Herodotus (V 18,4) has handed down
this story: Persian envoys who had come, before the Persian wars, to Macedonia
with demands for Macedonian submission to the Persian king, insisted upon the
presence of Macedonian women at the dinner given in their honour. The women
were brought in, but seated opposite the envoys, who then complain that these
girls could better have been kept out than to be put there as ἀλγηδόνας σφίσι
ὀφθαλμῶν. There is no doubt, in my opinion[16], that Plutarch makes Alexander
jestingly (παίζων!) point to this episode with a pun.
   A special category of exemplary reference is the sayings of famous people.
The genre was already popular in Antiquity as can be seen from collections
brought together by (Pseudo-)Plutarch, Athenaeus, Stobaeus, etc., and it also
found its way into Byzantine literature in collections such as the *Loci Commu-*

*nes* or *Florilegium* handed down under the name of Maximos Confessor[17], or that of Antonios 'Melissa'[18], 'the bee'. These *florilegia* serve a moralistic purpose and the examples and sayings have been arranged according to headings which indicate the different fields of interest, such as 'about the fact that most is not always best'[19] or 'on blame and slander'[20], etc.

In each chapter most of the examples or sayings are taken from the Bible or the Fathers, but also a number comes from ancient literature, among which several quotations are ascribed to Alexander. In 37 ('about the fact that most is not always best') Antonios quotes e.g. Luke XXI (the Widow's mite), I Cor. XIV (summarized as: five sensible words outdo a thousand senseless ones), etc. Two quotations are taken from the Alexander tradition: 'Alexander, on hearing that Darius conveyed 300.000 men in his army, said: 'One butcher is not afraid of many sheep'. The same said, as a scout reported to him that Darius' men outnumbered them: 'The sheep, more in number, are conquered by one wolf or two'.[21]

In the chapter I,53 ('on blame and slander') Antonios brings these two Alexander passages: 'Alexander received a letter in which his physician was accused of preparing an attempt on his life. At that very moment he had to swallow a medicine, but he disbelieved the slanderer so much, that he, along with reading the letter, drank the medicine. The same is said, when one of his intimates was being slandered, to have carefully stopped one of his ears with his hand, in order to keep it unbiassed for the absent one.' The heading of I,70 runs 'on fortune and misfortune'. Here we read: 'King Alexander saw Diogen lying in a barrel and said: 'Oh barrel full of thought!' The philosopher stood up and said: 'You greatest king'.[22] The second book of the 'Melissa' opens with a long chapter 'on a good and just king, on rulership and power'. A wealth of quotations is displayed from both Old and New Testaments, but also from Euripides, Xenophon, Plato, Plutarch, etc.; even Cato is mentioned. Here we find Alexander's saying that the best king binds his friends with attentions and turns his foes into friends with presents. Another reference is made to Alexander's reaction on his cupbearer's sadness about a golden cup which could easily be interpreted as an example of Alexander's arrogance, is obviously taken by Antonios in a positive way as an example of his non-materialism, and as such of royal behaviour.

The eleventh chapter of Melissa's second book deals with 'children who honour their parents and all goods which fall to their share by being obedient to them'.[23] The examples of Alexander presented here are somewhat remarkable in this respect: 'on the question, whom he loved more, his father Philip or (his teacher) Aristotle, Alexander said: his teacher; for, the first had wrought his existence, the second his right existence'.[24]
The second example pictures rather a naughty than an obedient boy, though there is perhaps more mockery than unwillingness involved; 'The same (Alexander) said, when his mother assigned him a somewhat awkward task, 'Mother, a bitter fee for a nine month's stay is what you ask'.[25]

In 2,69 a chapter entitled 'on slanderers and on wantonness', Alexander spares a slanderer of Philip in order to prevent him from even more backbiting; besides, he sees even in negative critics a stimulus to greater achievement.[26] The last quotation of Alexander is in chapter 74, dealing with 'arrogant, haughty, pretentious and conceited people.'

The story tells: 'Recovered after a lasting illness Alexander said he was in no way worse off: the illness reminded us not to be haughty, being mortals'.[27] The next, probably anonymous, quotation plays the theme 'pride with a fall'.[28]

It is clear that in these sayings and quotations Alexander functions as an example. From a stylistic point of view one may make the following statement: the fact that almost all Alexander quotations open with the name Ἀλέξανδρος points to the circumstance that in all probability Antonios Melissa took them from a collection or collections in which the sayings were represented in alphabetical order, as e.g. in the Wiener Apophthegmen Sammlung (Wachsmuth).[29] If one compares Plutarch's collections of sayings of kings and commanders, of Romans, Spartans, women, etc., one observes that in the latter the name or the quality of the person whose sayings are presented only appears in the first saying, whereas the other sayings open with a subordinate clause, an absolute genitive, the name of an 'opponent', etc. In the alphabetical collections the name of the person concerned is placed in front, referring already to the main clause.

It is, of course, obvious that the author of a collection of sayings is obliged to give a minimum of data which are indispensable for the understanding of the sayings, no less than the composer of an 'exemplum' must bring in the ingredients of his story, if his story is to be effective as a basis for comparison. The composition of the saying, c.q. the 'exemplum' is, as such, of less relevance, where the exemplary effect is concerned. Returning to the story of Alexander and the cupbearer who lost the golden cup, we can find this also applied in a less favorable way: Nicetas Choniates[30] gives, after the description of the death of Henry VI of Germany a comparison of this German king with Roman emperors, like the Antonines and the Augustinian dynasty (in that order!), whose impulse for expansion he gladly imitated. 'And,' continues Niketas, 'he was not far from Alexander's saying 'be it here or be it there, it is all mine'.' In his story of the emperorship of Isaac Angelus, Niketas brings yet another comparison of a western warrior with Alexander. In chapter 1, par. 2 Niketas relates the capturing of two important generals of the western crusader army, namely Richard, brother-in-law of Tancred, and count Alduin, a man of low origin but come into the king's favour by his strategic capacities (Van Dieten 1975: 359, 19ff). This man boasted on account of some victories over the Byzantines to be a better general than even Alexander the Great had been. True, he did not show off, like him with his breast hair, in the shape of the beak and the wings (of an eagle?),[31] but he considered his achievements greater than Alexander's because they were gained in no time and without bloodshed. It is strange that Niketas puts an otherwise unknown[32] and rather absurd comparison in the mouth of the Sicilian general, without giving any indication from where Alduin could possibly have taken this piece of information, unless Niketas coined this absurdity in order to give a further typification of the ignorance of this Occidental.

Another exemplary use of Alexander is to be found in the *Annales* of Eutychius, Patriarch of Alexandria (Sa'id ibn Batrik, 10th C). In the first place we see Alexander characterised as a Christian ruler: in his correspondence with Darius Alexander calls himself 'servant of God'.[33] He uses the same term in his farewell letter to his mother on his deathbed,[34] further he labels the day of his death as the last on earth and the first of his future life, which may console his mother.[35] Olympias, however, finds her consolation only after having invited a number of guests whose admission is made dependent on whether they ever experienced deep sorrow or not: nobody enters the dining-room! Eutychius ends his Alexander account with the story that his body was laid in a golden coffin, which, according to yet another tradition, was filled with honey. Then the coffin was placed on a square in Alexandria, in order to let people march past the bier and say a last fare-well. Philosophers start the ceremony:[36] (a) The wise Philemon remarks that this day shows a great exemplum: his fortune, which had (always) been ahead of him, has left behind. The wise Plato (!) also appears and says: (b) 'Alas, acting with violence you conquered what cheated you and slipped away from your hands: consequently the blame is yours, the profit will be other man's prey'. Then comes Aristotle (who makes not his most brilliant remark) saying: (c) 'Alexander left us speaking, but returned to us silent.' He is followed by the wise Naren who says: (d) 'Tell Alexander's flock, 'this is the day on which the flock herds its herd'. Other wise men follow, some mentioned by name, others not, and in some sayings the idea 'exemplum' is introduced. Thus someone said: (e) 'This may suffice as an example: yesterday gold was a treasure for Alexander, today it is his grave'. Another pronouncement reads: (f) 'The dead of kings is an adequate example for the people, the death of people an adequate reminder for kings.' In similar terms: (g) 'The most illustrious document which Alexander edited is his death.' Straightforwardly critical are pronouncements like that of the philosopher Lotas: (h) 'Let us not wonder that a man who had nothing to tell us during his lifetime, made at last his message clear by his death! A certain wise Sis makes the statement: (i) 'This man made many people die lest he should die himself; nevertheless, he died; how could it be that he was not able to repel death by death?', a no less critical statement than Lotas's. In the same way a wise Demetrius expresses himself: (j) 'Oh you, whose rage meant death, why did not you vent your rage on death?'. And thus follows a whole series of rather critical sayings. It should, however, be borne in mind that this kind of uttering often has more to do with reflections on death in general than with a specific condemnation of Alexander's behaviour as such.

Apart from these critical remarks towards Alexander on his bier, there are also other passages in which the person or the behaviour of Alexander or his realm is criticised. Within the framework of the four world-empires Anastasius Sinaita has a very sharp qualification for Alexander's empire: where the empires of Babylon and Persia are defined as glorious and remarkable, the Macedonian or Greek empire of Alexander is called 'piratical' and 'hard to attack'.[37] An incident, which procured Alexander bad publicity, was the destruction of Thebes. We find a reference in Photios *Bibliotheca* 243, where Alexander's successes are ascribed to his great efficiency, which made him appear before a town or on the battle-field sooner than expected, as is the case with lightning and thunder, and this efficiency also caused the calamitous fall of Thebes, a city in the umbilicus of the earth. Another author in Photios *Bibliotheca* 250,8 (Henry 1959) complains that it is very hard for rhetors and poets to say something in favour of people (i.e. Philip and Alexander) who devastated towns such as Olynthus and Thebes. Should these calamities be mentioned in covert terms, or openly? Nikephoros Gregoras, ῾Ρωμαϊκὴ ῾Ιστορία 16,3,4, mentions a Turkish general who conquered and demolished Roman (= Byzantine) cities more cruelly than Alexander destroyed Thebes.[38]

In a passage to be found in Niketas Byzantinus' *Confutatio Mohamedis* 17,76 criticism of Alexander is brought in an unusual way. Niketas is referring to an explanation in the Koran (18:83 and 18:90,91) concerning Dhul-Qarnain = Alexander the Great.[39] Alexander is said to have journeyed to the West where he saw the sun setting in a pool of black mud; then, going to the East 'he saw the sun rising upon a people whom We had utterly exposed to its flaming rays'. Then follows the story of the untidy peoples Gog and Magog being locked behind an indestructable iron wall, in which molten brass has been poured. Niketas gives his own abstract of this passage, writing: 'Then he mentions Alexander the Great and he says: 'He went away until the place of sunset and he found the sun setting into warm water,' and: 'In the North he walled off Og and Magog', and 'Alexander believed in the rule of the One, as did Abra(a)m, and was no heathen,' and he adds 'We tell before you this story in truth.'' Then comes his conclusion: 'How true truth is in these matters, everybody knows even when we are silent. Thus, he finishes his story with his usual rotten nonsense'.[40]

Of course, Niketas attacks his adversary as sharply as possible. The interesting thing is, however, that he clearly disapproves of a story of Alexander which was obviously appreciated and widespread in the Byzantine world, witness the adaptions of the Alexander romance, the Alexander passage in Pseudo-Method, George the Monk, Nikephoros Presbyter, etc. Moreover, he rejects the idea of a monotheistic Alexander. Next to this theological criticism we find a philosophical one in a letter of Eusthathius of Salonica to the emperor,[41] who is praised because he shows a deeper appreciation for his philosopher (Eustathius) than Alexander demonstrated towards Aristotle and Dionysius towards Plato.

Finally, it may be useful to note two different reactions to Alexander in relation to the Turks. The first is based on the message that (Constantine IX) Monomachos had Macedonians in his army because it was rumoured that in this way the Turks would be defeated as once the Persians by Alexander the Great. These pieces of information are provided by George Cedrenus and M. Glykas p. 599 (Bonn) and are, probably, the result of combining on the one hand linking of the Macedonian dynasty to the ancient Macedonians (cf. Const. Porphyr. *De Thematibus*[42]) with on the other hand the presence of a considerable contingent of Macedonians in Constantinople at the time of Constantine IX Monomachus, who revolted against him under Leo Tornices. The second dates from the end of the Byzantine empire. In his *De rebus peloponnesiacis Oratio* 2,2 Gemistos Pletho[43] remarks that the Greeks pay now, albeit late, the price for the fact that Alexander on his India campaign defeated the Paropamisades (obviously interpreted as being a Turkish tribe).[44] Theodorus of Gaza[45] refers to this passage in Pletho saying *expressis verbis* that Pletho considers the Paropamisades to be Turks. One may assume that the philosopher intended rather to indicate the long cycles of certain happenings in history than to criticise Alexander's campaigns; nevertheless his remark clearly points to a sceptical disapproval of this kind of campaign.

When we now return to more theoretical grounds, we have to conclude that the Alexander material, such as has been presented above, does not fit very well in the definition proposed for the medieval *exemplum* by Bremond-Le Goff-Schmitt (1982: 37). This is on the one hand the result of the limited material (especially sermons) which served Bremond c.s. as a starting-point, on the other hand it may be due to the different character of the Byzantine literature as such, c.q. the treatment of the Alexander material in that literature. If we follow the nine criteria enumerated in the first chapter of *L'exemplum* (36-7) we have to conclude that the narrative element is mostly lacking in the Byzantine Alexander exempla. That is to say, the reference to Alexander implicitly includes the story, which is presumed to be known. In the reference there must also be an indication of the situation or context: Alexander and the women of Darius, Alexander and the Amazones, Alexander, ruler of the third world empire. The second point ('la brièveté de la narration') is not relevant in correlation with point one. The reference itself can be of extreme shortness. As to the truth or authenticity of the example (the third point), one may assume that the narrator takes this for granted or at least presents it as being so, unless the improbability of the event itself must serve as an example, (e.g. Alexander at the far end of the world). The fourth criterion has been worded as follows: 'La dépendance relative de l'*exemplum* par rapport à un discours dans lequel il vient s'insérer comme un élément formant un tout, mais un tout subordonné à un ensemble englobant: c'est un *collage*'. With the restriction indicated in the first point, one may endorse this statement, which is generally valid for all extra-argumental elements like similes, excurses, dicts and sayings, anecdotes, etc. But, as we have seen in the works of Antonios Melissa, the factual argument can be reduced to the simple title of a chapter, in which the different examples figure as demonstration material. Point five: the Alexander material which I had at my disposal came mostly from sources other then sermons or comparable literature. As to the sixth point: the element of *persuasion* and the *rhetoric of persuasion* is more adherent to the homiletic genre, of course, but it often plays its role in other contexts as well. The persuasion can apply to the person or the act itself (Alexander was a just king, see his behaviour towards the women of Darius) or be in service of a message (avoid contact with women, see Alexander's behaviour towards the women of Darius). The seventh point is again the consequence of the restricted position of the homiletic literature, which, indeed, supposes a distinct auditoire. The Alexander examples occur in various contexts, which in theory imply various audiences/readers. One may ask, however, whether one should make the coupling of a special context and a special audience so strict. The direct contact between preacher and believers demands, of course, a special rhetorical approach which may affect the composition, c.q. presentation of the example; in the indirect contact of author and reader the application of an example, be it short story of simple reference, aims *mutatis mutandis* at the same effect: persuasion, demonstration, diversion, contrast, comparison, etc. Points eight and nine are equally bound to the homiletic context. Broadly interpreted an example will often be didactical or pedagogical, and various degrees of explicitness are thinkable. To say that most of the Alexander examples find their application in the perspective of the eternal salvation of the reader/auditor would reach much too far. There are, indeed, such applications: I think that Antonios Melissa's examples should be seen in that light. On the other hand, it is no more than a Christian extension of the antique idea of morality. In these cases where Alexander is fully presented as a Christian king, obedient to God's decrees, one may assume that the whole story or the examples taken from it have been placed in some eschatological perspective. But it is by no means necessary that either story or example be adapted to serve this end. In that respect one may assume, too, that the Byzantine readers of the abstracts of the Alexander historians in Photios' *Bibliotheca* simply understood them otherwise than the readers intended by the Alexander historians themselves.

It will be clear that the definition of Bremond c.s. is impractical for applications to the Alexander examples, as also to a broader range of exempla, broader, at least, than that which found its way into sermons. The title of the book is certainly misleading and should have run 'L'exemplum en forme de récit' or 'L'exemplum dans les sermons médiévaux' or something similar. A broader definition, applicable to the Alexander material, might be: an exemplum is a reference to a person or circumstance considered paradigmatic, in order to underline a conviction or to strengthen a persuasion. A similitudo, at last, applies an exemplum in a comparative way.


NOTES

1.      See e.g. Romanos the Melodist (ed. Grosdidier de Matons) I p. 412 Hymn on Ninive, where successively the sinner (Mary Magdalene) St. Peter, David and the inhabitants of Ninive are mentioned as 'exempla' of persons who were healed in the 'hospital of contrition'.

2.      See Leontios of Neapolis, *Vita Symeonis Sali* (V.S.S.) (Ryden 1963: 145, 19). Symeon's entrance in Emesa reminds of Jesus' entry in Jerusalem, his kicking down the tables of the cake-sellers, Christ's rage against the money-changers and other traders (Matth. 21,12). Also simply in the choice of terms: V.S.S. 163,7 ἦν δὲ πάλιν ἄπαξ καθήμενος μετὰ ἀδελφῶν καὶ θερμαινόμενος - Mark. 14.54: καὶ (ὁ Πέτρος) ἦν συγκαθήμενος μετὰ τῶν ὑπερετῶν καὶ θερμαινόμενος πρὸς τὸ φῶς.

3. See e.g. Gleixner 1961,35 (Malalas), 38 (Georgios Monachos), 40 (Georgios Kedrenos), 89 ff. (Alexander romance), 103 ff. (Alexander in folklore).

4. I thank these *anonymi* of the Workshop of Bergeyk for their accuracy in this real 'monk's work'.

5. These figures are approximate, doublets and triplets included.

6. Others, too, had their problems with defining (the difference between) *exemplum* and *similitudo*; see Bremond - Le Goff - Schmitt 1982: 31, note 11.

7. 'Εθέλω γὰρ καὶ μικρὸν ἐκ τῶν πάλαι προσθεῖναι τῷ λόγῳ διήγημα, τῇ ὑποθέσει πάνυ τοι σφόδρα προσῆκον . 'Αλέξανδρόν φασιν, ἐκεῖνον τὸν Μακεδόνα, μετὰ τὸν πολὺν ἐκεῖνον δρόμον καὶ τὰ μεγάλα τρόπαια, ἐπειδήποτε ῥαστώνης ἕνεκά τινος καὶ θυμηδίας ἐπιβὰς τριήρους ἔπλει περισκοπῶν καὶ ποταμὸν τὸν Εὐφράτην, ἐκπίπτει τῆς αὑτοῦ κεφαλῆς, συμβὰν οὑτωσί πως, ἡ βασιλικὴ καλύπτρα περὶ μέσον τὸν ποταμόν· ἣν τάχιστά τις τῶν ναυτῶν εἰλήφει διανηξάμενος· καὶ αὐτὴν μὲν τῇ χειρὶ βασ-τάζειν ἅμα καὶ νήχεσθαι μὴ ἔχων, τῇ ἑαυτοῦ κεφαλῇ περιθεὶς ἐξενήξατο κομίζων ταύτην τῷ βασιλεῖ· ὅ γε μὴν βασιλεύς, ὅτι μὲν τὴν βασίλειον καλύπτραν αὐτῷ διεσώσατο, τάλαντον ἐδωρήσατο· ὅτι δ'αὐτὴν ἀναξίως τῇ ἑαυτοῦ κεφαλῇ περιέθηκεν, ἀφαιρεῖται τῆς κεφαλῆς τὸν ἄνθρωπον.

8. Not mentioned in Cary (1956). The episode is related by Arrian, Anabasis VII 22. See also Aristoboulos in F. Jacoby (1927: 139, fr. 55).

9. One may even postulate that the mere mention of Alexander as the ruler of the third world empire is exemplary as such.

10. S. Andreas Cretensis, *rationes* 15 (PG 1121D - 1124A): οὐκ ἤκουσας τὸν Φιλίππου 'Αλέξανδρον, ἐπὶ ταῖς Δαρείου θυγατράσιν προσενεχ-θείσαις αὐτῷ πρὸς συνουσίαν, βασιλικῶς δυσφορήσαντα, καὶ τί μέγα καὶ σωφροσύνης μεστὸν ἐπιφθεγξάμενον πρόσρημα:"Αἰσχρὸν ἡμᾶς, ἄνδρας νικήσαντας, ὑπὸ γυναικῶν ἡττηθῆναι;"

11. Photios, *Epistolarum Liber* I 8,96:'Αλέξανδρος ὁ Μακεδών, 'Ασίας κύριος δόρατι γεγονώς, τὰς Περσίδας ἔλεγεν βολίδας ὀμμάτων εἶναι· ὁ δὲ σώφρων ὡς ἀληθῶς ἀνὴρ καὶ Δεσποτικῶν φύλαξ ἐντολῶν οὐ τὰς Περσίδας μόνον, ἀλλὰ καὶ πάσης γυναικὸς ὄψιν ὡς ὀξὺ ψυχῆς βέλος καὶ θανατηφόρον φεύξεται καὶ ἀπο-στραφεῖται.

12    See Achilles Tatius, with a translation by S. Gaselee (1961: I 4,4): κάλλος γὰρ ὀξύτερον τιτρώσκει βέλους καὶ διὰ τῶν ὀφθαλμῶν εἰς τὴν ψυχὴν καταρρεῖ· ὀφθαλμὸς γὰρ ὁδὸς ἐρωτικῷ τραύματι.

Cf. also Eur. *Hipp.* 525 Ἔρως, Ἔρως, ὁ κατ' ὀμμάτξων/στάζων πόθον ..., Dig. Akrit. (Grottaferrata, ed. Mavrogordato) IV 276,277 οὗ (leg. τὸ ) γὰρ κάλλος ὀξύτατον καὶ τὸ βέλος τιτρώσκει·/καὶ δι' αὐτῶν τῶν ὀφθαλμῶν εἰς ψυχὴν ἐπανήκει· .... See also Heliod. *Aeth.* III 7 and Const. Manasses τὸ κάλλος γὰρ ὀξύτατον τιτρώσκει καὶ βελέμνου/καὶ δι' ὀμμάτων εἰς ψυχὴν ἐπιρριζοῦν εἰσρέει.

13.    *De abstinentia a colloquio cum mulieribus* PG 89, 1480 B:
ἡ γὰρ τῆς γυναικὸς ὄψις βέλος ἐστὶ πεφαρμακευμένον. Ἔτρωσε τὴν ψυχὴν καὶ τὸν ἰὸν ἐναπέθετο καὶ ὅσῳ χρονίζει τοσοῦτον τὴν σῆψιν ἐργάζεται· ὁ δὲ φυλασσόμενος οὐκ ἐμπέσῃ εἰς αὐτὴν καὶ οὐ μὴ τρωθῇ ὑπὸ τῶν βελῶν αὐτῆς.

14.    Ἠκούσατε ὅτι ἐρρέθη· οὐ μοιχεύσεις. ἐγὼ δὲ λέγω ὑμῖν ὅτι πᾶς ὁ βλέπων γυναῖκα πρὸς τὸ ἐπιθυμῆσαι αὐτὴν ἤδη ἐμοίχευσεν αὐτὴν ἐν τῇ καρδίᾳ αὐτοῦ.

15.    *Sacra parallella* II par. 10 (PG 96,245 C-D):
Τουτὶ γὰρ εἰς ταὐτὸν ἐκεῖνο φέρει· Ὁ ἐμβλέψας πρὸς ἡδονὴν γυναικί, κἂν μὴ τῷ ἔργῳ τὴν μοιχείαν ἐπιτελέσῃ, ἀλλὰ τό γε τὴν ἐπιθυμίαν τῇ ψυχῇ παραδέξασθαι, οὐκ ἀφεῖται τοῦ ἐγκλήματος.

16.    In his commentary on Plutarch's *Alexander*, Hamilton (1969: 21,4) hesitates unnecessarily at this point.

17.    On Maximus Confessor, see Beck (1959: 440) and Buchwald - Hohlweg-Prinz (1982: s.v.). For other *florilegia* of sayings see also Wachsmuth.

18.    See Buchwald - Hohlweg - Prinz (s.v.); PG 136, 265-1244.

19.    Ant. Mel. I 37: περὶ τοῦ ὅτι οὐκ ἀεὶ τὸ πλεῖστον ἄριστον. Same title in Max. Conf. *Loci communes* 71 (= PG 91, 1018 C).

20.    *Ibid.* I 53: περὶ ψόγου καὶ διαβολῆς.

21.    *Ibid.* I 37: Ἀλέξανδρος, ἀκούσας ὅτι Δαρεῖος τριάκοντα μυριάδας εἰς παράταξιν ἄγει, ἔφη· "Εἷς μάγειρος οὐ φοβεῖται πολλὰ πρόβατα" Ὁ αὐτὸς κατασκόπου λέγοντος αὐτῷ πλείους εἶναι τοὺς Δαρείου ἔφη· "Καὶ τὰ πρόβατα, πλείονα ὄντα, ὑφ' ἑνὸς ἢ δευτέρου λύκου χειροῦνται". The same examples in Max. Conf. *l.c.* (note 23). See also Wachsmuth (no. 10 and 11). In the Alexander romance I[2]

similar similes are used by Nectanebo: καὶ γὰρ εἷς λέων (L: κύων) πολλὰς ἐλάφους ἐθηρεύσατο (L: ἐχειρώσατο), καὶ εἷς λύκος (L: λύκος εἷς) πολλὰς ἀγέλας προβάτων ἐσκύλευσεν (L: ἀγέλην ποιμνίων ὠλέσατο). In the Byzantine Alexander Poem (ed. S. Reichmann) 113,114: εἷς λέων ἐχειρώσατο πλείονας τὰς ἐλάφους, /ἐσκύλευσε δ'ἀγέλας τε λύκος εἷς τῶν ποιμνίων.

22. *Ibid.* I 70: (title περὶ εὐτυχίας καὶ δυστυχίας) ᾿Αλέξανδρος ὁ βασιλεὺς ἰδὼν Διογένην κοιμώμενον ἐν πίθῳ ἔφη· ᾿Ω πίθε μεστὲ φρενῶν. ῾Ο δὲ φιλόσοφος ἀναστὰς ἔφη· ᾿Ω βασιλεῦ μέγιστε,... (here the text has a lacuna). ((θέλω τύχης σταλαγμὸν ἢ φρενῶν πίθον, πρὸς ὅν τις ἀντέφησε τῶν φιλοφρόνων· ῾Ρανὶς φρενῶν μοι μᾶλλον ἢ βυθὸς τύχης ἧς μὴ παρούσης δυστυχοῦσιν αἱ φρένες)). See also Wachsmuth (no. 2).

23. Title: περὶ παίδων τιμώντων γονεῖς καὶ ὅσα ἕπεται ἀγαθὰ τοῖς ὑπακούουσιν αὐτοῖς.

24. Ant. Mel. 2,11: ᾿Αλέξανδρος ὁ βασιλεὺς ἐρωτηθεὶς τίνα μᾶλλον ποθεῖ, τὸν πατέρα Φίλιππον ἢ ᾿Αριστοτέλην τὸν διδάσκαλον ἔφη· <τὸν διδάσκαλον·> ὁ μὲν γὰρ τοῦ γενέσθαι, ὁ δὲ τοῦ καλῶς γενέσθαι αἴτιος. See also Wachsmuth no. 16; cf. no. 134. In the edition of Ant. Mel. the second <τὸν διδάσκαλον> is missing.

25. *Ibid.*: ῾Ο αὐτὸς βαρύ τι ἐπιτατούσης αὐτῷ τῆς μητρὸς ᾿Ολυμπιάδος, ἔφη· ᾿Ω μῆτερ, πικρόν με ἐνοίκιον τῆς ἐννεαμηναίου ἀπαιτεῖς.
Both passages also in Max. Conf. 23 = 860B under the title περὶ τιμῆς γονέων καὶ φιλοτεκνίας.

26. *Ibid.* 2,69, title: περὶ καταλαλούντων καὶ περὶ ὕβρεως. Text: Φίλιππον τὸν ᾿Αλεξάνδρου πατέρα ἐλοιδόρει τις τῶν κακογλώττων ἀνθρώπων· καὶ παρῄνουν οἱ φίλοι διώκειν τὸν λοίδορον, ὁ δὲ ἔφη· οὐκ ἔστι καλὸν τοῦτο ποιῆσαι, ἵνα μὴ ἐν πλείοσι περιεχόμενος κακῶς λέγῃ ἡμᾶς. ῾Ο αὐτὸς ἔλεγεν, ὅτι χάριν ἔχω τοῖς λοιδοροῦσί με, ὅτι βελτίονα ποιοῦσιν. ᾿Εγὼ γὰρ σπουδάζων ψευδεῖς αὐτοὺς ἀπελέγχειν, εἴ τι φαῦλον ποιῶ, μεταβάλλομαι.

27. *Ibid.* 2,74: ᾿Αλέξανδρος νοσήσας μακρὰν νόσον, ὡς ἀνέρρωσεν οὐδὲν ἔφη διατεθῆναι χεῖρον· ὑπέμνησε γὰρ ἡμᾶς ἡ νόσος μὴ μέγα φρονεῖν θνητοὺς ὄντας. See also Max. Conf. 34 = 896C.

28. Ibid. 2,74: ᾿Εὰν ἴδῃς πονηρὸν εἰς ὕψος αἰρόμενον,
      Λαμπρῷ τε πλούτῳ καὶ τύχῃ γαυρούμενον,
      ᾿Οφρύν τε μεῖζον τῆς τύχης ἐπαίροντα·

Τούτου τάχιον μεταβολὴν προσδόκα,
Ἐπαίρεται γὰρ μεῖζον, ἵνα καὶ μεῖζον πέσῃ.

29. The series opens with the name Ἀλέξανδρος (31 quotations, of which some begin with ὁ αὐτός, 25, 26, 28-31), then follow Ἀνταγόρας, Ἀναξαγόρας, Ἀλέξις ὁ τῆς κωμῳδίας ποιητής, etc.

30. Van Dieten (1975: 497,44 ff). The words which Van Dieten was not able to identify are rather certainly an allusion to the story of Alexander and the cupbearer who lost a golden cup. Alexander's answer is θάρσει, ὦ παῖ· ὅπου γὰρ ἂν εἴη, ἡμετέρα ἐστί : 'be quiet, boy, whereever it is, it is ours.' Thus Ant. Mel. *Sent.* 2,1 = 1005 D.

31. The text runs: οὐ κατ' ἐκεῖνον τρίχας δεικνὺς ῥάμφους καὶ πτερῶν εἰκασίαν ὑπεμφαινούσας. Grabler translates 'nur dass ihm nicht wie jenem auf seiner Brust Haare in der Form von Adlerflügeln und -krallen wuchsen' and adds in a note (zu pag. 470,2): 'Derartiges muss in volkstümlichen Darstellungen der Alexandersage, die weitverbreitet waren, gestanden haben. Die Adlerflügel sind natürlich Symbol der Weltherrschaft.' The translation is incorrect and too suggestive. Firstly ῥάμφους are no Krallen ('claws'), but 'beak'. It is possible that there is an allusion to the wings and beak of an eagle, but this eagle is not mentioned and can only be 'construed' from the idea 'ῥάμφος'. There is, nowhere else, as far as I know, an allusion to impressive breast hair of Alexander, on the contrary, one gets the impression from Plut. *Alex.* 4,2 that Alexander had a light, rosy complexion and was not very hairy, except for his lion-like mane. The Alexander romance I 13 gives him differently coloured eyes and teeth like a serpent in addition to lion-like hair.

32. Beck (1959: 93-4; 154-5). See also PG 111, p. 889-904. Migne gives the Latin translation from the Arabic, made by Edward Pococke, an Oxford professor of Hebrew and Arabic, and edited in Oxford 1658.

33. PG 111, 968D: *Ab eo qui a Deo rex constitutus est, Alexandro servo Dei, et Graecorum rege ad Darium praecelsum.*

34. PG 111, 971C: *Ab Alexandro servo Dei ... ad Olympiadem matrem suam benignam, ...*

35. PG 111, 972A: *Scriptae sunt ad te litterae istae meae, die huius mundi ultimo, futuri primo: hac spe ut tibi ad consolationem inserviturae sint, grataeque futurae.*

36. The texts run in Latin as follows:
a) 972D: *Dixit ergo Philemon sapiens: Magnum hic dies exemplum ex hi-*

*bet. Praecessit malum eius, quod a tergo erat; et retro abiit bonum eius, quod praecesserat.*

b) *ibid.:* *Plato sapiens: Heus! qui per vim [omnia] agebas, collegisti quod te decepit, et a te recessit; ita ut tibi adhaereat reatus eius, utilitas autem ad alium redierit.*

c) *ibid.:* *Aristoteles sapiens: Abiit a nobis Alexander loquens, reversus est ad nos silens.*

d) *ibid.:* *Naren sapiens: Dic gregi Alexandri, Hic est dies in quo custo-dit grex pastorem suum.*

e) *973C:* *Alius: Sufficit hoc in exemplum: heri fuit aurum Alexandro thesaurus, hodie Alexander in auro reconditus.*

f) *973C:* *Dixit alius: Sufficit vulgo in exemplum mors regum; et sufficit regibus in commonitionem mors vulgi.*

g) *ibid.:* *Dixit alius: Non aliud edidit Alexander documentum illustrius morte sua.*

h) *973A:* *Dixit Lotas philosophus: Ne miremini eum, qui cum in vita sua nos non instituerit, nobis tandem se morte sua monitorem praebuit.*

i) *ibid.:* *Dixit Sis sapiens: Hic multos morte affecit ne moreretur, at mortuus est; quomodo non potuit a se mortem morte repellere?*

j) *ibid.:* *Dixit Demetrius sapiens: Heus tu! cuius ira mors fuit, cur non ipsi morti iratus es?*

37. Anastasius Sinaita *Adv. Jud.* PG 8, 1213C: Τέσσαρας δὲ βασιλεῖς λέγει τὰ ἔνδοξά τε καὶ ἐπίσημα Βαβυλωνίων, Μήδων, καὶ τὸ τρίτον ληστρικὸν καὶ δυσεπιχείρητον τὸ Μακεδονικὸν Ἀλεξάνδρου, ἤγουν τῶν Ἑλλήνων.

38. Cf. ibid. 28,1 (56,1).

39. The Koran (Dawood 1974: 98-9).

40. PG 105, 767B: εἶτα μέμνηται Ἀλεξάνδρου τοῦ Μακεδόνος καί φησιν ὅτι· Ἀπῆλθεν ἕως δυσμῶν ἡλίου καὶ εὗρε τὸν ἥλιον δύναντα εἰς θερμὸν ὕδωρ· καὶ ὅτι εἰς τὸν βορρᾶν ἀπετείχισε τὸν Ὤγ καὶ Μάγωγ· καὶ ὅτι μοναρχίτης ἦν τὸ σέβας Ἀλέξανδρος κατὰ τὸν Ἀβρὰμ καὶ οὐχ Ἕλλην. Καὶ προστίθησιν ὅτι· Ἡμεῖς

διηγούμεθα ἐπάνω σου τὴν ἐξήγησιν ταύτην ἐν ἀληθείᾳ. Ὁποία δὲ ἐν τούτοις ἀλήθεια πρόσεστιν, καὶ ἡμῶν μὴ λεγόντων, πάντες ἴσασι· τὰ δὲ συνήθη αὐτῷ σαπρολογήσας ἔστη τοῦ μύθου.

41. PG 136, 1318B-C = Tafel, *Eust. Opuscula* 351, 78-82.

42. PG 113, 56C-57C.

43. PG 160, 841C-844A

44. This tribe is mentioned by Arrian *Anabasis* IV 22,5, V 3,2 ff. They are localised by ancient authors in the Caucasus, by modern scholars in Afghanistan (Hindu Kusj), see Tarn (1950: 178, 239, 241, etc. and map). Cf. also *Der kleine Pauly*.

45. *De origine Turcorum* PG 161, 1000D-1001A.

# BIBLIOGRAPHY

BECK 1959
Beck, H.G., *Kirche und Theologische Literatur im byzantinische Reich*. München 1959.

BREMOND-LE GOFF 1982
Bremond, Cl., Le Goff, J., Schmitt, J.Cl., *L'exemplum*, Turnhout 1982.

BUCHWALD-HOHLWEG-PRINZ 1982
Buchwald, W., Hohlweg, A., Prinz, O., *Tuskulum-Lexikon griechischer und lateinischer Autoren*. München-Zürich 1982[3].

CARY 1956
Cary, G., *The Medieval Alexander*. Cambridge 1956. Edited by D.J.A. Ross. (Reprinted 1967)

DAWOOD 1974
Dawood, J., *The Koran. Translated with notes*. Middlesex 1974[4].

GASELEE 1961.
Gaselee, S., *Achilles Tatius, with an English Translation*. London-Cambridge, Mass. 1961[3].

GLEIXNER 1961
Gleixner, H.J., *Das Alexanderbild der Byzantiner*, München 1961.

GRABLER 1958
Grabler, F., *Abenteurer auf dem Kaiserthron. Die Regierungszeit der Kaiser Alexios II., Andronikos und Isaak Angelos (1180-1195) aus dem Geschichtswerk des Niketas Choniates übersetzt, eingeleitet und erklärt*. Graz-Wien-Köln 1958.

GROSDIDIER DE MATONS 1981
Grosdidier de Matons, J., *Romanos le Mélode, Hymnes; introduction, texte critique, traduction et notes*. Paris 1981.

HAMILTON 1969
Hamilton, J.R., *Plutarch, Alexander, a Commentary*. Oxford 1969.

HENRY 1959
Henry, R. (ed.), *Photios biblotheca*. Paris 1959.

JACOBY 1957
Jacoby, F., *Fragmente der griechischen Historiker*. Leiden 1957[2].

MAVROGORDATO 1956
Mavrogordato, J., *Digenes Akrites, edited with an Introduction, Translation and Commentary*. Oxford 1956.

DER KLEINE PAULY 1964
*Lexikon der Antike auf der Grundlege von Pauly's Realenencyclopädie ...* herausgegeben von Konrat Ziegler und Walther Sontheimer. Stuttgart 1964.

REICHMANN 1963
Reichmann, S., *Das byzantinische Alexandergedicht*. Meisenheim am Glan 1963.

RYDEN 1963
Ryden, L., *Das Leben des heiligen Narren Symeon von Leontios von Neapolis*. Stockholm 1963.

TARN 1950
Tarn, W.W., *Alexander the Great II*. Cambridge 1950.

VAN DIETEN 1975
Van Dieten, J.L. (ed.), *Nicetae Chroniatae Historia*. Berlin 1975.
WACHSMUTH
Wachsmuth, C., *Die Wiener Apophtegmensammlung (Cod. Vind. theol. 149)*. Wien 1882.

L.J. Engels

# Aspekte der Anwendung von Exempla bei Petrus Damiani

1. Dieser Beitrag behandelt einige Aspekte der Anwendung von *exempla* im Prosawerk des Petrus Damiani (1007-1072).[1] Damianis Platz in der Entwicklung des Exempels ist von Jacques Le Goff (im Anschluss an Welter 1927: 32f.) knapp und vorläufig wie folgt charakterisiert: 'Plus sûrement (als in den *Collationes* des Odo von Cluny, LJE) des anecdotes proches de l'*exemplum* proprement dit, dont une partie est empruntée aux auteurs païens de l'Antiquité, une autre aux fables d'animaux, une autre encore à des faits contemporains pour la plupart tirés de l'expérience et de l'information propre de l'auteur (par exemple des récits de visions) apparaissent dans l'oeuvre de Pierre Damien ... Ici encore une étude s'imposerait' (Bremond-Le Goff: 51).

Dieser letzten Anregung wird hier gefolgt, jedoch ohne eine vollständige Behandlung des Themas zu beanspruchen. Zuerst wird (in 2) eine Skizze von Damianis Anwendung verschiedener Arten von *exempla* gegeben, die durch eine Weiterführung von antiken, teilweise patristischen rhetorischen Konventionen gekennzeichnet wird. Anschliessend wird ein bestimmter *exemplum*-Typus im Mittelpunkt stehen, und zwar derjenige der sich des besonderen Interesses der Forschungsgruppe um Jacques Le Goff und Jean-Claude Schmitt erfreut und der von Le Goff vorläufig folgenderweise definiert worden ist: 'un récit bref donné comme véridique et destiné à être inséré dans un discours (en général un sermon) pour convaincre un auditoire par une leçon salutaire' (Bremond-Le Goff 1982: 37f.). Anhand von *opusc.* 19 wird (in 3) ein Eindruck vermittelt von der Weise in der Damiani Berichte und Erzählungen über Ereignisse aus seiner eigenen Zeit oder aus der nahen Vergangenheit verarbeitet hat in seinen auf Beweisführung und Überredung abzielenden Erörterungen; darauf werden (in 4) Aspekte der Anwendung dieser Kategorie von *exempla* analysiert. Zum Schluss folgen (in 5) einige Folgerungen die mit beabsichtigen die Befunde um Damianis Verwendung von *exempla* in einen grösseren Rahmen einzuordnen.

2. Unterscheidet man die bei Damiani vorkommenden *exempla* nach ihrer Herkunft in drei Typen (Bremond-Le Goff 1982: 41), dann kann man folgendes bemerken.

Die erste und grösste Gruppe ist die der jüdisch-christlichen und frühchristlichen *exempla*. Diese Kategorie hätte also in Le Goffs oben angeführter Charakterisierung der Verwendung von *exempla* bei Damiani auf jedem Fall erwähnt werden müssen. Die *exempla* aus der Bibel, mit der Damiani so intim vertraut ist (Leclercq 1960: 212ff.; Calati 1978), findet man zerstreut in allen Schriften, manchmal ausführlich interpretiert und breit ausgesponnen, manchmal, wenn es sich handelt um bekannte Personen mit einer gefestigten Exempelfunktion, gestaltet als Kurzexempel (Erwähnung des Namens und der im Kontext wichtigen Tat, (Un)Tugend oder Äusserung). Der Hagiographie entlehnte *exempla* treten vor allem in den Predigten über Heilige stark in den Vordergrund (Lucchesi 1975; Identifizierung der hagiographischen Quellen in den *Monita* von Lucchesi 1983); in den Briefen und Brieftraktaten spielen sie eine bescheidene Rolle. Den Kirchenvätern, der Kirchengeschichte, den päpstlichen Dekreten und den Konzilsakten werden vom Juristen Damiani (Dressler 1954: 194; Ryan 1956; Leclercq 1960: 206-211; Cantin 1975: 505-34) zahlreiche, of wortgetreu angeführte Präzedenzfälle, *testimonia* und *auctoritates* entnommen, selbstverständlich vor allem in Werken die sich dazu vom Thema her eignen, u.a. die *Disceptatio synodalis* (*opusc.* 4) und der *Liber gratissimus* (*opusc.* 6).

Die zweite Gruppe - *exempla*, die aus dem heidnischen Altertum stammen oder darüber handeln - ist bei Damiani am seltesten vertreten; wenn man die kurzen Erwähnungen als Präzedenzfall oder Kurzexempel und die Anspielungen auf die Mythologie ausser Acht lässt, bleiben etwa vierzig übrig (sowohl *facta* als auch *dicta*).[2] Sie sind grösstenteils der Historiographie entlehnt. Diese wird in der Regel angedeutet als kollektiver Fonds (*annales*, *historia* oder *historiae*, mit Bezeichnungen wie *authentica*, *Romana*, *vetus*, *gentilium* und *veterum*). Damiani nennt verhältnismässig selten Namen antiker Autoren, und es würde sich lohnen in jedem Einzelfall zu untersuchen, inwiefern direkte oder indirekte Rezeption vorliegt (die Erwähnung Herodots in *opusc.* 40, 654B, und die Zuschreibung an Gellius einer bei diesem unauffindbaren Anekdote über Alexander den Grossen, in *opusc.* 33, 561B, lässt zweifeln ob Damiani Sallust, den er in *opusc.* 18.1, 388D, erwähnt, selbst eingesehen hat; auf jedem Fall meint er mit Eutropius die teilweise auf diesem basierenden *Historia Romana* des Paulus Diaconus). Die Anwendung antiker *exempla* beschränkt sich praktisch auf die Briefe und Brieftraktate. Abgesehen von der üblichen Anführung von Vespasian und Titus in der Erklärung von *4Reg.* 2.23f. (auf sie und die Zerstörung von Jerusalem weisen die zwei Bären hin, die zweiundvierzig der Jünglinge zerreissen die den Propheten Elisaeus verspotten, s. z.B. *serm.* 39, 74ff.) finden sich in den Predigten nur zwei antike *exempla*, beide in *serm.* 28.[3]

Die dritte Gruppe, die der zeitgenössischen, auf eigener Erfahrung oder mündlicher Überlieferung beruhenden *exempla*, ist gross - gelegentlich handelt es sich dabei um zwar schriftlich überlieferte, Damiani nur aber durch mündliche Information bekannte Geschichten.[4] Wenn man die vielen Wundererzählungen in der

Sphäre der Hagiographie und die zahlreichen Beispiele der Verzichtleistung oder der Frömmigkeit in asketischem Kontext ausser Acht lässt, bleiben immerhin etwa hundertfünfzig übrig. Sie erscheinen immer in der Gestalt einer kurzen Erzählung, die meistenfalls durch eine Angabe der Lehre, die man ihr entnehmen soll, eingeführt oder abgeschlossen wird. Man findet sie ausschliesslich in den Briefen und Brieftraktaten; in den Predigten (in denen zwar viele Wundererzählungen vorkommen, aber fast immer aufgrund schriftlicher Quellen)[5] fehlen sie völlig. Ich werde unten ausführlich auf diesen *exempla*-Typus eingehen.

Es stellt sich also heraus, dass Damiani nicht alle Sorten von *exempla* gleich oft in allen Arten von Schriften verwendet. Die zeitgenössischen Exempel fehlen ganz und die antiken fast gänzlich in seinen Predigten. Auf der anderen Seite werden in den Briefen und Brieftraktaten *exempla* von verschiedener Herkunft mit einander verknüpft; die antiken *exempla* gehen Hand in Hand mit den biblisch-christlichen, und die zeitgenössischen mit den antiken und den biblisch-christlichen.[6] Dies deutet auf eine Ähnlichkeit in Funktion und einen Unterschied in Brauchbarkeit.

Zum Abschluss dieser Übersicht über die ihrer Herkunft nach zu unterscheidenden Kategorien von *exempla* sei hier zur Vermeidung von Missverständnissen (wo Welter 1927: 32, von 'contes d'animaux' redet und Le Goff in dem oben gegebenen Zitat von 'fables d'animaux') bemerkt, dass die Tierfabel in Damianis Arsenal keinen Anteil hat und die Fabel nur einen geringen. Die zahlreichen zur Belehrung erwähnten Eigenschaften und Gewohnheiten der Tiere (durch das ganze Werk verstreut, aber angehäuft in *opusc.* 52) rühren nicht von Fabeln her, sondern von den antiken *naturarum rimatores*, an erster Stelle Plinius, den Kirchenvätern (vor allem Ambrosius und Augustinus) und vom Physiologus (Cantin 1975: 535-94; Frugoni 1980). Aus den Fabeln wird m.W. nur einmal geschöpft (*epist.* 1.16, 236B-D, der Wettkampf zwischen Sonne und Wind, Thompson 1955-8, L 351). Vielleicht ist es kein Zufall, dass Damiani unmittelbar darauf folgen lässt: *Sed ut e scripturis sacris honestius proferatur exemplum*, und dann dieselbe Lektion nochmals aus der Bibel heraus stützt, mit dem handfesten aber wenig erfolgreichen Auftreten des Roboam (*3Reg.* 12.1-19 und *2Par.* 10.1-19), und aus der *natura* des Nashorns (*rhinoceros*),[7] das nur gefangen werden kann, wenn eine Jungfrau es besänftigt hat (236D).

In der Verwendung von *exempla* zeigt sich Damiani also stark beeinflusst von Ambrosius, Augustinus, Hieronymus und Gregor dem Grossen. Die zwei erstgenannten haben seine Aufmerksamkeit auf die Schöpfung - vor allem die Tierwelt, aber auch andere Naturerscheinungen, wie die Jahreszeiten und die Sterne - als *mirabile* und *spiritualis figurae sacramentum* gelenkt (Cantin 1975: 535-94). Mit Hieronymus (Pétré 1961: 1890f.) hat Damiani gemeinsam, dass er, obwohl die Bibel und die christliche Tradition den übergrossen Teil der *exempla* liefern (im patristischen Sprachgebrauch werden diese auch *nostra* genannt), keinesfalls an den *exempla* aus der nichtchristlichen Antike (den *aliena*) vorübergegangen ist. Teils in der Spur Gregors des Grossen (Le Goff 1981) hat er, wie bereits Welter (1927: 33) bemerkt hat den in seiner Umgebung umlaufenden Erzählungen über, wunderbare, lehrreiche Ereignisse einen wichtigen Platz eingeräumt.

In Damianis Verwendung von *exempla* widerspiegelt sich weiter seine Vertrautheit mit der Rhetorik (Dressler 1954: 185ff.; Leclercq 1960: 168-76; Cantin 1975: 291-374). Mit Ausnahme eines Teiles der sich auf mündliche Überlieferung stützenden, mehr zeitgenössischen Erzählungen (worauf ich in 3 und 4 zurückkommen werde) werden die *exempla* im allgemeinen in Übereinstimmung mit den Vorschriften der antiken Argumentationslehre verwendet, welche die genau genommen lose mit der Sache zusammenhängenden Argumente (wie überzeugende Präzedenzfälle, schlagende Parallellen und massgebende Sprüche) unter dem Sammelnamen *exempla* zu den Kunstmitteln der Beweisführung rechnet - neben den wahrnehmbaren Zeichen (*signa, indicia, vestigia*) und den rationellen, der *causa* selbst entlehnten Beweisen (*argumenta*; s. Lausberg 1960: 227ff.).[8] Die Berücksichtigung der literarisch-rhetorischen Konventionen ist ein Faktor, der trotz ihrer verschiedenen Herkunft eine unverkennbare Einheit in der Verwendung von *exempla* bringt.

Wie sich aus den Bemerkungen ergibt die die Übergänge vom einem zum andern Redetypus markieren, ist Damiani sich des Unterschieds zwischen rationeller Beweisführung einerseits (charakterisiert mit Ausdrücken wie *argumenta, argumentatio, assertio, ratio* und *ratiocinatio*), und Beweisführung und Überredung mit Hilfe der verschiedenen Sorten von *exempla* anderseits (der *rei (ut) gestae commemoratio*, der *auctoritas*, der *similitudo* u.ä.) sehr wohl bewusst.[9] Ferner findet man bei ihm die übliche Auffassung, dass die Wirkung von *exempla* grösser sei als die von *praecepta, verba* usw. (Bremond-Le Goff 1982: 48f.). Selbst bringt er diese Auffassung nicht nur in seinen Schriften, sondern auch im alltäglichen Leben in Verwendung, und er kennt die mit dem paulinischen Katalog der *testes fidei* aus dem Alten Testament (*Hebr.* 11) verbundene Interpretation der Seile (*funes*) und der Lappen (*panni*), mit deren Hilfe der Prophet Jeremias aus dem Brunnen gezogen wurde (*Jerem.* 38.1-13), als *figura* der *praecepta* und *exempla* die die Heilige Schrift enthält.[10] Weiterhin ist Damiani sich, wie wir unten, im 4. Teil, sehen werden, von der grossen Effektivität der *exempla* aus der eigenen Umwelt (*domestica*) bewusst. Die zweifache Funktion die *exempla* von alters her haben - Beweisführung und pädagogische Beeinflussung (Lumpe 1966: 1230f.) - wird bei ihm ebenfalls klar sichtbar, wie sein Wortgebrauch zeigt. Im ersten Falle werden Funktion oder Effekt des Exempels angedeutet mit Wörtern wie *approbare, astruere, convincere, corroborare, declarare, demonstrare, firmare,* und *monstrare*, sowie in Licht-Metaphern;[11] im zweiten Falle findet man regelmässig (positiv) *cohortari, compellere, confortare, incitare, invitare, provocare*, (prohibitiv) *caveri, compescere* und dergleichen; weiter ist gelegentlich die Rede von *consolatio* und *delectare*, und werden *aedificare* und *aedificatio*, die auch ausserhalb der Sphäre von den *exempla* manchmal als Zielsetzung von Petrus' Schriften genannt werden (Cantin 1975: 16, 318), auffällig oft benützt.[12] Wie Cantin (1972: 104, 297f.) gezeigt hat, wendet Damiani die Regel an, die den *exempla* ihren Platz vor allem nach den *argumenta* und in der Schlussrede zuspricht.

Das Gewicht das Petrus Damiani all diesen *exempla* beimisst, ist nicht gering. Dies wird zusammenhängen mit seiner Zurückhaltung der Dialektik gegenüber, deren Argumentationsweise und Spekulationsart er zwar beherrscht, aber als verdächtig betrachtet (Cantin 1972: 197; 1975: 375ff. und 572ff.). Aber es ist auch ein deutlicher Unterschied in Gewicht zwischen Kategorien von *exempla* zu spüren, der mit ihrer Herkunft zusammenhängt. Selbstverständlich wiegen die *exempla* aus der Bibel, die auch zahlenmässig überlegen sind, am schwersten; die höchste *ratio* ist für Damiani die *sacri eloquii auctoritas*.[13] Darauf folgen die Heiligen, die *patres* und *pontifices* aus der Spätantike und der Übergangszeit zum Mittelalter, und die von ihnen handelnde Geschichtsschreibung und Hagiographie; letztere ist übrigens nicht immer über Zweifel erhaben.[14] Oft wird eine Ausführung ausschliesslich durch *exempla* aus diesem Teil des Fonds unterstützt. Letzteres kann man nicht behaupten von den *exempla* aus dem heidnischen Altertum, aus der Gegenwart und der nahen Vergangenheit und aus der Tierwelt. Diese spielen meistens eine untergeordnete Rolle, was auf ein geringeres Gewicht hinweist. In einigen Werken haben sie allerdings ein derartiges Übergewicht, dass sie die Schrift als ganzes prägen (so in *epist.* 1.20 die antiken *exempla*, in *opusc.* 34.1 und 34.2 die zeitgenössischen, und in *opusc.* 52 die der Tierwelt entnommenen).

Zur Abrundung dieser Orientierung noch einige Bemerkungen zum Gebrauch des Terminus *exemplum*. Dieser weist interessante Aspekte auf, die eine tiefer schürfende Studie zu rechtfertigen scheinen; das Folgende sei nur eine erste Sondierung. Das Wort *exemplum* kommt bei Damiani sehr oft vor, meistens in der Bedeutung 'Beispiel'; Synonyme in der Umgebung des Wortes sind dann *forma*, *norma* und *speculum*.[15] Von den speziellen Bedeutungen ist '(massgebendes) Zitat' bei Damiani am häufigsten; sie hängt sehr eng zusammen mit der Art seiner Argumentation, die ja wimmelt von Zitaten. In der Umgebung des Wortes *exemplum* findet man in diesem Falle vor allem *testimonium*, *sententia* und *dictum* als Termini mit verwandter Bedeutung. Meistens handelt es sich um Anführungen aus der Bibel; in ungefähr fünfundzwanzig Prozent der Fälle sind Zitate aus den Werken der Kirchenväter und Aussagen der Päpste oder aus Kanones im Spiel. Die Nuancen können variieren. Manchmal geht es lediglich darum, dass zitiert wird, so dass mit *exemplum* allein angegeben werden soll, dass die Worte einer massgebenden Quelle entnommen sind ('Zitat, angeführter Passus'). Manchmal wird dagegen der Inhalt des Zitates betont ('angeführte Aussage, Auffassung oder Mitteilung'). In beiden Fällen befindet sich der Wortgebrauch in der Sphäre des rhetorischen Fachausdruckes, der wie gesagt auch die *auctoritas*, die Richtungweisende Aussage und den Präzedenzfall umfasst.[16] Im gleichen Rahmen passt der bei Damiani übrigens verhältnismässig seltene Gebrauch von *exemplum* in der Bedeutung von *similitudo*.[17] Nahe verwandt hiermit scheint der Gebrauch in der Sphäre der Exegese als Synonym von *imago* en *umbra*.[18] Die Bedeutung 'Exempel, lehrreiche oder beweiskräftige Erzählung', von der man angenommen hat, dass sie erst im 12. Jahrhundert aufgekommen sei (Bremond-Le Goff: 1982, 27), findet sich bereits bei Damiani, allerdings seltener als man aufgrund der in seinen Schriften vorkommenden Zahl zeitgenössischer *exempla* erwarten könnte. Letzteres scheint mit der Tatsache zusammenzuhängen, dass er die zeitgenössischen Exempel meistens mit Formeln einleitet, die auf die

Lektion oder die Herkunft hinweisen und in denen die Geschichte mit einem Pronomen (*hoc, illud, quod* u.d.) angedeutet wird. Ausserdem werden die Exempel *casus, gestum, historia, miraculum* und *signum* genannt.[19] Gerade in diesem Punkt weichen die Überschriften der Kapitel übrigens stark vom Wortgebrauch im Text ab; dort gibt es das Wort *exemplum* ziemlich oft in der Bedeutung 'beispielhafte Geschichte', und sie scheinen eine spätere Phase in diesem Gebrauch des Terminus *exemplum* widerzuspiegeln. Damit bestätigt dieses Detail die Auffassung, dass diese Überschriften nicht Damiani zugeschrieben werden dürfen, es sei denn er teilt explizit mit, dass er sie selber für angebracht gehalten hat (Brezzi 1943: 203; Leclercq 1960: 153 und 158; Cantin 1972: 310).[20]

3. Zur Veranschaulichung der Weise in der Petrus Damiani auf mündlicher Überlieferung beruhende Geschichten in seinen Schriften verarbeitet hat, und als Beispiel einiger Besonderheiten in derer Präsentation kann *opusc.* 19 nützlich sein.

In diesem langen Brief aus dem Anfang des Jahres 1060 reicht Petrus, der sich nur widerwillig im Jahre 1057 zum Kardinal-Bischof hatte erheben lassen (Leclercq 1960: 75-80; Reindel 1983: 6), sein Rücktrittsgesuch bei Papst Nikolaus II. ein, damit er sich in Zukunft dem eigenen Seelenheil widmen könne. Nachdem er daran herinnert hat, dass er das ihm auferlegte Amt (*episcopatum non canonice traditum sed violenter injectum*) bereits früher habe niederlegen wollen, formuliert Damiani seinen Entschluss: *cedo jure episcopatus* (423B-D). Weil er voraussieht, dass man ihm vorhalten wird dass dies nicht erlaubt sei (*semel acceptum dimitti regimen non licere*), formuliert er seinen Standpunkt: Viele bleiben in Amt und Würde auf Kosten ihres Seelenheiles, während man fest darauf vertrauen darf, dass alle diejenigen die mit lauterer Absicht, notgedrungen oder aus gutem Grund, abgedankt haben, in die ewige Seligkeit eingegangen sind (424B). Zur Begründung listet Damiani eine lange Reihe von Präzedenzfällen aus der frühen und jüngeren Kirchengeschichte an. Zuerst hat er die Absicht es bei zwanzig Fällen bewenden zu lassen (436C), aber über vierundzwanzig (die Zahl der *seniores* in *Apoc.* 4.4: 440A) erhöht er ihre Zahl schliesslich auf dreissig (441A); danach folgen noch einige 'Zugaben' (441B-442B) bevor der Brief endet mit einer Peroration (442B-C), in der Petrus *horum ... aliorumque patrum auctoritate suffultus* seinen Entschluss wiederholt.

Die Reihe von Präzedenzfällen wird nach dem ersten Dutzend einige Male unterbrochen. Zuerst geschieht dies beim dreizehnten Fall der sich auf einen Bischof bezieht,[21] der abdankte und die Mönchskutte annahm, nachdem er in einer Vision das jämmerliche Schicksal des Papstes Benedikt VIII. im Jenseits erblickt hatte und nachdem er in dessen Auftrag seinem Bruder Johannes XIX. berichtet hatte, dass eine bestimmte, nicht durch Raub sondern rechtmässig erworbene Summe den Armen geschenkt werden sollte. Diesem Präzedenzfall geht eine Erzählung von abscheulichen Vögeln voran, die sich von Samstagabend spät bis Montagmorgen früh in der Nähe von Puteoli (also in der Gegend des Vesuvs), wie aus Fesseln befreit und den Jägern ungreifbar, ergötzen bis sie sich, von einem Raben so gross wie ein Geier ermahnt, wieder ins schwefeldampfende Wasser stürzen. Manche halten sie unter Berufung auf Prudentius für unglückliche Seelen die den Strafen der Hölle verfallen sind, am Sonntag jedoch und während der angrenzenden Nächte eine erquickende Verschnaufpause (*refrigerium*) geniessen *pro Dominicae resurrectionis gloria* (427B-D). Nachdem Damiani diese ihm von Humbert von Silva Candida erzählte Geschichte aufgezeichnet hatte, sah er sich mit der Verwerfung derselben durch Abt Desiderius von Montecassino konfrontiert. Weil ein Gespräch zwischen Humbert und Desiderius keine Klarheit gebracht hat, lässt er wegen beider *auctoritas* die Sache dahingestellt sein (427D-428A).[22] Dem anschliessenden Präzedenzfall (in dem, wie wir gesehen haben, die Rede war von einer Vision, die einen Bischof zur Abdikation veranlasste) folgen erstens eine Beschreibung einer anderen Vision, aus der sich das elende Los des unwürdigen Papstes Benedikt IX. herausstellt (dieser büsst, in Erwartung des jüngsten Tages an dem seine Verdammnis besiegelt werden soll, in der Gestalt eines Bären mit Eselsohren und einem Eselsschwanz, *quia*, wie er erklärt, *bestialiter vixi*: 428C-D) und zweitens ein *miraculum* das dazu führt, dass es mit einem in schweren Sünden gestorbenen Mönch doch noch ein gutes Ende genommen hat (dieser wird, wieder zum Leben erweckt, nachträglich zum Einkehr gebracht und stirbt dann unverzüglich abermals: 429B-430B).

Die drei Erzählungen, die den Präzedenzfall, weshalb alles angefangen hat, einrahmen, haben einen gemeinsamen Gewährsmann: Humbert von Silva Candida, *summae auctoritatis vir* (427B), *cujus nimirum verba velut apostolica videntur veritate fundata* (430B). Die Geschichte der Seelenvögel ist ausdrücklich als eine Einführung zum Präzedenzfall gemeint,[23] der ja auch von einem Verstorbenen handelt, der sich ausserhalb des Jenseits zeigt. Die Hinzufügung der Vision über Benedikt IX. als verdammtes *monstrum* wird nicht erläutert; das *mysterium* jedoch, die tiefere Bedeutung auf die seine Gestalt verweist, wird erklärt.[24] Der Grund weshalb die dritte Geschichte, das *miraculum*, erzählt wird, stellt sich als wenig tiefschürfend heraus: Damiani sagt, dass er sie hinzufügt, weil sie durch ihren glücklichen Ausgang mit der Vision über Benedikt IX. kontrastiert, der ja ein schlimmes Ende gefunden hat.[25] Die Schlussfolgerung, die Petrus mit dem *miraculum* zu verbinden weiss, hätte ihn zu seinem Thema zurückführen können: Wenn eine so schwere Strafe jenem sündigen Mönch drohte, der bloss die Verantwortung für seine eigene Seele trug, wie könnte dann ein unwürdiger Bischof wie ich zuversichtlich sein, der sich ja für jede Seele zu verantworten hat die durch seine *negligentia* oder *prava exempla* verloren geht (430B)? Trotzdem wird die Aufreihung der abdankenden Bischöfe nicht gleich wieder aufgenommen.

Bereits der folgende Präzedenzfall (der des Silvanus, der den Sitz von Philippopolis in Thrazien aufgab, weil er der dort herrschenden Kälte nicht gewachsen war, aber der später den Sitz von Troja annahm, wo seine Heiligkeit sich nicht durch die Abdankung angegriffen zeigte, wie das Wunder, das er vollbracht, beweist: 430C-431C[26]), veranlasst zu einer neuen Digression. Zuerst konfrontiert Petrus die Lebensumstände des Silvanus in Thrazien mit seinen eigenen in Rom, wo das Klima nicht nur ungesund ist für seinen Körper (*Roma ferax febrium*) sondern auch für seine Seele (431D-432D). Vielleicht hat dies verursacht, dass seine Gedanken abschweifen zu Hildebrand, dem späteren Gregor VII., dem er seine Erhebung verdankt.[27] Wie dem auch sei, es folgen nun zwei Geschichten die Petrus aus Hildebrands Mund vernommen hat. Die erste bezieht sich nur indirekt auf das Thema des Briefes: In Frankreich sind von einer Synode unter dem Vorsitz von Hildebrand als *apocrisiarius* des Papstes Viktor II. (1055-1057) sechs durch Simonie zum Amt geratene Bischöfe abgesetzt worden (433A-B); einer von ihnen war von Gott gestraft worden mit der Unfähigkeit, die Worte *Spiritus sanctus* auszusprechen. Die zweite bemerkenswerte Geschichte (*insigne*) des *prudentissimus vir* Hildebrand beschreibt wie unrechtmässiger Besitz kirchlichen Gutes bestraft wird: Eine Vision hat aufgedeckt, dass die Angehörigen eines gräflichen Geschlechtes in Deutschland, wie fromm sie selber auch gelebt haben mögen, bis in die zehnte Generation dafür büssen, dass einer der Vorfahren dem heiligen Stephan von Metz ein Grundstück entwendet hat; nach ihrem Tod müssen sie, einander auf einem Leiter folgend, qualvoll in die Hölle hinabsteigen, indem sie jedesmal, wenn der nächste dahingeht eine Stufe hinuntergehen (433B-434A).

Von dieser Geschichte, von Damiani *exemplum* genannt, gibt der Autor selber zu, dass sie etwas ausserhalb der Reihe fällt.[28] Er entschuldigt die Einschiebung aus seiner Zielsetzung heraus, die nicht die Befolgung der strengen Regeln der Komposition, sondern die Dienstbarkeit an der Erbauung (*aedificatio*) der Mitbrüder im Auge hat. Er rechtfertigt die Aufnahme des Exempels an dieser Stelle, indem er auf die Vergessenheit weist, in die es geraten könnte falls es nicht aufgezeichnet würde, und er gibt Argumente für dieses Vorgehen, die zwar bloss locker mit der Sache zusammenhängen, aber seine Entscheidung verständlich machen. Sie sind der alltäglichen Praxis entnommen (wer zum Fischen auszieht, verschmäht deshalb noch nicht ein Stück Wild oder einen Vogel falls der Zufall diese auf seinen Weg führt) und dem Evangelium (auf dem Wege nach dem Hause des Vorstehers der Synagoge, dessen Tochter er auferwecken wollte, hat der Herr dennoch zuvor die Frau geheilt, die blutflüssig war: *Matth.* 9.18 ff.).[29] Trotzdem stellt sich heraus, dass auch dieses Exempel, einmal erzählt, eine Lehre enthält die zur Beweisführung (*ad propositum*) zurückführt: wenn ein so rechtschaffener Graf verdammt wird wegen irgendeines einst von einem Vorfahren entwendeten Kirchenbesitzes, was stehe dann wohl einem Bischof in Aussicht der, obgleich unwürdig, nicht auf den Besitz eines ganzen Bistums verzichtet (434C)?

Dieses Mal wird der Exkurs expressis verbis abgeschlossen (*iam itaque post diverticulum ad propositum revertamur*) und wird die Reihe von Präzedenzfällen tatsächlich mit einem Zehnergruppe fortgeführt. Bei der Besprechung des vierundzwanzigsten Falles stellt sich heraus, dass Damiani daran zweifelt ob, der fragliche zurückgetretene Bischof, Liutulphus von Cagli, die durch Abdikation erworbene Gelegenheit, hinfort zu büssen, auch wirklich ausgenutzt hat (437A). Das veranlasst auszuführen, dass der Mensch für alle seine Freveltaten büssen wird, entweder noch in diesem Leben oder im Jenseits. Dies wird untermauert mit einem Exempel: Ein Mönch des Klosters Clivus Scauri in Rom (dort aufgewachsen als Oblat, dann jedoch in die Welt zurückgekehrt und verheiratet, aber erkrankt und wieder ins Kloster zurückgekommen) wurde auf seinem Sterbebett, wie er den Umstehenden, die es jedoch nicht wahrnehmen konnten, mitteilte, wie aber nachträglich die Striemen, die man auf seinem zerbleuten Körper fand, bewiesen, vom Apostel Andreas und vom Papst Gregor dem Grossen (dem Schutzherrn bezw. dem Stifter des Klosters) ausgepeitscht, so dass er büsste für seine Untaten vor seinem Tode und ihm die Höllenstrafen erspart blieben (437B-438B). Die Lehre aus dieser von zuverlässigen Mitbrüdern vernommenen Geschichte (*quod fida fratrum relatione cognovimus*) wird anhand eines Ereignisses aus derselben Quelle (*ut ibidem didicimus*), das sich gleichfalls im Andreaskloster zugetragen hat, verdeutlicht: Ganz gewiss strafen die Heiligen die die Welt richten werden (*Sap.* 3.7f. und *Matth.* 19.28) Menschen die mit Vernunft ausgestattet sind; denn sie schonen nicht einmal ein *brutum animal*, wie das Schicksal einer trächtigen Hündin zeigt, die tot niederfiel noch bevor sie in der nach dem Stifter des Klosters benannten Krypta aus der Quelle trinken konnte oder ihre Junge auf der steinernen Ruhestatt gebären konnte, auf der der heilige Gregor im Sommer zu ruhen gewohnt war (438B). Die nachträgliche Betrachtung dieses Vorfalles mündet erneut aus in den Gedanken, dass Gott, falls er nicht sofort oder noch in diesem Leben straft, den Sünden auf jeden Fall der ewigen Rache im Jenseits unterwirft (438C).

In dieser Phase der Redaktion von *opusc.* 19[30] hatte Petrus, wie er mitteilt, den Abt Desiderius von Montecassino zu Besuch, einen sehr zuverlässigen Gewährsmann,[31] der ihm etwas erzählt hat, das perfekt zu diesem Zusammenhang passt und deshalb aufgezeichnet wird (*quod ipsa ratio persuadet ut scribam*, 438D). Es folgt die Geschichte eines Mannes Gottes in der Nähe von Neapel, der in einer Nacht zusah, wie eine grosse Menge Heizmaterial von Teufeln herbeigeführt wurde, weil man sich in der Hölle auf die Ankunft des soeben verstorbenen *princeps Capuae* Pandulphus und des *magister militum* von Neapel, Johannes, dessen Tod demnächst erwartet wurde, vorbereitete. Letztgenannter - vergebens vom Eremiten gewarnt - starb tatsächlich kurz darauf, wonach der Vesuv Flammen ausspie (438D-439C). Damit will einerseits untermauert sein, dass Sündern, denen es hier auf der Welt gut geht, Strafe im Jenseits droht, und andrerseits wird, eindringlicher als oben anlässlich der Geschichte der Seelenvögel, angedeutet, dass der Versuv ein Platz ist wo das Höllenfeuer sich oft einen Weg zur Erdoberfläche bahnt (*unde... gehenna frequenter eructat*). Diese zweigliedrige Funktion hat ebenfalls die anschliessend erzählte Anekdote von einem *Salernitanus princeps*, der die Aktivität des Vesuvs zwar richtig interpretierte, nämlich als ein Zeichen dass bald ein sündiger Reicher (*sceleratus dives*) sterben würde, aber nicht erkannte, dass es sich um ihn selbst handelte, und der in der nächsten Nacht in den Armen seiner Geliebten (*dum securus cum meretrice concumberet*) seinen letzten Atem aushauchte. Es folgen darauf noch zwei kurze Erzählungen, die ausschliesslich den Vesuv als Eingangsstelle zur Hölle dokumentieren (ein Priester, der im Messgewand übermutig auf Erkundung ging, ist verschollen: 439D,[32] und ein anderer Priester hörte auf der Reise in der Nähe von Neapel, als Flammen aus dem Vesuv auflderten, seine Mutter die er krank in Beneventum zurückgelassen hatte, wehklagen, und hat nachher festgestellt, dass sie in dieser Stunde gestorben war: 439D-440A).

Möglicherweise verdankt Petrus auch diese vier Erzählungen vom Vesuv ein und demselben Gewährsmann, Desiderius von Montecassino, aber anders als oben im Falle von Humbert und Hildebrand sagt er es nicht aus. Er kehrt zu seinem Thema zurück (*Ut igitur ad superiora redeamus* ..., 440A), führt weitere Präzedenzfälle für die Niederlegung des Amtes an, und bringt ohne weitere Digressionen seine Darlegung zu Ende.

4. Wie gesagt ist *opusc.* 19 in vielen Hinsichten representativ für die Weise, in der Petrus Damiani in seinen Schriften viele Erzählungen von wunderbaren und lehrreichen Ereignissen aus der jüngeren Vergangenheit anwendet.

Erstens wird beim Verwenden dieser Exempel die Zuverlässigkeit der mündlichen Überlieferungen mit den nötigen Gewährleistungen umgeben. Wenn es sich nicht um ihm aus schriftlichen Quellen bekannte Daten[33] oder persönliche Erlebnisse[34] handelt, berichtet Damiani meistens auch an anderen Stellen in seinen Schriften, von wem er eine Geschichte vernommen hat. Manchmal gibt er nur den Status von Gewährsmännern an (*seniores*, *fratres*, ein *abbas*, *diaconus* oder *presbyter*),[35] aber gewöhnlich nennt er auch ihren Namen. Meistens handelt es sich um Klosterbrüder und Geistliche verschiedenen Ranges;[36] Laien fehlen nicht, aber sie haben nur einen bescheidenen Anteil.[37] Die meisten Informanten werden nur einmal genannt. Unter den öfter als zweimal genannten sind Hochstehende auffällig stark vertreten. Oft handelt es sich um Personen aus den Kreisen der von Dressler (1954: 86-174) beschriebenen Reformkurie, wie Alfanus von Salerno, Desiderius von Montecassino (den späteren Victor III.), Hildebrand (den späteren Gregor VII.), Hugo von Cluny, Humbert von Silva Candida, Bischof Rainald von Como und Kardinal Stephan.[38] Die *auctoritas* (*opusc.* 19, 427A) der Gewährsmänner beruht teils auf ihrem Rang,[39] teils auf ihrer *opinio* und *fama* (*opusc.* 34.1, 573D) die aus ihrer Frommheit, Rechtschaffenheit oder Gelehrsamkeit hervorgeht,[40] teils auf ihrer Wahrheitsliebe.[41] Weiter wird in diesem Zusammenhang offenbar Wert gelegt auf Anwesenheit von Zeugen bei der Weitergabe der Erzählungen,[42] sowie auf eine weite Verbreitung des Überlieferten, auf die Tatsache dass es mehr als einen Informant gab oder dass die Geschichte mehrere Male vernommen wurde und dergleichen.[43] Dieses Interesse für Authentifizierung ist nicht eine persönliche Eigenart des Damiani, wenn er auch als Hagiograph und Prediger die Wahrheit ebenfalls hochhält und sorgfältig mit seinen schriftlichen Quellen umgeht (Cantin 1975: 468-83). Auch seine Gewährsmänner nennen ihre Quellen oder verbürgen jedenfalls deren Zuverlässigkeit,[44] und sie melden ob sie etwas mit mehr oder weniger Verbürgung erzählen.[45] Hieraus dürfen wir folgern, dass das sich hier zeigende Bedürfnis nach Verbürgung für die Authentizität der Geschichten kennzeichnend ist für das Milieu, in dem diese zirkuliert haben, und dass auch Damianis Leser Authentifizierung geschätzt haben. Dies war das Mittel, wodurch das mündlich Überlieferte eine ähnliche Glaubwürdigkeit bekommen konnte wie das schriftlich Überlieferte (Bremond-Le Goff 1982: 41s.).

Zweifel an der historische Richtigkeit der Erzählungen oder an der naturwissenschaftliche Plausibilität dessen, was man einander erzählt, begegnen wir nur selten in Damianis Schriften. Er hat vor allem, genau so wie bei der Bibelinterpretation, Interesse am tieferen Sinn, an der Moral oder der Lehre, die in den Erzählungen steckt. Es geht ihm bei den *mirabilia* und den *exempla* nicht in erster Linie um das 'signe', sonder um das 'signifié' (Cantin 1975: 572ff.).[46] Dieser Sinn, diese Lehre und Moral werden denn auch, wie wir gesehen haben, in der Regel explizitiert, vorher oder nachher. Weil dem mündlich Überlieferten die selbstverständliche Autorität der schriftlichen Tradition fehlt, wird neben der Lehre auch der Fundierung der Überlieferung grosse Aufmerksamkeit gewidmet.

Auch der eigenen Ansicht nach ist übrigens für Damiani nicht alles was er schriftlich weitergibt über jeden Zweifel erhaben. Regelmässig bringt er seine Skrupel zum Ausdruck über die Zuverlässigkeit der Geschichten, die er seinen Lesern weitererzählt. Gelegentlich scheint er seinen Gewährsleuten nicht ganz zu vertrauen[47] oder bringt ihn eine Meinungsverschiedenheit über das Überlieferte, wie diejenige zwischen Humbert und Desiderius, in Verlegenheit. Aber in weitaus den meisten Fällen, in denen er einen Vorbehalt macht, handelt es sich um seinen eigenen Wert als Zwischenglied in der Überlieferungskette: Nicht immer hat er genau Notiz genommen von dem was ihm erzählt wurde;[48] viel hat er im Vorbeigehen gehört und dann hat er den Verlauf der Geschehnisse besser behalten als die Namen der Beteiligten.[49] Kurzum, wiederholt entlastet Damiani sein Gewissen mit dem Geständnis, dass er nicht für die absolute Zuverlässigkeit der Geschichten, die er niederschreibt, einstehen kann, und vor allem bezweifelt er, ob er sich auf sein Gedächtnis verlassen kann.[50] In diesem Zusammenhang fällt es auf, dass er so oft berichtet, dass er, was er niederschreibt, vor kurzem[51] oder gar erst beim Verfassen der betreffenden Schrift[52] vernommen hat. So weckt er den Eindruck, dass es seine Absicht war, die Erzählungen, die er hörte und die ihm der Aufzeichnung wert schienen, so schnell wie möglich in seinen Schriften einzuarbeiten, damit sie ihm nicht entfallen und so seinen Lesern vorenthalten blieben würden. Vielleicht finden wir hier die Erklärung der bereits oben bemerkten auffälligen Tatsache, dass *exempla* in Damianis Ausführungen, zwar in der Regel eine argumentative oder persuasive Funktion haben, dass sich namentlich bei den zeitgenössischen Exempeln Ausnahmen finden. Dass Petrus grundsätzlich die Regeln der Argumentationslehre auch für diese Kategorie von *exempla* gelten liess, geht klar hervor aus der Häufigkeit und der Weitläufigkeit, mit der er den Verstoss gegen die Konvention entschuldigt, und aus der Tatsache dass er meistens der Regel folgt. Dass er nur dann die Regel verletzt, wenn es sich um zeitgenössische *exempla* handelt, macht es plausibel, dass dies mit den spezifischen Merkmalen dieser Kategorie in Zusammenhang steht. Deshalb scheint es weniger auf der Hand zu legen, dieses Phänomen ganz Damianis Vorliebe für *disiunctio* (Cantin 1972: 301ff.), dem Vermeiden allzu straffer Kontinuität der Ausarbeitung und Beweisführung, zuzuschreiben. Dort, wo Damiani nicht ordungsmässig verfährt, bringt er öfters die Gefahr der *oblivio* als Grund vor um etwas zu erzählen, obwohl es eigentlich ausserhalb des Rahmens fällt: Das mündlich überlieferte Exempel vergleicht er dann mit irgendeinem Gegenstand, der auf den Wogen eines Stromes davonzuschwimmen droht (*res fluctivaga* oder *fluctivagum quid*) und der mit dem Seil der Schrift (*styli* oder *scriptionis funiculus*) wie an einem Pfahl (*paxillus*) befestigt werden soll damit er nicht verloren geht im Mahlstrom der Vergessenheit.[53] Selbstverständlich könnte hier ein Gemeinplatz vorliegen, aber es scheint doch nicht unberechtigt,

Damianis Worten Glauben beizumessen und daraus zu folgern, dass er es mit den mündlich überlieferten Exempeln in diesem Punkt weniger genau genommen hat, weil er es für wichtiger hielt, sie wie auch niederzuschreiben als dabei die Regeln der Argumentationslehre zu beachten. Dies könnte auch erklären, wieso er, wenn es sich um diese Art *exempla* handelt, so oft seinen Assoziationen nachgibt (Cantin 1972: 307f.) und Gruppen von Anekdoten bietet, die den Gewährsmann oder den Zeitpunkt, an dem sie ihm bekannt geworden sind, den Ort der Handlung, die beteiligte Person oder das Thema gemeinsam haben.[54] Es ist aber durchaus denkbar, dass die etwas lockere Vorstellung der zeitgenössischen Exempel einen Mangel an Struktur jener Gespräche widerspiegelt in denen man sie einander weitererzählte, oder dass sie eine Folge der grossen Vorliebe ist, die man in Damianis Umgebung für sie hatte.

Damiani hat ja viele von den in seiner Umgebung mündlich umlaufenden Exempeln dem bereits in der Literatur verfügbaren Bestand hinzugefügt, indem er sie mit oder ohne Unterbrechung der Argumentationslinie niederschrieb.[55] Ab und zu könnte man den Eindruck bekommen, dass das Niederschreiben von solchen *exempla* für ihn ein Grund an sich gewesen sei, um das eine oder andere Werk zu verfassen, und dass er sich, abgesehen von der Anwendung der *disiunctio*, in einigen Schriften gar nicht um die Argumentationslinie gekümmert hat. Derartige kompositorische Schwächen finden sich jedoch nur selten in Damianis Werk, und dann meistens nur scheinbar (Leclercq 1960: 169; Cantin 1972: 301ff.); vor kurzem z.B. hat man dargelegt dass *opusc. 52, De bono religiosi status*, eine in diesem Zusammenhang wichtige Schrift, mehr ist als die planlose Reihe von (dem Buche der Natur entliehenen) *exempla,* für die man es bisher gehalten hat.[56] Es ist natürlich sehr wohl möglich, dass Damiani ein besonderes Vergnügen am Erzählen lehrreicher Geschichten aus der eigenen Zeit und dem eigenen Milieu hatte - er stört sich tatsächlich oft nicht an der Regel, die die Häufung von *exempla* untersagt (Lumpe 1966: 1245). Es kann aber kein Missverständnis darüber geben, dass er auch einen besonderen Grund gehabt hat, Exempel aus der 'modernen' Zeit zu verwenden. Dieser ist bereits von Leclercq (1960: 204) treffend wiedergegeben: 'les exemples plus rapprochés, dans le temps et l'espace, touchent davantage nos âmes'. Wir begegnen hier wieder der literarisch-rhetorischen Tradition, jetzt in der Form einer Adaption des römischen Unterschieds zwischen *exempla* aus der eigenen nationalen Vergangenheit und denjenigen anderer Herkunft, von denen man die ersteren für wirkungsvoller hielt als die letzteren, die *externa*. In der frühchristlichen Literatur wurde dies umgesetz in die Opposition biblisch-christlich versus heidnisch (Pétré 1961; Lumpe 1966). Damiani explizitiert und benutzt auch die in diesem Gegensatz enthaltenen anderen Aspekte der Nähe. Die Nähe in der Zeit (die dazu veranlassen kann, die Namen der Beteiligten zu verheimlichen)[57] wird genannt als wichtiges Moment für die Wirksamkeit eines Beispiels in *opusc.* 15 (361C): *efficacius ... modernorum cohortantur exempla quam veterum* (man kann diese ja nicht damit abtun dass die Zeiten sich geändert haben). Andere Formen der Nähe (räumlich, qua Milieu oder durch Verwantschaft) werden in Übereinstimmung mit der antiken Tradition (Kapp-Meyer 1939, *passim*) zum Ausdruck gebracht durch die Benutzung von Qualifikationen wie *domesticus* und *vernacu-*

*lus.*[58]

Die ungefähr hundertfünfzig aufgrund mündlicher Überlieferung oder eigener Erfahrung von Damiani aufgezeichneten Geschichten über wunderbare und lehrreiche Ereignisse aus der jüngeren Vergangenheit sind ungleichmässig über das Werk verteilt. Sie fehlen, wie oben bereits angedeutet, in den Predigten - und das ist eine nicht unwichtige Gegebenheit in Zusammenhang mit dem Gewicht das die Pariser Forschungsgruppe dem Vorkommen des Exempels in Predigten in der von ihr vorgeschlagenen Definition beimisst (Bremond-Le Goff 1982: 36ff.). Sie sind weiter auch in den Briefen nicht immer gleich stark vertreten. In den kürzeren (die *epistolae* nach der Einteilung von Gaietano; s. Anm. 1) sind sie in der Regel wenig häufig. In den Traktatbriefen sind sie manchmal zahlreich oder zumindest ziemlich stark repräsentiert, manchmal spärlich vertreten oder ganz abwesend. In den früheren Schriften scheint ihre Frequenz im allgemeinen geringer als in den späteren (Cantin 1975: 323); etwa achtzig Prozent der *exempla* dieser Sorte findet sich in den Werken die aus der Zeit von Petrus' Kardinalat stammen.

Diese bemerkenswerte Streuung muss man wahrscheinlich in Zusammenhang mit Sachen wie Gattung, Thema und intendiertem Publikum sehen sowie mit der dadurch beeinflussten Behandlungsweise des Stoffes und den Ausbeutungsmöglichkeiten dieser Kategorie von *exempla*. Damianis Predigten sind sehr stark biblisch-exegetisch oder hagiographisch orientiert und enthalten kaum Anspielungen auf Aktualitäten (Lucchesi 1975; Leclercq 1960: 161-163).[59] In Zusammenhang mit der von Le Goff vorgetragenen Definition (S.19) ergibt sich dann auch die Frage ob man darin nicht besser von einer bestimmten Art von Predigten als von Predigten im allgemeinen sprechen sollte. Der *Antilogus contra Judaeos* (*opusc.* 2/3) beschränkt sich zielgemäss auf die *testimonia prophetarum* und auf einen einzigen Fall von *ratiocinatio* (ed. Reindel 1983: 99). Die *Disceptatio synodalis* (*opusc.* 4), in der die Beweisführung von formalen Argumenten getragen wird, enthält ebenfalls wenig Erzählungen aus der eigenen Zeit. Im vor allem vom kanonischen Recht genährten *Liber gratissimus* (*opusc.* 6) und dem durch Konfrontation von *rationes* gekennzeichneten Traktat *De divina omnipotentia* (*opusc.* 36) finden sich, trotz des nicht geringen Umfangs, nur wenige. In pastoralen Traktaten jedoch, wie *De eleemosyna* (*opusc.* 9), *De frenanda ira* (*opusc.* 40), *De fide Deo obstricta non fallenda* (*opusc.* 42.1) und *De castitate* (*opusc.* 47, von dem noch die Rede sein wird), sind sie verhältnismässig zahlreich. Dies scheint eine Bestätigung der Auffassung zu sein, dass diese Sorte von *exempla* vor allem in dem Bereich der persuasiven Rhetorik eine wichtige Funktion ausgeübt hat (Bremond-Le Goff 1982: 37). Das nimmt jedoch nicht weg, dass sie bei Damiani auch, sei es weniger oft, die demonstrative Funktion erfüllen, um die es sich in der Argumentationslehre handelt.[60] Schliesslich ist bemerkenswert, dass man den grössten Häufungen zeitgenössischer *exempla* in Brieftraktaten begegnet, die an Papst Nikolaus II. (*opusc.* 19, s. oben), (unter anderem) Hildebrand (*opusc.* 20) und Desiderius von Montecassino (*opusc.* 33 und 34.1) gerichtet sind, das heisst an Repräsentanten des Milieus, zu dem offenbar auch Damianis am meisten genannten Informanten gehören.

Damit berühren wir einen interessanten Punkt. Zweifellos war bei der bislang beschriebenen Verwendungsweise von *exempla* die Rede von einem Weitergehen auf dem von Gregor dem Grossen eingeschlagenen Wege (Le Goff 1981), und spielt dabei der grosse Einfluss, den Gregor auf Petrus Damiani persönlich ausgeübt hat (Leclercq 1960: 172f.), eine nicht zu vernachlässigende Rolle. Aber es ist ebensosehr klar, dass Damiani diesbezüglich ein Milieu repräsentiert, in dem man ein grosses Interesse an solchen Geschichten hatte. Dieses in erster Linie monastische Milieu und seine Mentalität sind in Damianis Werk deutlich greifbar, nicht nur im Stoff von dem die Geschichten handeln, in den genannten Gewährsleuten und den intendierten Lesern,[61] sondern auch in Abschnitten, die zeigen, wie und in welchen Umständen man mit den Erzählungen beschäftigt ist, sie austauscht, sie auf ihren Sinn hin untersucht, und die Autorität der Gewährsleute prüft. Der Kreis, in dem die Anekdoten kursieren, umfasst, wie wir sahen, vor allem Geistliche, aber auch Laien. Das Exempel scheint, wenn wir uns auf Damianis Zeugnis verlassen dürfen, vor allem in informellen Situationen zu funktionieren. Nur in zwei Fällen ist expliziet die Rede von *exempla* die Damiani dadurch kennt dass sie von anderen in einer Predigt verwendet wurden[62]. Viel häufiger erfahren wir von Austausch von Geschichten bei wechselseitigen Besuchen und auf der Reise; sie bieten Stoff zur Diskussion anlässlich aktueller Fragen oder Schriften, an denen man arbeitet, und man befragt einander über die Deutung, die bei Damiani gelegentlich an die Weise erinnert in der die Bibel interpretiert und benutzt wird.[63]

In *opusc.* 47, vom Ende des Jahres 1066 oder Anfang 1067, lässt Petrus seinen Neffen Damianus und uns einen Blick tun in so ein Gespräch, an dem er am Tag zuvor teilgenommen hatte. Ausserdem zeigt der Brief, wie der Kreis, in dem die zeitgenössischen *exempla* kursieren offenbar beim Verfasser Damiani als Faktor in der *inventio*, als ein Auswahlkriterium, eine Rolle spielen kann. Es war Abend (*hesterno jam vespertini temporis elabente crepusculo*, 711B): etwas, das Damiani öfters als erwähnenswert erachtet, wenn er die Situation beschreibt, in der er eine Geschichte vernommen hat; vielleicht deutet es auf eine Funktion dieser Geschichten während Gespräche nach der Abendmahlzeit, eine Art *collationes* (Konferenzen, Lesungen mit Gedankenaustausch: Von Severus 1984).[64] Kaiserin Agnes und Petrus Damiani unterhielten sich bei der fraglichen Gelegenheit über Sachen die dem Seelenheil dienlich waren.[65] Die Kaiserin, immer interessiert an Tugenden aller Art, zeigte ein besonderes Interesse an erlauchte Vorbilder der Keuschheit (*vernantis flosculi*[66] *castitatis*). Sie erzählte (*illa hoc in medium protulit*), wie vor ungefähr einem Jahrhundert eine der Töchter Berengars II. (der im Jahre 966 in Bamberg im Exil starb) sich und ihrer Schwester während der Gefangenschaft die Freier vom Leibe gehalten hatte durch den Gestank von Hühnerfleisch, das sie zwischen ihren Brüsten verfaulen liess (711C-712A).[67] Auch war die Rede von anderen Dingen: Agnes erzählte Damiani an jenem Abend (*eadem mihi tunc venerubilis regina narravit*) von einem in Worms geschehenen Wunder mit einer Hostie, die durch Nachlässigkeit zu lange aufbewahrt und in Fleisch verwandelt war (712B). Damiani selber, der derartigen Geschichten als Verfasser nicht verschmäht, wird wohl tüchtig mitgehalten haben, obwohl er darüber nichts aussagt. Nichts in der Darstellung deutet darauf hin, dass die übrigen in *opusc.*47 vorkommenden Erzählungen ebenfalls bei dieser Gelegenheit ausgetauscht worden sind. Sie entstammen jedoch alle demselben Kreis um Agnes, und Damianis Arbeitsweise in diesem Brief bestätigt sehr schön, was oben über sein Vorgehen beim assoziativ Aneinanderreihen von *exempla* gesagt wurde. Was die Kaiserin an jenem Abend erzählte veranlasst Damiani dazu, an dieser Stelle in seinem Brief eine ähnliche Wundergeschichte aufzuzeichnen, die vom Bischof Rainald in diesem Milieu (*dum adesset*) erzählt worden ist (das in dessen Kirche in Como geschehene Wunder mit dem verschütteten konsekrierten Wein: 712B-D). Hierauf folgt eine Geschichte die Hildebrand laut der Einführung einmal (wahrscheinlich vor dem Jahre 1064) in Anwesenheit von Agnes, Damiani und Rainald erzählt hat (vom einfaltigen Mönch Marinus in Aachen, der sich vom Teufel, der ihm in der Gestalt eines Engels erschienen war einreden liess, dass er mit keinem mehr sprechen dürfe: 713A-C).[68] Die eine Geschichte vom Teufel ruft dann die andere hervor: Damiani lässt folgen, was Agnes vor Jahren von Papst Leo IX. (der ja im Jahre 1054 gestorben war) (*quid praefata regina retulerit audisse ex ore beati Leonis noni Romanae ecclesiae pontificis*) über dessen vom Teufel besuchte Tante vernommen hatte(713C-714B). Damit beschliesst er die Ermahnungen durch *exempla*, den er seinem Neffe vorhält.[69] Er fügt jedoch als Aufmerksamkeit dessen Prior gegenüber noch ein ebenfalls von der Kaiserin Agnes vernommenes Exempel hinzu (*illi conveniens exemplum profero... Nam et eadem Agnes regina quae supra inquit etiam...*), das den Prior zur Gastlichkeit und Freigebigkeit den Armen gegenüber anspornen soll (in Alemannia sah sich ein Mönch auf seinem Sterbebett für Hilfe belohnt, die er, als er noch in der Welt lebte, während der Jagd zwei Frauen in Not geleistet hatte: 714C-715C). Und der Brief werd erst echt beendet nachdem noch eine vom Kaplan der Kaiserin, Stephan, vernommene Geschichte erzählt worden ist (*id quod Stephanus ejusdem reginae capellanus, vir videlicet honestus et prudens, enarravit*), die lehrt, dass eine einzige edle Tat die Waage eines ganzen Lebens in die gute Richtung ausschlagen lassen kann (in Gallicia haben drei Prostituierte auf der Weigerung beharrt, den Sarazenen ihre Dienste zu leisten und sind von Christus in einer Vision gestärkt, den Märtyrertod gestorben, *de meretricibus martyres* geworden, 715C-716C).

5. Zusammenfassend kann man sagen, dass Petrus Damiani über ein umfangreiches und reichschattiertes Arsenal von *exempla* verfügt. Den wichtigsten Anteil darin haben die Exempel von jüdisch-christlicher Herkunft (aus der Bibel, der frühen Kirchengeschichte, den Kirchenvätern, der Hagiographie und den Konzilsakten). Die zeitgenössischen, mündlich überlieferten *exempla* kommen an zweiter Stelle und übersteigen die antiken (die grösstenteils der Historiographie entlehnt zu sein scheinen) zahlenmässig und an Wichtigkeit. Die Verwendung der verschiedenen Kategorien von *exempla* fügt sich in bemerkenswertem Masse den antiken und patristischen literarisch-rhetorischen Konventionen. Dies schafft Einheit in der Verschiedenheit.

Die Verwendung zeitgenössischer Exempel unterscheidet sich auf den ersten Blick ziemlich stark von der der jüdisch-christlichen und antiken. Es stellt sich jedoch heraus, dass die Unterschiede oft zusammenhängen mit spezifischen Merkmalen der zeitgenössischen *exempla*, und manche der Einzelheiten bestätigen dass im Grunde für diese Gruppe dieselben Konventionen gelten als für die übrigen. Die Authentifikation gleicht den Nachteil der mündlichen Überlieferung aus; sie bezweckt dem mündlich Überlieferten dieselbe Autorität zu verleihen, wie sie das schriftlich Dokumentierte durch Tradition besitzt, so dass die einleitend oder abschliessend formulierte Lehre auch tatsächlich die erwünschte Beweis- oder Überzeugungskraft besitzt. Auch bei den zeitgenössischen *exempla* ist Einfügung in eine Beweisführung die Regel, aber, anders als im Falle der antiken und jüdisch-christlichen *exempla* (wo diese Regel keine Ausnahme kennt) werden die zeitgenössischen ziemlich oft ausserhalb der Argumentationsordnung erzählt. Die Tatsache, dass Damiani fast immer selber darauf aufmerksam macht und sich so oft dafür entschuldigt, bestätigt, dass Einschaltung in die Beweisführung auch für diese Kategorie von *exempla* zur literarischen Konvention gehört. Der Verstoss kann die Folge verschiedener Faktoren sein: Petrus selber malt die Gefahr des Vergessens (*oblivio*) aus und beruft sich auf seine Zielsetzung (*aedificatio*), aber auch seine Vorliebe für *disiunctio* und seine damit zusammenhängende Neigung zu einer assoziativen Beweisführung kann im Spiel sein, und schliesslich kann man nicht ganz und gar ausschliessen, dass seine Arbeitsweise in diesem Punkt die Wirklichkeit, in der diese *exempla* funktionierten - in diesem Falle den Verlauf der Gespräche in denen man sie einander erzählte - widerspiegelt.

Damit ist ein wichtiger Punkt angesprochen. Die Anwendung zeitgenössischer *exempla* in Damianis Schriften ist einerseits bestimmt durch verschiedene Aspekte seiner Persönlichkeit (auch als Schriftsteller mit einer gediegenen rhetorischen Schulung und mit Kenntnis der literarischen Tradition). Aber andererseits kann man sie nicht werten, ohne das Milieu, in dem er lebte, in Betracht zu ziehen. In seiner Umgebung spielten derartige Geschichten eine wichtige Rolle: Er nennt seine Gewährsmanner, er erwähnt und beschreibt die Situationen, in denen er die Geschichten, die er aufzeichnet, vernommen hat, und er vermittelt einen Eindruck der Weise, in der man sie in diesem Kreis handhabte. Es scheint lohnenswert, dieses Milieu und seine kollektive Mentalität einer näheren Untersuchung zu unterziehen und es mit anderen zu vergleichen, in denen dieser Typus von *exempla* früher (man denke an Gregor den Grossen) und später (in der Zeit auf die sich die Pariser Forschungsgruppe konzentriert) in den Vordergrund tritt. Die Linie, die von Gregor dem Grossen bis zu Petrus Damiani führt (Le Goff 1981) und später von Damiani zu Helinand von Froidmont (s. Anm. 55), ist nicht nur eine Linie von Autor zu Autor, sondern auch eine von Milieu zu Milieu.

Wenn wir Petrus Damiani in dieser Perspektive als Vorboten späterer Entwicklungen betrachten, ist folgendes auffällig. Das zeitgenössische Exempel beruht in seiner Zeit noch fast ganz auf mündlicher Überlieferung; Damiani ist einer der Begründer der schriftlichen Tradition. Die zeitgenössische Erzählung fehlt ganz und gar in seinen eigenen Predigten, während auch Predigten anderer Leute nur selten von Damiani als Quelle der Kenntnis einer Geschichte genannt werden. Ersteres lässt einsehen, dass, wenn man (nach dem Vorschlag von Le Goff) das Vorkommen in Predigten als Kennzeichen in der Definition des späteren *exemplum* von diesem Typus aufnehmen möchte, beachtet werden soll, dass es sich dabei handelt um einen bestimmten Predigttypus. Das zweite steht im Einklang mit der Tatsache, dass das zeitgenössische *exemplum* in Damianis Milieu oft in vielerlei informellen Situationen zu funktionieren scheint, in denen im Alltag die Fragen zur Sprache kamen, auf die die Erzählungen eine Antwort geben; daneben gibt es Hinweise auf eine besondere Funktion dieser *exempla* in dem auf geistliche Sachen gerichteten Abendgespräch. Die Sphäre, in der die Exempel funktionieren, ist überwiegend, aber nicht ausschliesslich, spirituell-persuasiv. Der Klerus spielt zwar in dem von Damiani skizzierten Milieu eine Hauptrolle im Weitergeben und Interpretieren der Erzählungen, aber Laien von Rang spielen auch eine aktive Rolle, als Gewährsleute und als Gesprächs-teilnehmer; es ist noch nicht die Rede vom späteren Einbahnverkehr.

Schliesslich erhebt sich aufgrund unserer Befunde die Frage, ob man der Geschichte des *exemplum* im Mittelalter gerecht wird, wenn mann, wie die Pariser Forschungsgruppe in ihren Veröffentlichungen zu tun geneigt scheint, den hier vor allem besprochenen Typus als das mittelalterliche Exempel schlechthin bezeichnet und sich dazu verleiten lässt, es zusehr an sich zu betrachten und die anderen Sorten *exempla*, die gleichzeitig daneben weiterkursierten, unberück-sichtigt zu lassen. Auf der einen Seite läuft man damit das Risiko, diesem Typus von *exempla* Merkmale zuzuschreiben, die nicht oder nur in geringerem Masse distinktiv sind (z.B. die Form der Kurzgeschichte), oder über Funktionen hin-wegzugehen, die er auch haben kann (z.B. die demonstrative Funktion),[70] und Zusammenhänge und Wechselwirkungen zwischen der Anwendung unterschied-licher Sorten von *exempla*, wie sie bei Damiani deutlich wahrnehmbar sind, zu übersehen. Auf der anderen Seite droht die Gefahr, dass man allzusehr eine lineare chronologische Entwicklung, eine zeitliche Abfolge von Phasen in der Evolution des mittelalterlichen *exemplum* suggeriert, obwohl wir in Wirklichkeit mit einer bunten Mischung von Tradition und Erneuerung zu tun haben. Im 11. Jahrhundert verwendet Petrus Damiani, als Vertreter eines bestimmten Milieus und einer gelehrten Tradition, *exempla* sehr verschiedener Herkunft, deren Anwendung von einer und derselben literarischen Konvention beherrscht wird. Im 12. Jahrhundert werden Repräsentanten des Schulmilieus, z.B. Petrus Abaelar-dus und Johannes von Salisbury,[71] die Tradition der antiken *exempla* weiterfüh-ren alsob sie keine Ahnung hätten von den zeitgenössischen Exempeln die einer grossen, zur gleichen Zeit vorbereiteten Zukunft entgegen gehen, einer Zukunft die jedoch nicht das Ende der anderen Sorten von *exempla* bedeutet hat.


ANMERKUNGEN


1.    Literatur zum *exemplum* passim in der Bibliographie dieses Bandes. Die Beschränkung auf die Prosaschriften ist eingegeben durch den Wunsch, das Dossier hinsichtlich der repräsentierten Gattungen einigermassen einheitlich zu halten; es sei vor allem hiermit nicht suggeriert, dass *exempla* in Dichtung etwa fehlen würden (s. z.B. Abaelards *Carmen ad*

*Astralabium:* vv. 283ff., 391f., 945ff. und 993ff., ed. Rubingh-Bosscher 1987). Für eine kurze Beschreibung von Damianis Leben und Werk und für eine ausführliche Bibliographie s. Reindel 1983 und Calati 1985. Die Predigten werden nach Lucchesi 1983, die Heiligenleben und Briefe nach Migne PL 144 und 145 zitiert, wenn nicht explizit anders erwähnt. Weil für die Mehrzahl der Briefe noch keine moderne Ausgabe zur Verfügung steht, werden hier der seit der Ausgabe von Constantino Gaietano (1568-1650) eingebürgerte Unterschied zwischen (kürzeren) *epistolae* und (längeren) *opuscula*, wenn auch prinzipiell unrichtig (Reindel 1983: 12 und 30f.), und die herkömmliche Nummerierung dieser Werke aus praktischen Gründen beibehalten (für eine Konkordanz der alten und der nach Vollendung der Ausgabe von Reindel zu bevorzugenden neuen Nummerierung, s. Reindel 1983: 54ff.); in Übereinstimmung mit Reindel ist auf eine Einteilung der Briefe nach Kapiteln verzichtet.

2. *Die Zahl der kurzen Erwähnungen ist ziemlich gross, weil Damiani zweimal eine Reihe von Präzedenzfällen gibt (in opusc.* 23, 474B-C, dreizehn Namen von römischen Kaisern die durch das Schwert ums Leben gekommen sind, und in 56, 816A-817B, siebenunddreissig Fälle von Fürsten und Feldherren, die vom Glück im Stich gelassen worden sind, von denen in dreiunddreissig Fällen kaum mehr als der Name erwähnt wird). Wenn wir Kurzexempel (wie in *opusc.* 12, 258A: *Croesus et Amyclas, diversi quidem possessores, sed non diversas circa haec, quibus fruuntur, exhibent voluntates,* und 13, ed. Brezzi 1943: 308: *nec cum Sardanapalo plumis innatare pensilibus inhiat, qui pervigiles cum Macario noctes ducere in orationibus intentus anhelat*) ausser Betracht lassen, bleiben etwa vierzig antike oder wenigstens über die Antike handelnde *exempla* übrig (ein Beispiel der letztgenannten Kategorie ist die Geschichte vom Tempel des Romulus in *opusc.* 36, ed. Cantin 1972: 458, die vor allem bekannt ist durch die *Mirabilia Romae* 6, ed. Valentini-Zucchetti 1946: 21). Die meisten dieser vierzig füllen nicht mehr als einige Textzeilen aus, und nur sieben erreichen einen Umfang der es rechtfertigt, von einem in die Beweisführung eingeflochtenen narrativen Ganzen zu reden(s. Anm. 70). Anspielungen auf mythologische Gestalten, wie Saturnus, Juppiter und Danaë (die Ausgabe bietet in *epist.* 3.6, 294D-295A, *Diana*) und Ikarus, sind wenig zahlreich.

3. Es handelt sich um den ersten Sieg der Römer in einer Seeschlacht (bei Mylae, 260 v.Chr.), eine *victoria gloriosa quia nova* wie der Sieg des heiligen Alexius (263ss.), sowie die (auch in *opusc.* 48, ed. Reindel 1983: 242ff., sich befindende) Probe des Mutes vom Konsul Marcellus im Kampf gegen die Gallier, der Alexius, *noster iste Marcellus,* gleichkam (300ss.).

4. *Serm.* 2, 50ss. *Quamquam beati Fredelini Vita, in qua haec referri perhibetur historia, in manus nostras nequaquam deuenerit, sed quod hic scriptum est indicio nobis fraternae relationis innotuit; opusc. 19 (435A)*

*sicut veridica fratrum relatione didicimus, qui descriptam ejus* (sc. Arnulphi Mettensis) *se lectitasse testantur historiam*; 34.1 (578B) *Adraldi nempe prudentis et religiosi viri, qui Bremetensi praeminet monasterio, didici relatione quod scribo, quod etiam inditum litteris esse dicebat*; weiter *vita Mauri* 1 (946C) und wahrscheinlich *opusc*. 9 (220D); 19 (426D); 36 (ed. Cantin 1972: 458); 57.1 (823B). In derartigen Fällen scheinen Grenzfälle zwischen 'mode écrit' und 'mode oral' (Bremond-Le Goff: 1982, 41) vorzuliegen, aber die Darstellungsweise ist klar die des 'mode oral'.

5.  Ich habe in den Predigten nur ein auf mündliche Überlieferung beruhendes *miraculum* vorgefunden, das des Schauers der auf wunderbarer Weise einen Brand löscht, der die Abtei von Montecassino bedroht (8, 67ss.). Vielleicht ist es kein Zufall, dass in der Predigt über den heiligen Donatus (38) einer doch erbaulichen Anekdote, die Damiani in Arezzo beim Donatusfest vom Kanzel herab gehört hat, keine Erwähnung getan wird (*opusc*. 34.1, 574D-575C, Einleitung zitiert in Anm. 62).

6.  Antike *exempla* gehen Hand in Hand mit biblisch-christlichen in *epist*. 6.9 (390B-C); 7.3 (437C-438A, 439B-D, 439D-440A); *opusc*. 13 (ed. Brezzi 1943: 328ss.); 18.1 (388C-D); 48 (720B-C). Zeitgenössische Exempel werden mit antiken kombiniert in *opusc*. 56 (816A-818A); mit biblischen in *epist*. 4.7 (ed. Reindel 1983: 145f.), 6.32 (429C-432A), 7.17 (456B-457D), 8.5 (470B-472C), opusc. 34.1 (576C-577D); mit biblischen und frühchristlichen in *epist*. 4.9 (315A-316D), *opusc*. 6 (ed. Von Heinemann 1891: 41ff.), 57.1 (821B-823B); mit biblischen und antiken in *opusc*. 40 (652D-654C); und mit biblischen, frühchristlichen und antiken in *opusc*. 39 (645C-648C).

7.  In *opusc*. 52 (783C) dieselbe Information, nun hinsichtlich des Einhorns (*unicornis*).

8.  Für die *ornatus*-Funktion des antiken *exemplum* s. Lausberg 1960: 699.

9.  Vgl. *epist*. 5.12 (ed. Reindel 1983: 121) *Sed ne argumentationi potius quam solidae veritati videamur insistere, hoc quod proposuimus per sacrae scripturae, non pigeat exempla monstrare; opusc*. 2/3 (ed. Reindel 1983: 99) *Nunc igitur, Iudaee, si tot sacrae scripturae testimonia ad fidem te Christi non attrahunt, si omnium te prophetarum tam perspicua et clara dicta non flectunt, libet adhuc postpositis scilicet prophetarum exemplis sola tecum ratiocinatione contendere...*; (ibid. 101) *Non coloratos rhetoricae facundiae flosculos, non acuta dialecticorum ponere argumenta curavi... Nolui te prolixis argumentorum distinctionibus onerare. Quapropter dum nuda pene tibi scripturarum exempla proposui, velut sagittarum fasciculum in pharetram misi*; 16 (ibid. 367) *Libet nunc... postpositis patrum exemplis cum adversario...propriis assertionibus disputare, ut, qui tam gravi tam multiplici canonum auctoritate*

*confunditur, nostris etiam rationibus probabiliter superetur...*; 38 (642B) *Possemus adhuc nonnulla scripturarum exempla congerere, nec impossibile esset nostris allegationibus egregios catholicae fidei defensores cum suis argumentationibus adhibere...*; 51 (751D) *ubi ratiocinandi copia suppetere desiit, ad sanctorum mox exempla confugimus, ut illis saltem fides habeatur, quorum auctoritas ad probationem cujuscunque negotii incunctanter admittitur.*

10.     *Opusc.* 53 (792D-793C) *Duo ... sunt, quae si vigilanter attendimus, facile violentorum quorumlibet insolentias injuriarumque molestias superamus, praecepta videlicet et exempla, quia et scripturae sanctae nos ad poenitentiam cohortantur, et electi quique quidquid a furiosis diaboli membris inferri potuit aequanimiter pertulerunt. Nam quod divinis admonitionibus et praecedentium exemplis adjuti de profundo nobis illatae tribulationis eripimur, recte in Jeremia propheta de puteo prodeunte signatur... Quid enim funibus nisi praecepta dominica figurantur quae, quia nos in mala operatione positos et convincunt et eripiunt, quasi ligant et trahunt, coarctant et levant ? Sed ne ligatus his funibus, dum trahitur, incidatur, simul etiam panni veteres deponuntur quia, ne divina praecepta nos terreant, antiquorum patrum nos exempla confortant, ut ex eorum nos comparatione facere praesumamus quod ex nostra imbecillitate formidamus...* (diese Interpretation von *Jerem.* 38.1-13 bietet auch Abaelard, *Comm.Rom.*, prol. 22ff., ed. Buytaert 1969: 41). Für die Opposition *exempla/praecepta, verba* vgl. weiter u.a. *epist.* 6.27 (416B) *Cum ergo non modo vetustae legis auctoritas, sed evangelica gratia verborum plagas modo per praecepta modo per exempla commendet...*; 8.3 (467C) *Sed dum veterum congerimus testimonia scripturarum, etiam novi casus apponere non gravemur exemplum, ut saltem ostensa divinae justitiae vindicta <non> praetereat quos mandatorum coelestium cingula non refrenant; opusc.* 6 (ed. Von Heinemann 1891: 40) *ut quod sermone proferimus firmemus exemplo;* 15 (336C) *cum ad perfectionis culmen praecepta quidem moveant, sed exempla compellant;* 17 (386A) *Quod... ille docebat verbis, ad hoc tu... multo deterius invitas exemplis;* 19 (436A) *non me minus exhortatus est verbo quam provocabat exemplo;* 45 (ed. Brezzi 1941: 172) *sed quoniam ad poenarum perferenda tormenta efficacius aedificaverunt martyrizando quam praedicando, postponentes verbum reliquere sequentibus imitationis exemplum;* 47 (711B) *ut apud animum tuum non tam laciniosa loquendi prolixitas quam insignis exempli dignitas convalescat.* - In *epist.* 6.19 (401C-402C) erzählt Damiani, wie er, als er krank war, dank eines Exempels seine Mitbrüder davon abgehalten hat, ihn zu nötigen, Fleisch zu essen.

11.     *Approbare*: *opusc.* 4 (ed. Von Heinemann 1891: 88), cf. *probatio* in 51 (751D, s. Anm. 9); *astruere*: *epist.* 7.18 (459A); *convincere*: *opusc.* 2/3 (ed. Reindel 1983: 80); *corroborare*: *opusc.* 49 (744B); *declarare*: *epist.* 7.4 (442D); *opusc.* 1 (25D); 4 (ed. Von Heinemann 1891: 81, s. Anm. 16); 38

(636D, s. Anm. 16); *demonstrare*: *epist.* 5.12 (ed. Reindel 1983: 121, s. Anm. 4); *firmare*: *opusc.* 6 (ibid. 40, s. Anm. 5); *monstrare*: *epist.* 5.12 (356A); *superare*: opusc. 2/3 (ed. Reindel 1983: 72). Lichtmetaphorik in *serm.* 37.174 *ut exemplo facilius possit elucere quod dicimus; opusc.* 2/3 (ed. Reindel 1983: 88) *post tam perspicuam exemplorum lucem*; 19 (435A) *ignorantiae nostrae tenebras per exempli sui radios abigit et nostris allegationibus inexpugnabiliter robur attribuit.*

12.   *Aedificare: opusc.* 33 (570B), 45 (ed. Brezzei 1941: 172, s. Anm. 10); *ae-dificatio* in Zusammenhang mit *exemplum* (u.a. der Ausdruck *aedificationis exemplum*) *serm.* 14, 248f.; 28, 4f.; 32, 195; *opusc.* 19 (434A-B, s. Anm. 29); 20 (448C); 34.1 (581C, s. Anm. 50); 56 (811D und 813B); 57.1 (813B und 825A, s. Anm. 50); 57.2 (828B, s. Anm. 48); *caveri epist.* 4.7 (ed. Reindel 1983: 146); *cohortari*: *serm.* 50,35f.; *opusc.* 15 (361C); 19 (431D); 49 (724D); *compellere*: 15 (336C, s. Anm. 5); *compescere*: 36 (ed. Cantin 1972: 466); *confortare*: 53 (793B, s. Anm. 10); *consolatio* 36 (ed. Cantin 1972: 484); *delectare*: 47 (714C, s. Anm. 69); *incitare*: *serm.*49, 26; 50, 25f.; *invitare*: *opusc.* 17 (386A, s. Anm. 10); *provocare*: *epist.* 8.5 (471C); *serm.* 15, 63f.; *vita Romualdi* 15 und 27 (ed. Tabacco 1957: 37, 56); *opusc.* 19 (436A, s. Anm. 10); 56 (815A).

13.   *Opusc.* 11 (240A) *Quod si quis adhuc his etiam nostris disputationibus calumniator exstiterit,... ut non tam verbis quam rationibus acquiescat, exemplum damus quod ex sacri eloquii auctoritate didicimus.* S. auch einige der in Anm. 9 zitierten Passus.

14.   Dies ergibt sich aus einer kritischen Randbemerkung (*si tamen rei fides est adhibenda quae dicitur*) in *serm.* 34, 46f. anlässlich Informationen aus der *Passio Florae et Lucillae* (BHL 5017).

15.   Forma: *epist.* 2.12 (282B) *ut exemplum praebeat...; formam ... praebens*; 5.2 (342C-B) *quatenus... formam... exprimeret ... et... praebere posset exemplum; serm.* 33, 285s. *tam egregii praeliatoris imitemur exemplum, istius formam*; 64, 147ff. *quatinus ... subeundi martyrii ceteris praeberet exemplum...;... secuturis martyribus esset constantiae forma; opusc.* 12 (289A) *alter... teres forma coenobitarum, alter imitandum eremiticae conversationis exemplum*; 57.2 (829B-C) *quid aliud quam nostri redempto-ris imitabatur exemplum ? ... ut rex angelorum formam daret rectoribus hominum*; norma: *serm.* 42, 32ff. *quatinus quisquis sacris altaribus appro-pinquat, apostolicae sibimet rectitudinis exempla proponat... Et quid mirum, si nos...beatorum apostolorum... iubeamur imitari normam...? opusc.* 6 (ed. Von Heinemann 1891: 22) *sancta aecclesia ab ipso suo capite huius normam institutionis arripuit... Immo, cur ad accipiendum sacerdotale fastigium dominicae aetatis adhiberetur exemplum...?* speculum: *opusc.* 57.2 (830C) *Hunc tibi... quasi speculum statue aliorumque tibi... exempla propone.*

16. Testimonium: *epist.* 8.3 (467C, s. Anm. 10) ; *opusc.* 2/3 (ed. Reindel 1983: 69) *si cuncta, quae nobis ex tuis libris* (d.h. aus dem Alten Testament) *testimonia suppetunt, ad hoc affirmandum colligere volumus, prius forsitan lingua fatiscente deficimus quam exemplorum copia careamus*; (ibid. 88) *qui post tam perspicuam exemplorum lucem adhuc testimoniis indiget, restat, ut ad contemplandum radiantem ei in meridie solem lucernae lumen efflagitet*; (ibid. 99, s. Anm. 9); 4 (ed. Von Heinemann 1891: 81ff.) *Ea, quae proposuisti, scripturae declarentur exemplis... Recte plane cuncta, quae proposueras, perspicuis roborasti testimoniis scripturarum*; 16 (ed. Reindel 1983: 364) *si cuncta sacrae scripturae testimonia, quae huic assertioni congrua reperiuntur, tentaremus apponere, ante fortasse dies quam exemplorum copia numerosa deficeret*; 38 (636D) *nec res testimoniis indiget, cum hoc ipsum et ea quae supra posuimus evidenter exempla declarent*; 42 (678D) *Sed jam ab his supersedendum est, ne, dum propositionem nostram pluribus nitimur scripturarum testimoniis allegare, videamur in epistolari compendio lacinias texere. His igitur tantisper instructus exemplis diligenter attende...* Sententia: *epist.* 1.13 (222A-B) *Possemus et alia quamplurima catholicorum patrum exempla congerere* (im Vorangehenden sind päpstliche Aussagen buchstäblich zitiert worden), *nisi perspicue cognosceremus nequaquam hoc epistolari compendio convenire. His itaque sanctorum pontificum aliisque sententiis manifeste convinceris...*; 8.8 (481D) *Idcirco autem... non tam mea verba quam sacri eloquii tibi exempla propono, ut... prudentia vestra... vel sanctorum testimonia divinitus inspirata non dedignetur audire. Has igitur... pluresque alias sacrae scripturae sententias intra mentis tuae armarium collige...; opusc.* 6 (ed. Von Heinemann 1891: 68) *Ne quis autem nos involuti voluminis arguat, dum admisceri his prolixiora canonum fortassis exempla conqueritur, hanc noverit procul dubio causam, quia nimirum hos, cum quibus agimus, ad inspiciendos sacros canones sepissime suadendo vel exhortando compellere non valemus. Atque idcirco hic adponendas sanctorum patrum sententias ducimus, ut...* (auch *opusc.* 24, 482C, sieht Damiani ein, dass er eigentlich recht ausführlich - in diesem Falle aus Augustin - zitiert: *Nimius fortasse fuerim in protelando beati hujus doctoris exemplo*); 22 (469C) *Sic, juxta scripturae sententiam* (Iudic. 9.15), *egressus est ignis de rhamno, et devoravit cedrum Libani. Sed et per hoc exemplum, quod nunc de scriptura posuimus, illud etiam non inconvenienter occurrit, quod ibidem in libro Judicum positum memoramus...* Dictum: *opusc.* 2/3 (ed. Reindel 1983: 99, s. Anm. 9). Schöne Beispiele für die Bedeutungen 'Auffassung' und 'Präzedens' in *opusc.* 8.2 (205D) bezw. 4 (ed. Von Heinemann 1891: 79).

17. *Epist.* 2.19 (ed. Reindel 1983, 138) *Nam et ipsum mei capitis oculum non video, per quem video, utilitate tamen ministerii eius nichilominus fruor; et quia oculus mihi in proferendis exempli verbis occurrit, tu mihi in hac parte sis oculus...; serm.* 37, 174ff. *Et ut exemplo facilius possit elucere quod dicimus, numquid... qui hoc anno auenam siue lolium seminauerat,*

*tritico se replere modo cellarium sperat ? opusc.* 1 (25C-26A) *Quod quia
... manifestis comprehendi nequit indiciis, a catholicis saepe doctoribus
visibilium rerum declaratur exemplis... Ecce iterum aliud praebet* (sc.
Augustinus) *exemplum: In sole calor et splendor in uno radio sunt, sed
calor exsiccat, splendor illuminat... 16* (ed. Reindel 1983: 350)
*Quapropter post illam summae auctoritatis epistolam hoc etiam
opusculum suscipe... quatinus illa ac si validus vomer... pectoris arva
proscindat. Hoc quasi vilis sarculus subsequens glebas frangat, immo ut
exemplum congruentius proferatur, hoc velut orator manifesti criminis
reos esse convincat, quos illa auctoritas velut arbiter praesidens canonici
vigoris censura coerceat.*

18. *Opusc.* 2/3 (ed. Reindel 1983: 92) *Tunc ... mandata legalia veraciter
adimplentur, cum iuxta spiritalem intelligentiam ad quam instituta sunt,
fiunt. Nam tunc erant vacua, umbra scilicet et imago rei, non ipsa res,
cum carnaliter servabantur. Vis audire, quomodo erant vacua et vana, et
non veritas ipsa, sed veritatis exempla ? ... Quod... Moyses vidit in
monte, sancta aecclesia est, ipsa rei veritas est. Tabernaculum autem
illud... umbra et imago eiusdem aecclesiae est, ad cuius exemplum factum
est. Est scilicet homo ad cuius imaginem fit sigillum, sed in comparatione
vicaria, homo quidem res et veritas dicitur, cum sigillum similitudo
tantum rei et forma videatur.*

19. Für *exemplum*-'illustrative Geschichte (aus der Gegenwart)' s. z.B. *epist.*
1.21 (253A und 254A); 4.7 (306C); 6.32 (430A); *opusc.* 19 (433C); 47
(714C); 57.2 (827D). Muster der Formeln mit denen Damiani Exempel
einleitet oder abschliesst, findet man u.a. in den Anm. 23, 25, 28, 42, 44,
45, 62 und 65. Für *casus* s. epist. 8.3 (467C, zitiert in Anm. 10) und
*opusc.* 51 (761C) *terribilem nihilominus et alterius monachi casum praete-
reundum esse,* wo *casus* übrigens auch geleichbedeutend sein kan mit
*lapsus*); *gesta: opusc.* 6 (ed. Von Heinemann 1891: 66) *ne tamen res adhuc
in dubium pendeat, si et gestorum quoque auctoritas non accedat, de
aecclesiastica hystoria prebeamus exemplum...;* 16 (ed. Reindel 1983: 369)
*cuncta exempla veterum, omnia gesta patrum;* historia: *epist.* 6.20 (404A)
*audisti, frater, historiam; esto providus ad cautelam; opusc.* 33 (567A, s.
Anm. 50); miraculum: *epist.* 2.12 (280D) *miraculum celebri memoria dignum
sibi dudum contigisse narravit; opusc.* 19 (429B, s. Anm. 25); signum:
*epist.* 8.5 (471C) *ut ad explendum quod bene coepisti non exhortatio sola
verborum sed et ostensum divinae virtutis te provocet signum.*

20. In Kapitelüberschriften in Werken in denen Damiani bezeugt, diese selber
angebracht zu haben (*opusc.* 50: 750C und 51: 764A) kommt die Bezeich-
nung *exemplum* nicht vor. In den Überschriften von anderen Werken
findet man dagegen Formulierungen, die einen stark erinnern an jene in
späteren Exempelsammlungen, die aber weit entfernt sind von Damianis
Wortgebrauch: *exemplum de* (562B), *exemplum* mit dem Namen der betei-

ligten Person (573D *Arnaldi*, 574D *Tedaldi*, 727A *Zeuxidis*) und der Typus *exemplum mulieris quae...*, der den Inhalt kurz zusammenfasst (568B, 575C, 816B en 817B). Nur die Überschrift *terribile exemplum cujusdam hominis desperati ac interficientis seipsum* (582A) erinnert an Petrus' Formulierung *sic itaque per Pharulphi monachum deludentis exemplum deterioris evasi confusionis opprobrium* (epist. 6.19, 402C).

21. Damiani nennt ihn unter Vorbehalt (laut der Ausgabe von Migne) Bischof von Capri (*qui ..., si recte teneo, Capraeis praeerat*: 428A); bei Helinand von Froidmont (s. Anm. 55) handelt es sich um einen *episcopus Capuanus* (PL 212, 935C-D).

22. *Sed quoniam personae istae, Desiderius videlicet et Humbertus, tantae auctoritatis sint ut neutri eorum fides debeat denegari, ego quoque, quod scripsi, procaciter non affirmo, sed utrum verum sit necne,legentium inquisitioni relinquendum esse decerno* (428A). - Für die Sonntagsruhe für Seelen in Hölle und Fegefeuer und für die Lokalisierung des Eingangs zur Hölle bei Vulkanen s. Deneke 1987: 330. Auf den Vesuv als Höllenmündung kommt Damiani in *opusc.* 19 noch zurück (439D); vgl. auch epist. 1.21 (248D) und *Vita Odilonis* 935C-937A (übereinstimmend mit *opusc.* 9, 220C-D).

23. Wie sich aus den einleitenden Worten ergibt (*ut igitur illud inferam, propter quod ista praemisi...*, 428A).

24. Der Esel als *animal luxuriosum* (Bezug nehmend auf *Ezech.* 23.30) und der Bär als *figura* der *carnalitas* (weil *a physicis traditur* [s. z.B. Plin. *nat.* 8.54. 126f.], dass die Bärin ein Fleischklümpchen gebärt, das sie darauf leckend zu einem Bärenjung formt; s. auch *opusc.* 52, 784B).

25. *Sed quia hoc triste* (das Los Benedikts IX.) *praetulimus, aliud pietatis divinae miraculum, quod nimirum laetos habuit exitus, ex ejusdem Humberti narrationibus subnectamus* (429B).

26. Wörtlich nach Epiphanius-Cassiodorus, *Hist. eccles. tripart.* 12.8.21-27 (CSEL 71, 675f.).

27. Unter anderem an Hildebrand ist *opusc.* 20 gerichtet, das hinsichtlich des Themas und teilweise auch hinsichtlich des Inhalts mit *opusc.* 19 verwandt ist. Damiani nennt darin Hildebrand seinen *blandus tyrannus* und *sanctus satanas*, beschenkt mit einer *Neroniana pietas* (444A-B).

28. *Porro autem, quia prudentissimi illius viri semel incidit mentio, aliud etiam insigne quod retulit, etiam si non magnopere ad propositum thema pertineat, non silebo. Nam dum de praediis ecclesiarum injuste possessis,*

*sub praesentiae vestrae conspectu, venerande papa, in Aretina conciona-*
*retur ecclesia, intulit congruenter exemplum...* (433B-C); s. auch Anm. 29.

29.    434A-B: *Quia igitur nos non tam districtae scribentium regulae quam*
    *aedificationi fraternae cupimus deservire, rem veluti ab intentione propo-*
    *siti operis extraneam apposuimus; ut quodammodo fluctivagum quid, ne*
    *oblivio funditus raperet, styli funiculo stringeremus. Nam cum quis pisca-*
    *turus egreditur, si casus attulerit feram repente vel volucrem, capit,*
    *etiamsi nil de venatione vel aucupio proposuerit. Praeterea, ut nostris*
    *assertionibus etiam evangelica non desit auctoritas, Salvator noster cum*
    *domum principis synagogae, filiam ejus resuscitaturus aggreditur, mulieri*
    *fluxum sanguinis patienti, velut absque ea quam coeperat, intentione*
    *medetur. Quid igitur mirum, si scribentes aliquando quod coeptum est*
    *intermittimus, nec omittimus; illud videlicet inserentes, quod nihilominus*
    *ad aedificationem pertinere sentimus?*

30.    *Porro dum styli hujus exaro dictator articulum, ecce Desiderius religiosus*
    *Casinensis monasterii abbas accedit* (438D); vielleicht handelt es sich um
    den Besuch, wobei es zu einer Meinungsverschiedenheit kam in Bezug auf
    die Vögel bei Puteoli. - Für die Praxis des Schreibens, u.a. die Verwen-
    dung von *notarii* s. Leclercq 1960: 151-57, und Cantin 1975: 325-35.

31.    Mit dem Propheten Daniel ist Desiderius durch seinen Namen verwandt
    (vgl. *Dan.* 9.23 et al.: *vir desideriorum*) wie durch seine Wahrheitsliebe
    (*sicut beato Danieli cognatione jungitur nominis, sic eum ab illo non*
    *separat assertio veritatis,* 438D). Für Petrus' Verbindung mit Desiderius s.
    u.a. Leclercq 1960: 135-38, und Cantin 1972: 49-63.

32.    Dies erinnert mutatis mutandis an das Schicksal von Plinius dem Älteren
    am 24. August des Jahres 79: Plin. *epist.* 6.16.

33.    Was die Präzedenzfälle aus früherer Zeit anbelangt, wird in *opusc.* 19 oft
    angegeben, dass sie schriftlichen Quellen entnommen sind (424C, 425C,
    426A, 427A, 430C, 434C, 436A, 436B, 440D; vielleicht bezieht sich auch
    der Ausdruck *antiqua traditio,* 425A, auf schriftliche Überlieferung). Weil
    Damiani es normalerweise andeutet, wenn er durch mündliche Überliefe-
    rung Kenntnis hat von literarischen Traditionen (s. Anm. 4) und bei
    mündlich erworbener Information fast immer seine Gewährsmänner nennt
    (in *opusc.* 19 z.B. 426D, 435A), indiziert die Weise, in der er über A-
    thanasius, Valerius von Hippo, Martinus von Tours (424B, 425B, 440B-C)
    und andere redet, dass er diesbezüglich aus schriftlichen Quellen schöpft.

34.    In *opusc.* 19 z.B. 425B, 435D, 436C, 437A-B, 441B. Für persönliche Er-
    fahrungen in anderen Werken s. u.a. *epist.* 4.7 (ed. Reindel 1983: 149f.);
    6.32 (430A-432A); *opusc.* 13 (ed. Brezzi 1943: 274ff. und 304ff.); 18.2
    (409B-D); 20 (454B-455A); 34.1 (575C-576B und 581D-582A); 40 653B-

654A); 42.1 (668D-669D, 670D-671D und 672B-673D;) 45 (ed. Brezzi 1943: 188); 50 (742D-744B); 53 (793D-796A); 54 (798B-D) = 55 (804D-805B).

35. *Epist.* 1.20 (243C); 6.5 (385A); 6.32 (429A); *opusc.* 10 (ed. Reindel 1983: 166); 19 (435A en 437B); 20 (451B); 36 (ed. Cantin 1972: 462); 52 (782B).

36. S. passim in diesem Beitrag und Leclercq 1960: 204f.

37. *Epist.* 6.25 (413C) *Rainerius iudex, vir ... insignis et facundiae lepore conspicuus*; 8.2 (465B) *excellentissimus dux Gothifredus; opusc.* 9 (218 D) *Berardus marchio*; (220D) *Gothfredus ... clarissimus dux et marchio*; 33 (568C) *Atto piae memoriae Auximanus cives, prudens ... et honestus vir*; 42.1 (671D) *Guarimpotus senex, vir ... honestissimus, apprime litteris eruditus ac medicus*; 43 (681D) *Petrus de Burgo, vir ... clarissimus*; 47 (711B, 712B, 713C und 714C) *imperatrix Agnes, olim ... aureo quidem diademate coronata, nunc autem multo felicius et incomparabiliter eminentius in regis aeterni thalamo collocata* (für Agnes s. auch infra); 57.1 (823B) *comes Ubaldus, vir ... disertus ac prudens*.

38. Alfanus: *epist.* 8.5 (471C: *vir ... verax ac prudens*); *opusc.* 40 (656A-657A, drei Anekdoten); Desiderius: *epist.* 8.5 (472); *opusc.* 19); 40 (656A: *religiosissimus ac veracissimus*); Hildebrand: *opusc.* 19; 20 (446C-447C, zwei Erzählungen); 47 (713A); Hugo: *opusc.* 9 (220B-D, zwei Geschichten); 34.1 (582A und D, ebenfalls zwei); Humbert: *opusc.* 19; Rainald: *opusc.* 34.2 (587C-590A, drei Erzählungen) 47 (712B: *veridicus enarrator*, s. Anm. 65); Stephan: *opusc.* 19 (426D); 33 (562B: *vir religiosus et prudens*, und 564B).

39. *Epist.* 8.3 (467C) *ex ore ipsius Alexandri venerabilis papae; opusc.* 20 (447B); 47 (713C).

40. Beispiele in den Anmerkungen 37 und 38.

41. Beispiele in den Anmerkungen 31 und 38.

42. *Opusc.* 6 (ed. Von Heinemann 1891: 41): *Rozo namque, qui dicitur magister cantorum, Florentinae aecclesiae diaconus, vir adprime litteralibus studiis eruditus, in magno clericorum suorum conventu, presente quoque reverentissimo domino Gerhardo suo episcopo* (der spätere Papst Nikolaus II.), *hoc mihi per ordinem retulit ...*; 19 (433B, s. Anm. 28); 34.1 (573B); 34.2 (586B); 47 (712B und 713A).

43. *Opusc.* 9 (217C) *referri frequenter audivi*; (218A) *celebri solet redolere memoria*; (218D) *quod ... saepius referebat*; 33 (567C) *mihi saepe narravit*; 34.1 (573C) *Stephano Romano pontifici, me praesente, sub jurejurando saepe testatus est*; (582D) *quod nunc dicturus sum, et ex relatione jam dicti Cluniacensis abbatis* (sc. Hugo), *et ex ore illius cui res ipsa conti-*

*gerat, frequentius audivi*; 36 (ed. Cantin 1972: 458) *celebri fama vulgatur*; 40 (655A) *celebri ... relatione vulgatur*; (656B) *idem Salernitanae rector ecclesiae* (sc. Alfanus) et ... *Casinensis monasterii abbas Desiderius uno mihi, ut ita loquar, ore dixerunt*; 57.2 (830B) *celebri redolere memoria frequenter audivimus.*

44.  *Epist.* 6.25 (414B) *hoc se certis quorundam relationibus didicisse narravit*; 6.29 (420D) *certa se relatione didicisse narravit; opusc.* 20 (446D) *ut enim te retulisse memini, haec tibi ... Novariensis Ecclesiae narravit episcopus*; (447B) *beato Leone sedis apostolicae praesule referente cognoveras*; 33 (567C) *quod ipse ... fratrum a Comani lacus confinio venientium relatione cognovit*; 34.2 (587C) *quod ... ab Humberto venerabili sanctae Ruffinae quondam episcopo se didicisse perhibuit*; 47 (713C) s. infra; (715C) *ait enim quod Stedelandus imperator Galliciae retulit ...*

45.  *Opusc.* 33 (564B) *Idem ... aliud mihi retulit, quod tamen non adeo certum tenebat, sicut aliud, quod supra digessimus*; 34.2 (590A) *Ignorabat tamen hujus rei relator episcopus utrum ille frater* (der von der heiligen Jungfrau vor Gottes Richterstuhl freiplädiert worden war) *ad nos reversus, an aliis in hac vita degentibus ista retulerit.* Vgl. auch *epist.* 8.5 (471D); *vita Mauri* 1 (946B-C).

46.  Neben der Meinungsverschiedenheit zwischen Desiderius und Humbert, die in *opusc.* 19 ans Licht kommt (s. supra), ist in diesem Zusammenhang Damianis eigener Vorbehalt angesichts Daten aus der hagiographischen Literatur bemerkenswert (s. Anm. 14). Bedürfnis nach experimenteller Verifikation zeigt *epist.* 1.16 (236D-237A), wo Damiani bemerkt, dass es ihm nicht bekannt ist ob Jäger bestätigen können, was von den *naturarum rimatores* über das Benehmen des Bibers überliefert wird (dass dieser nämlich, erkennend dass man ihn jagt wegen der Heilkraft seiner Testikel, sich deren entledigt und sich aufrichtet um zu zeigen, dass es zwecklos ist, ihn weiter zu jagen; s. auch *opusc.* 52, 769C-D).

47.  Z.B. *epist.* 6.7 (420B); *opusc.* 10 (ed. Reindel 1983: 167); 33 (572B, s. Anm. 50); 34.1 (581C); 36 (ed. Cantin 1972: 458).

48.  *Opusc.* 57.2 (828B) *scribere nonnulla possumus, quae forent aedificationi procerum profutura; sed quia, dum nobis dicerentur, singula gestorum verba notare negleximus, ne, quod absit, aliquo fallamur in verbo, scribenda haec aliis delegamus.*

49.  *Opusc.* 20 (449B) *Idcirco autem nomina hominum non appono, quoniam ordo peractae rei facilius haesit animo; nomina vero, curis aliis intervenientibus, fateor, intercepit oblivio. Nec magnopere curamus videri aucupes nominum, dummodo non excidat series et ordo gestorum; quamquam et haec eadem gesta, quae scribimus, quia in transitu audire nos contigit,*

*utrum inoffensam fidei lineam teneant, certum per omnia non habemus. Ne igitur sine nominibus digesta narratio nares fastidiosis lectoribus contrahat, a talibus interim supersedeo...* Obwohl also die Leser offenbar Wert legten auf die Erwähnung der Namen der an diesen Geschichten Beteiligten, sind Redewendungen wie *cuius me ad praesens vocabulum fugit* in der Tat keine Ausnahme (*opusc.* 9, 424D; 20, 445A; 33, 562C; 40, 656B; 57.2, 829D). Es gab übrigens noch einen anderen Grund keinen Namen zu nennen; s. unten, Anm. 57.

50.     *Opusc.* 33 (566A) *nisi me fallat obliviosa memoria, fideliter narro; (567A) Non ... fortassis hanc, sed hujusmodi ... narravit historiam, cujus etsi prae oblivione verba non teneo, saltem in quantum mihi possibile est a relatis quadam similitudine non recedo. Confessionis igitur iste versiculus ad relata vel referenda mihi cuncta proficiat; meque in quibus ignoranter oberro, coram supernis obtutibus excusabilem reddat; (572B) Haec omnia, venerabilis pater, non sine magno timore describimus, ne vel per oblivionem propriam vel per infidae relationis audaciam a veritatis linea quantumlibet declinemus. Quamobrem haec nos non constanter astruimus; sed quia velut sub hoc relationis ordine ad nostram fuerint perlata notitiam, opinamur;* 34.1 (581C) *Haec ego, venerabilis pater, et alia quamplurima non sine magnae formidinis angore conscribo; ne videlicet vel relatores mei merae veritatis semitam non tenuerint, vel ipse quoque relationum in quolibet immemor oblivione deliquerim. Verum tamen teste conscientia non haec mentiendi voto sed aedificationis affectu, prout melius possum narrata recolere, satago schedulis adnotare. Si quid mihi tamen in his oblivionis obrepsit, ... divina mihi pietas tuis orationibus in memoriam revocet ac digne lugere permittat;* 57.1 (824D-825A) *Hoc autem ego non ut constanter verum fuisse perhibeam retuli; sed quod mihi cursorio sermone relatum est, in quantum non intercepit oblivio, praelibavi. Verum tamen nunquam hoc usque ad nos antiquitas fama vulgante transmitteret, si non ad aedificationis exemplum prodesse posteris credidisset.* In Einklang mit seinem ständigen Appell an die *oblivio* sind Klauseln wie *si rite teneo* (*epist.* 4.7, ed. Reindel 1983: 147; *opusc.* 9, 218C; 18.2, 409C; 19, 428A, s. Anm. 21; 34.1 573A; 36, ed. Cantin 1972: 462; 42.1, 669A; 45, ed. Brezzi 1943: 184; 57.2 828A); vgl. auch das Vergessen von Namen (Anm. 49).

51.     Zum Beispiel *nuper* (*epist.* 4.7, ed. Reindel 1983: 146; 6.25, 413C - vgl. 414A; *opusc.* 10, ed. Reindel 1983: 164; 34.2, 586B; 40, 656A; 43,681D); *necdum tres menses elapsi sunt* (*vita Rodulphi,* 1020C); *necdum emenso, ut ita loquar, mense* (*opusc.* 52, 789C); *vix ante sex dies* (*vita Rodulphi,* 1017C = *opusc.* 50, 747C); *ante quintum fere diem* (*opusc.* 33, 562B); *pridie post vesperam* (*epist.* 8.3, 467C); *hesterna relatione* (*epist.* 4.8, 309D); *hesterno die* (8.10, 483C); *hesterno jam vespertini temporis elabente crepusculo* (*opusc.* 47, 711B). Wo von schriftlichen Quellen die Rede ist, findet man eine solche Mitteilung über jüngst erfolgte Kennt-

nisnahme nur äusserst selten (so wird in *opusc.* 20, 453C, auf eine Hieronymusstelle verwiesen die Damiani noch vor weniger als eine Stunde gelesen hatte).

52.  *Epist.* 6.29 (420A) *dum haec coram eo scriberem*; für *opusc.* 19 (438D) s. Anm. 30.

53.  Vgl. *opusc.* 19 (434A-B, zitiert in Anm. 29); 20 (446C) *quanquam non magnopere hujus videatur esse negotii, quod versatur in manibus, tamen dum quomodolibet hoc apicibus tradimus, ne vorago funditus oblivionis absorbeat, quasi rem fluctivagam paxillulis alligamus*; 51 (762A) *Hoc autem et si praesenti stylo usquequaque non congruat, idcirco tamen inter haec apicibus mandare curavimus, ut rem memorabilem, ne oblivio tolleret, quasi ad paxillum funiculo stringeremus...* Der Ausdruck *funiculus scriptionis* in *epist.* 6.20 (403A).

54.  Gewährsmänner: *epist.* 6.29 9420A-D); 7.17 (456C-D); 8.10 (483C-484D); *opusc.* 19 (s. supra und Anmerkungen 25 und 28); 34.1 (578B-579D); 34.2 (585B); 47; Gelegenheit, bei der das Exempel vernommen wurde: *epist.* 6.25 (414A) und *opusc.* 47 (s. infra; Handlungsort: *epist.* 6.32 (430A-432A); *opusc.* 19; 20 (452D); beteiligte Personen: *epist.* 8.5 (472C-473B), *opusc.* 10 (229A-230A), 33(570B-572B), 57.2 (827D-830C); Thema und Tendenz: *opusc.* 19 (s. supra; 20 (447D-449A, 449C-450D und 452A); 47 (s. infra); 50 (743D-744D); 51 (761A-762D); 52 (789B-790B).

55.  Die Erforschung der Rezeptionsgeschichte dieser *exempla* könnte nicht nur einen Beitrag zur Kenntnis der Wirkung von Damianis Schriften leisten, sondern auch zu einer besseren Sicht auf die späteren Milieus, in denen dieser Typus von *exempla* eine bleibende Funktion erfüllte. In Anbetracht des mächtigen Aufschwungs, den die Verwendung von *exempla* dieser Kategorie seit dem Ende des 12. Jahrhunderts genommen hat, wird es wohl kein Zufall sein, dass insoweit bis jetzt bekannt (Welter 1927: 32, Anm. 51, und 111ff.) namentlich die zeitgenössischen Exempel Damianis rezipiert worden sind und dass der Rezeptionsprozess mit Helinand von Froidmont (c. 1160-nach 1229) in eine entscheidende Phase getreten ist, der mehr als vierzig deren in seine Predigten und vor allem in sein *Chronicon* (PL 212, 774AB, 935C-936B, 951C-952A, 952D-953A und 964D-975B) aufgenommen hat, aus dem sie ihren Weg ins einflussreiche *Speculum Historiale* des Vinzenz von Beauvais gefunden haben (23.75, 25.21, 25.35 und 25.52-64 in der Ausgabe Douai 1624, anast. Graz 1965). Der Weg, über den Helinand Damianis *exempla* kennengelernt hat wird von M.M. Woesthuis (Fachgruppe Mediaevistiek, Rijksuniversiteit Groningen) untersucht.

56. Als Beispiele von Briefen in denen die grosse Zahl der *exempla* die Ausführung versanden zu lassen scheint können *opusc.* 34.1 und 34.2 dienen, die in der Ausgabe von Gaietano die Überschrift *De variis miraculosis narrationibus*, bzw. *De variis apparationibus et miraculis* führen. Die von Frugoni (1980) aufgedeckte Struktur und Zielsetzung von *De bono religiosi status* zwingt zur Korrektur des Urteils von Leclercq (1960: 186: 'une longue épître inutile; ... l'opuscule en question n'a aucun but précis').

57. Gelegentlich unterlässt Damiani das Nennen der Namen, weil es ihm darauf ankommt, die *vitia* zu bekämpfen und nicht etwa an anderer Leute *infamia* oder *ignominia* Gefallen zu finden (*opusc.* 31, 536A; 45, ed. Brezzi 1943: 188; 52, 789D). Wo es sich um Beispiele handelt, die zur Nachahmung dienen, empfiehlt er als Verhaltensregel, den Namen der Personen aus dem eigenen Kreise nicht zu nennen, jedoch wohl die von *extranei* (*opusc.* 15, 361C); mustergültige (und folglich demütige) Asketen wünschen nicht, dass von ihren Leistungen viel Aufheben gemacht wird (*opusc.* 51, 755D und 759B-C; 54, 798D; 56, 813B). Für das Vergessen von Namen s. Anm. 49.

58. S. z.B. *epist.* 6.32 (430A); 7.18 (459A); *opusc.* 13 (ed. Brezzi 1943: 306); 19 (436C); 57.2 (827D).

59. Selbstverständlich enthalten die Predigten über Heilige auch *miracula* aus der jüngeren Vergangenheit, aber diese beruhen nur ausnahmsweise (*sermo* 8, 87ff., s. Anm. 5) auf mündlicher Überlieferung. Kennzeichnend für Damianis Auffassung von Predigten scheint weiter, dass er seine Ausführungen in *sermo* 73 (*Fratribus eremi de vitio linguae*) nicht mit Anekdoten untermauert, sondern mit Lebensweisheiten (oft in der Gestalt von *similitudines*), die der Bibel und Alltagslebenserfahrungen entnommen sind.

60. Für zeitgenössische *exempla* mit einer demonstrativen Funktion s. z.B. *epist.* 2.12 (280D-281B); 4.8 (309D-311A); 6.5 (385A-B); 7.17 (456B-457B); *opusc.* 6 (ed. Von Heinemann 1891: 41ff. und 60); 20 (446D-449A).

61. Für die wichtigsten Informanten s. supra und Anm. 38. - Damianis Briefe sind aus verschiedenen Gründen keine Massarbeit für die Personen, an die sie gerichtet sind; sie sind bestimmt für eine breitere Gruppe (Reindel 1975; Cantin 1975: 319-24). Dennoch kann Betrachtung des Adressaten als Repräsentanten des intendierten Publikums zu interessanten Hinweisen führen (Cantin 1975: 552-60).

62. *Opusc.* 19 (433C), zitiert in Anm. 28; 34.1 (574D): *Interea... illud in memoriam rediit, quod olim Tetaldus episcopus* (von Arezzo)..., *in festivitate beati Donati constitutus in pulpito, sermoni, quo concionabatur,*

*adjecit.*

63. Austausch von Geschichten bei Besuchen: *epist.* 6.22 (405B); 6.29 (420A, s. Anm. 52); *opusc.* 19 (438D, s. Anm. 30); im Ausland oder während der Reise gehörte Erzählungen: *epist.* 6.29 (420A); 10 (ed. Reindel 1983: 165); Austausch bei Gesprächen: *opusc.* 6 (ed. Von Heinemann 1891: 60) und 47 (s. infra); Unsicherheit oder Diskussion über die Lehre: *opusc.* 19 (427D-428A, s. supra); 40 (656B und C-D); 43 (681A-C); Damiani über die Bedeutung wunderbarer Ereignisse befragt: *opusc.* 34.1 (579C) und 50 (743D-744B). - Beim Lesen im Buche der Natur benutzt Damiani regelmässig Termini die eine technische Bedeutung in der Sphäre der Bibelexegese haben (z.B. in *opusc.* 52 *figura, imago, typus* und *designare, figurare, innuere* und *significare*). Dies begegnet weniger oft bei der Erklärung zeitgenössischer Exempel, aber die Fälle sind interessant. In *opusc.* 19 (428D-A) bezeichnet er den tieferen Sinn einer Vision mit *mysterium* und entschlüsselt er sie mit Hilfe von Bibelzitaten (s. Anm. 24). In *epist.* 6.5 (385A-D) spitzt er die Geschichte des von Venezianern aus dem Griff einer Schlange geretteten Löwen, der seine Dankbarkeit zeigte, indem er seinen Rettern über längere Zeit täglich die Haut eines erbeuteten Tieres anbot, gleichfalls unter Verwendung von Bibelzitaten zu auf die Beziehung zwischen den Mönchen von Cluny und ihmselbst (*hoc fortassis exemplum quadam vobis valeat ratione congruere*): sie schulden ihm die Haut ihrer Gebete. Man vergleiche die Weise in der er in *opusc.* 22 (469C-470A und 471D-472B) das *allegoriae mysterium* und die *historiae figura* anhand der Fabel vom König der Bäume (*Judic.* 9.8-15) erläutert.

64. S. *epist.* 2.12 (280D): *dum jam sol <ad> occasum vergeret*; 8.3 (467C): *pridie... post vesperam.*

65. Für Damianis Kontakte mit Kaiserin Agnes und ihrer Umgebung s. Dressler 1954: 165ff., und Leclercq 1960: 126ff. An jenem Abend umfasste die Gesellschaft neben Kaiserin Agnes und Damiani vielleicht auch Agnes' Kaplan Stephan und ihren Vertrauten, Bischof Rainald von Como. Die Anwesenheit von Rainald bei diesem Gespräch scheint jedoch fraglich angesichts der Formulierung, mit der Damiani ihn als Quelle für eine Wundergeschichte vorführt (*Rainaldus etiam venerabilis Cumanae ecclesiae pontifex dum adesset, quod sibi paulo ante contigerat, veridicus enarrator exposuit*: 712B). Dass Rainald aber an solchen Gesprächen teilgenommen hat, ist unzweifelhaft, weil später in *opusc.* 47 die Rede ist von einer Geschichte, die Hildebrand an Agnes, Damiani und Rainald berichtet hat (*interea dum haec loquor, et illud nunc ad memoriam redit, quod Hildebrandus Romanae ecclesiae archidiaconus eisdem qui superius memorati sunt et episcopo praesentibus retulit*: 713A). Für die Anwesenheit des Kaplans Stephan gibt es in *opusc.* 47 keine Hinweise.

66. Eine vergleichbare Bedeutung haben *flosculi* und *flores* in *epist.* 7.17 (420A) bezw. *opusc.* 54 (796C).

67. Vgl. für eine ähnliche Geschichte von den Töchtern des Herzogs Gisulf von Friaul, die am Anfang des 7. Jahrhunderts in die Hände der Avaren gefallen sind, Paulus Diaconus, *Hist. Langob.* 4.37.

68. Für die Einführung s. Anm. 65. Für Agnes' Bruch mit Hildebrand in 1064 s. Dressler 1954: 158ff.

69. 714B-C: *Ad hoc igitur... tibi proponuntur exempla, ut et ipse contra hostis callidi deceptoris insidias solerter evigiles et, dum te delectat aliorum cum hoste luctantium audire victorias, ipse te per languidi corporis ignaviam non remittas. Sed jam ista sufficiant.*

70. Sämtliche Kategorien von *exempla* können bei Damiani die Gestalt eines 'récit bref' annehmen. Sehe z.B. die antiken *exempla* in *opusc.* 33 (561D-562A: Phalaris und der Hersteller des Marterstiers), 36 (ed. Cantin 1972: 458: der Palast des Romulus), 40 (654B-C: Cyrus und der Cnydus, 658A-C: Tiberius und der Erfinder des unzerbrechlichen Glases), 49 (727A-C: Zeuxis und die Modelle für seine Diana), 56 (816C-D: das Schicksal des Valerianus nach der Niederlage gegen Sapor, 816D-817A: das sich wendende Kriegsglück des Hannibal nach Cannae). Für zeitgenössische *exempla* mit einer demonstrativen Funktion s. Anm. 60.

71. Für Abaelard s. Rauner 1987: 161 (unrichtige Charakterisierung, die wohl auf Welter 1927: 38, zurückgeht, bei Cantel-Richard 1961: 1893, und Chesnutt 1984: 594f.); für Johannes van Salisbury s. Von Moos 1984.

# BIBLIOGRAPHIE

BREMOND-LE GOFF 1982
Claude Bremond, Jacques Le Goff, Jean-Claude Schmitt, L''exemplum', Turnhout 1982.
BREZZI 1943
Brezzi, P. (Hrsg.), Nardi, B. (Übers.), *S. Pier Damiani, De divina omnipotentia e altri opuscoli*, Firenze 1943.
BUYTAERT 1969
Buytaert, E.M. (Hrsg.), *Petri Abaelardi opera theologica, I: Commentaria in Epistolam Pauli ad Romanos*, Turnholti 1969.
CALATI 1978
Calati, B., 'S. Pier Damiano maestro nella S. Scrittura', in: *Fonte Avellana nella società dei secoli XI e XII*. Atti del II Convegno del Centro di Studi Avellaniti, Fonte Avellana 1978: 305-20.
CALATI 1985
Calati, B., 'Art. Pierre Damiani', in: *Dictionnaire de Spiritualité*, Fasc.LXXX-LXXXII, Paris 1985: 1551-1573.
CANTEL-RICARD 1961
Cantel, R, Ricard, R., 'Art. Exemplum. Au moyen âge et à l'époque moderne'. In: *Dictionnaire de Spiritualité*, IV.2, fasc. XXX-XXXII, Paris 1961: 1892-1902.
CANTIN 1972
Cantin, A., *Pierre Damien, Lettre sur la toute-puissance divine. Introduction, texte critique, traduction et notes*, Paris 1972.
CANTIN 1975
Cantin, A., *Les sciences séculières et la foi. Les deux voies de la science au jugement de S. Pierre Damien (1007-1072)*, Spoleto 1975.
CHESNUTT 1984
Michael Chesnutt, Art. Exempelsammlungen im Mittelalter, in: Enzyklopädie des Märchens, IV, Berlin-New York 1984, 593-604.
DENEKE 1987
Deneke, B., 'Art. Fegfeuer.2: Volksglauben'. In: *Lexikon des Mittelalters*, IV, 2. Lief., München-Zürich 1987: 330f.
DRESSLER 1954
Dressler, F., *Petrus Damiani. Leben und Werk*, Rome 1954.
RUGONI 1980
Frugoni, Chiara, 'Letteratura didattica ed esegesi scritturale nel *De bono religiosi status* di S. Pier Damiani'. In: *Rivista di storia della chiesa in Italia* 34 (1980 7-59).
KAPP-MEYER 1939
Kapp, I., Meyer, G., Art. 'Exemplum'. In: *Thesaurus Linguae Latinae*, V.2, Leipzig 1931-53: 1326-50.
LAUSBERG 1960
Lausberg, H., *Handbuch der literarischen Rhetorik*, München 1960.
LECLERCQ 1960

Leclercq, J., *Saint Pierre Damien, ermite et homme d'Eglise*, Rome 1960.

LE GOFF 1981

Le Goff, J., "Vita' et 'pre-exemplum' dans le 2e livre des 'Dialogues' de Grégoire le Grand'. In: E. Patlagean, P. Riché (Hrsg.), *Hagiographie, cultures et sociétés, IVe-XIIe siècles*, Paris 1981: 105-116.

LUCCHESI 1975

Lucchesi, G., 'Il Sermonario di S. Pier Damiani come monumento storico, agiografico e liturgico'. In: A.M. Stickler e.a.(Hrsg.), *Studi Gregoriani per la storia della 'libertas Ecclesiae'* 10. Rome 1975: 7-67.

LUCCHESI 1983

*Sancti Petri Damiani Sermones ad fidem antiquiorum codicum restituti cura et studio Ioannis Lucchesi*, Turnhout 1983.

LUMPE 1966

Lumpe, A., Art.' Exemplum'. In: *Reallexikon für Antike und Christentum*, VI, Stuttgart 1966: 1229-57.

PETRE 1961

Pétré, Hélène, Art. Exemplum. 'Epoque patristique'. In: *Dictionnaire de Spiritualité*, IV.2, fasc. XXX-XXXII, Paris 1961: 1886-92.

RAUNER 1987

Rauner, E., Art.'Exempel/Exemplum, II. Mittellateinische Literatur'. In: *Lexikon des Mittelalters*, IV, 1. Lief., München-Zürich 1987: 161-3.

REINDEL 1975

Reindel, K., 'Petrus Damiani und seine Korrespondenten'. In: A.M. Stickler e.a. (Hrsg.), *Studi Gregoriani per la storia della 'libertas Ecclesiae'* 10, Rome 1975, 203-19.

REINDEL 1983

Reindel, K.(Hrsg.), *Die Briefe des Petrus Damiani*, Teil 1 (Nr. 1-40), München 1983.

RUBINGH-BOSSCHER 1987

Rubingh-Bosscher, José M.A.(Hrsg.), *Peter Abelard, Carmen ad Astralabium*, Groningen 1987.

RYAN 1956

Ryan, J.J., *Saint Peter Damiani and his canonical sources. A preliminary study in the antecedents of the Gregorian Reform*, Toronto 1956.

TABACCO 1957

Tabacco, G.,(Hrsg.), *Petri Damiani Vita beati Romualdi*, Rome 1957.

THOMPSON 1955-1958

Thompson, S., *Motif-Index of Folk Literature*, Copenhague 1955-58.

VALENTINI-ZUCCHETTI 1946

Valentini, R., Zucchetti, G., *Codice topografico della Città di Roma*, III, Rome 1946.

VON HEINEMANN 1891

Von Heinemann, L.(Hrsg.), *Petri Damiani Liber gratissimus, Disceptatio synodalis*, Hannover 1891: 15-94.

VON MOOS 1984

Von Moos, P., 'The use of *exempla* in the *Policraticus* of John of Salisbury.

In: M. Wilks (Hrsg.), *The World of John of Salisbury*. Oxford 1984: 207-61.

VON SEVERUS 1984

Von Severus, E., art. 'Collatio'. In: *Lexikon des Mittelalters*, III, 1.Lief., München-Zürich 1984: 33.

WELTER 1927

Welter, J.-Th., *L"exemplum' dans la littérature religieuse et didactique du Moyen Age*, Paris-Toulouse 1927 (hier zitiert: anast. Nachdruck Genève 1973)

P. von Moos

# Das argumentative Exemplum und die 'wächserne Nase' der Autorität im Mittelalter

Gegenüber kontroversen Fachtermini kann man sich nominalistisch oder realistisch verhalten oder, wie im alten Universalienstreit, Mittellösungen suchen. Man kann zum Beispiel einen etablierten Begriff wissenschaftsgeschichtlich ableiten und sachlich in Frage stellen und ihn dennoch in einem relativierten Sinn beibehalten, weil der Schaden der Begriffszerstörung für die wissenschaftliche Kommunikation grösser wäre als der Nutzen einer richtigen, aber einsamen Umbenennung. So sollte man es mit dem Exemplum halten. Grosse Autoritäten der antiken und mittelalterlichen Sprachtheorie sind insofern noch heute beherzigenswert; Abaelard sagt im *Sic et non*-Prolog[1]: 'Wie der Fürst der Grammatik und Ordner der Rede, Priszian, lehrt, muss man sich beim Unterrichten mehr um den *usus* (die Praktikabilität oder Konvention) als um die proprietas (die eigentliche Bedeutung) der Worte kümmern (Boyer-McKeon 1976: 89f). Er sagt: 'beim Unterrichten'. In der Forschung aber - so könnte man weiterdenken - gilt gerade das Umgekehrte. Hier möchten wir wenigstens 'etymologisch' wissen, wie ein bestimmtes Verhältnis von proprietas und *usus* zustande gekommen ist.

Sehen wir von allen allgemeinen Bedeutungen des Wortes 'Beispiel' ab, so bedeutet *exemplum* in der Fachsprache der Mediävistik und benachbarter Disziplinen vor allem zweierlei: 1. eine Erzählgattung und 2. eine rhetorische Funktion. An erster Stelle gilt als Exemplum das sogenannte Predigtmärlein, das heisst eine narrative Predigteinlage, wie sie die Bettelmönche des 13. und 14. Jahrhunderts verwendet haben. Diese in allen mediävistischen Fächern heimische Bedeutung ist wissenschaftsgeschichtlich nicht älter als das 1927 erschienene Standardwerk von J.Th. Welter.[2] Die lateinischen Termini des Mittelalters hierfür sind unabsehbar (*historia, narratio, gestum, fabula, parabola*); ebenso vielfältig sind die modernen Synonyma (etwa Histörchen, Erzähleinlage, Schwank, witzige Anekdote, erbauliche Geschichte, 'historiette', 'conte pieux et amusant', 'récit authentique et légendaire', 'edifying anecdote', 'popular homiletic tale' usw.).[3] Diesen narrativen Gattungsbegriff hat zuletzt Jacques Le Goff noch einmal repräsentativ vertreten, allerdings im pragmatischen Rahmen einer 'Typologie' der historischen Quellen und kaum in der Absicht, einen Beitrag zur literaturwissenschaftlichen Gattungsdiskussion zu leisten (Bremond-Le Goff 1982). Es handelt sich in Wahrheit um einen wissenschaftlichen Hilfsbegriff. Entstanden ist er wahrscheinlich durch eine Vermengung der Allgemeinbegriffe 'Vorbild' und 'Sinnbild', Modell und Symbol. *Exemplum* ist zwar tatsächlich ein Schlüsselwort in Predigten und Predigtlehren des hohen und späten Mittelalters, bedeutet dabei jedoch meist soviel wie *similitudo*, Zeichen, Verweis, sichtbare Repräsentation des Unsichtbaren - der Predigtforscher G.R. Owst sagt einfach: 'any kind of homiletic simile or illustration' (1933: 152).

Stofflich umfasst dieses '*exemplum*' schlechthin die ganze religiös signifikante Welt der Dinge und Ereignisse, den *liber creaturarum* und den *liber historiarum*, unter vielem anderen natürlich **auch** kuriose, sensationelle, lustige oder grauenvolle Geschehnisse, also jene eigenartigen Vorkommnisse, die im modernen Verständnis das Wesen und alleinige Faszinosum des Predigtexempels ausmachen.[4] Die Weite des mittelalterlichen Exemplumbegriffs zeigt gut folgende typische Stelle aus einer hochmittelalterlichen *Ars praedicandi*: Robert von Basevorn (Charland 1936: 314) empfiehlt bei der homiletischen Warnung vor Stolz die Erläuterung *per exemplum* zu entwickeln, und zwar auf mehreren Stufen: 1. *in natura*, 2. *in arte*, 3. *in figura*, 4. *in historia*. Dies heisst konkret: 1. *exemplum in natura*: ein allzu weit hervorragender Ast wird vom Wind abgerissen (Naturbeispiel); 2. *in arte*: ein allzu elegant gebautes Türmchen fällt vom Dach (Kunstbeispiel); 3. *in figura*: Jotams Fabel im Buch der Richter von der Wahl eines Baumkönigs durch die versammelten Waldhölzer, wobei die Erwählten die Ehre wegen der Gefahr einsamen Hervorragens ablehnen (allegorisches Beispiel); 4. *exemplum in historia*: der Traum Nebukadnezars im 4. Buch Daniel von der bevorstehenden Erniedrigung (Geschichtsbeispiel). Man sieht: Exemplum bedeutet soviel wie geistliche Illustration im allerweitesten Sinne. Immerhin kennt auch die homiletische Literatur die Unterscheidung von reinen Naturbeispielen und 'historischen', oder erzählenden Beispielen. Der Dominikaner Johannes von San Gimignano zum Beispiel betont im Prolog zu seiner allegorischbedeutungsenzyklopädischen Sammlung *Liber de exemplis et similitudinibus rerum*, er wolle nicht, wie so viele vor ihm, die genugsam bekannten *exempla historialia* aus Bibel, Heiligenleben und 'Taten der Heiden' sammeln, sondern die, wie er meint, bisher vernachlässigten Naturbeispiele des aussermenschlichen *res*-Bereichs, signifikante Tiere, Pflanzen, Steine und dergleichen.[5] Exemplum bedeutet in diesem Zusammenhang 'Sinnfälligkeit', 'Anschaulichkeit', *evidentia*[6] im Dienste geistlicher Zeichenhaftigkeit oder *significatio*; bezeichnet also weder eine literarische Gattung noch eine rhetorische Funktion, sondern eine semantische Kategorie. Es ist formal durch die spezifisch christliche Art symbolischer Bedeutsamkeit definiert und kennt thematisch keine Grenzen: Sein Stoffbereich ist die ganze Schöpfung und die ganze Geschichte. Darum kann auch manches, was seit der Antike in den Bereich des rhetorischen Exemplums fällt, ein Predigtexemplum hergeben.

Nehmen wir ein Alexander-Beispiel: Die Anekdote vom Piraten vor dem Welteroberer ist in der Form, wie sie Augustinus seinem grossartigen Sarkasmus gegen die Staatsgebilde als *magna latrocinia* dienstbar macht, oder wie sie Johann von Salisbury als politische Klugheitslehre über die pragmatische Harmonie zwischen kritischen Untergebenen und toleranten Herrschern einsetzt,[7] durchaus ein rhetorisches Exemplum, das auch Cicero noch als solches hätte empfinden können, nämlich ein argumentativer 'Ereignisvermerk' (wir kommen ausführlich gleich darauf zurück). Wenn aber die materiell identische Geschichte in den *Gesta Romanorum* zu einer Allegorie wird für die Kunst des priesterlichen Seelenführers, eines 'Alexander', den Sünder, das heisst den 'frechen Räuber', auf den rechten Weg zurückzuweisen (Oesterley 1872: 504f.; Cary 1956: 282), so ist dies ein Exemplum nur in dem metasprachlichen Sinn der Predigtlehrbücher, ein spirituelles *significans* auf der gleichen unspezifischen Ebene wie etwa die Bedeutung eines Raubtiers. Man kann natürlich alle Unterschiede aufheben und von drei Varianten des Exemplums, verstanden als 'illustrative Kurzgeschichte', sprechen, wenn man sich bewusst bleibt, dass man damit einen modernen narratologischen Beschreibungsterminus verwendet, der durch kein theoretisches Konzept der Antike oder des Mittelalters wirklich abgedeckt ist, und vor allem, wenn man nicht unterstellt, dieser *terminus technicus* entstamme einer alten Definition von didaktischer Unterhaltungsliteratur.

So wenig also der vermeintliche mittelalterliche Gattungsbegriff *exemplum* im Sinne des erbaulich-schwankhaften Predigtmärleins selbst legitimiert ist, so lässt sich doch verstehen, wie es zu der Begriffsverschiebung gekommen ist. Dieser mediävistisch fest etablierte Terminus beruht, logisch betrachtet, auf zwei Äquivokationen: einerseits auf einem unbewussten *totum pro parte*; denn das ganze 'Buch der Natur', die Erstoffenbarung, steht gewissermassen für ein darin aufgezeichnetes 'merkwürdiges Ereignis' mit spirituellem Hintersinn; andererseits auf einem unausgesprochenen semantischen Dimensionswechsel von der Ebene geistlicher Hermeneutik zur Nomenklatur literarischer Formen. So wurde die tropische Bedeutungsform *exemplum visibile invisibilia significans* mit dem Erzählmedium *historia* (allenfalls *fabula*) und mit der rhetorischen Beweisfigur *exemplum* heillos durcheinandergebracht. Vollends unentwirrbar wird das Konfusionskneuel, wenn man dieses formale *mixtum compositum* auch noch inhaltlich festlegt und es mit Le Goff an eine eschatologische 'leçon salutaire' im Rahmen einer Volkspredigt bindet (Bremond-Le Goff 1982: 36-8).

Mit der Kritik des mediävistischen Fachbegriffs *exemplum* soll natürlich keineswegs geleugnet werden, dass es das damit bezeichnete Phänomen, die anekdotische, sich an Gefühl und Sinne wendende Predigteinlage, tatsächlich gab. Insbesondere die in der neuzeitlichen Rezeption beliebteste Art, das schwankhafte Predigthistörchen, dürfte jedoch - unter den gleich darzulegenden argumentationsrhetorischen Gesichtspunkten - oft am allerwenigsten *exemplum* heissen. Denn diese Erzählform dient meistens nicht der Bestimmung, das zentrale in Frage stehende Anliegen, die *res dubia* überzeugend darzulegen, vom Zweifel zu befreien, in die *res certa* zu wandeln. Diese Erzählung zielt überhaupt nicht unmittelbar auf die Sache (*causa*), sondern auf das Publikum; sie will auflockernd, entspannend, aufweckend, unterhaltend vom Hauptgegenstand ablenken. Sie gehört mithin zu dem, was in der auch im Mittelalter bekannten ciceronischen Erzählarteneinteilung (*genera narrationum*) die 'sachfremde Erzählung', *narratio a (civilibus) causis remota*, heisst und was in mittelalterlichen Rhetoriken, seien es *artes dictandi, artes poeticae* oder *artes praedicandi* immer wieder vorzüglich im Rahmen der *insinuatio* oder *captatio benevolentiae* sowie der *digressio* behandelt wird, also bei den Techniken, mit denen der Adressat eingestimmt oder 'warm gemacht' werden soll.[8] Dieses Exemplum gehört nach einer anderen allgemeinen (bis auf Aristoteles zurückgehenden) Theorie zu den Mitteln der *aversio a materia*, mit denen der Redner scheinbar von etwas anderem redet als von seinem Vorhaben, um dann überraschend, 'schlagartig' darauf zurückzukommen. Es war darum eine technische Regel, im eigenen Parteiinteresse auf solch amplifikatorischem Gebiet des Guten - oder Unterhaltsamen - nicht zuviel zu tun, eine Regel, die schon längst galt, als sie in Predigtlehren geschwätzigen Mendikanten erneut eingeschärft werden musste. Authentische mittelalterliche Termini für diese rekreative Erzähleinlage, für dieses fälschlich so genannte 'Exemplum homileticum', sind etwa *apologus, fabula, iocus, novitas, res nova, res que risum moveat* und ändere (Lausberg 1960: Nr. 411ff. 848ff.; Von Moos 1987: Anm. 457). Doch solches soll uns hier gerade **nicht** beschäftigen.

An zweiter Stelle bedeutet Exemplum eine rhetorische Form oder Funktion, mit der vergangenes Geschehen in persuasiver Absicht auf einen gegenwärtigen Problemfall bezogen wird. Diese *a priori* unthematische, gattungsübergreifende Bedeutung ist so alt wie die abendländische Rhetorik und in der Klassischen Philologie seit je selbstverständlich (Von Moos 1987: 89ff.). Sie lässt sich a) unter stilistischem, b) unter argumentationstheoretischem Aspekt betrachten: In der *elocutio* ist das Exemplum eine stilistische Vergleichsfigur wie etwa die Metapher. Darüber hat zuletzt in der Mediävistik am eingehendsten Fritz Peter Knapp gehandelt (1975: 41-108). In der Stoffauffindungs- und Beweislehre (*inventio* und *probatio*) ist das Exemplum ein Vergleichsargument, das uns vor allem unter dem juristischen Begriff des Präzedenzfalls vertraut ist. Abgesehen von rechts- und philosophiegeschichtlichen Arbeiten gibt es hierzu wenig mediävistische Literatur. Nach Abschluss einer mehr literaturwissenschaftlich und mentalitätsgeschichtlich orientierten Arbeit über dieses Thema,[9] über das im eigentlichen Sinne 'rhetorische Exemplum', gehe ich im weiteren auf andere Exemplum-Bedeutungen nicht mehr ein. Man mag das Phänomen, diese Tatsache - Jacob Burckhardt nennt in der Einleitung zur Griechischen Kulturgeschichte 'die Denkweisen' Tatsachen - so oder so benennen, wenn nur bewusst bleibt, dass wir hier mit einer für das Verständnis des hohen und späten Mittelalters nicht unwichtigen **Denkform** zu tun haben, die, gemessen an der Bedeutung des volksliterarischen Predigtmärleins in der Mediävistik eher eine Aschenputtelrolle spielt. Während das homiletische Exemplum, zum Epochensignum hypostasiert, uns ein didaktisches und dogmatisches Mittelalter vor Augen führt, in dem eifrige Volksmissionare den *simplices* und *rudes* 'die Hölle heiss machen' und 'den Teufel an die Wand malen', führt das rhetorische Exemplum in eine helle, rationale Welt des intellektuellen Dialogs und Disputs, des spielhaften und ernsthaften Zweikampfs, in das Mittelalter der 'Dialektiker'.

Jedem Mittelalterforscher ist eine typische Form historischer oder mythologischer Anspielung vertraut, die aus einer knappen Erzählung, einem narrativen 'Kürzel', oder aus einer blossen Erwähnung, einem metaphorisch verwendeten

Namen bestehen kann. Diese Form der 'Erinnerung' (*commemoratio*) setzt einen hinreichend gebildeten Adressatenkreis voraus, der das gemeinte Ereignis aus Geschichte oder Mythos schon kennt.[10] Will jemand vor den Gefahren der Sinnlichkeit warnen, so erinnert er an Odysseus und die Sirenen; wer gegen feudale Sippenhabgier und Nepotismus zu Felde zieht, erwähnt das glänzende Gegenbeispiel eines Brutus, der aus Sorge für Gemeinwohl und Vaterland seine eigenen Söhne umbrachte.[11] Am einfachsten sind gewöhnliche biblische Tugend-chiffren, wie Job für Geduld, David für Demut, die Emmausjünger für Gast-freundschaft. Im Zusammenhang mit der *consolatio mortis* liessen sich eine Menge stereotyper Beispiele dieser Art systematisieren. Die trivialsten hat schon E.R. Curtius in eher spöttischer Weise als 'Trosttopik' charakterisiert: tenden-ziell unendliche Illustrationen der Weisheit: 'alle Menschen müssen sterben', jene litaneiartigen Paradigmenketten von Adam, den Patriarchen, über alle Heiligen bis hin zum gegenwärtigen *defunctus*, wie sie in der karolingischen Poesie besonders beliebt waren.[12] Daneben gab es heroische *exempla fortitudinis* für die Gefasstheit im Leid, wie Anaxagoras, Job oder die heilige Melania,[13] und an dritter Stelle *exempla iusti doloris* für die Berechtigung der Tränen, wie Caesar, David oder Bernhard von Clairvaux.[14] In vielen problemgeschichtlichen Untersu-chungen wurden die historischen Exempla in ähnlicher Weise zusammengestellt und thematisch geordnet, etwa in Arbeiten zu Fürstenspiegeln, Freund-schaftslehren und zur Liebeskasuistik, über Themen wie Reden und Schweigen, Schuld und Sühne und anderes mehr. Oft bieten gerade diese Exempla und Exemplakataloge die interessantesten, differenziertesten Aufschlüsse über die mittelalterliche Auffassung eines ethischen Problems.[15] Was die Intellektuellen des 12. Jahrhunderts über die Ehe dachten, erfahren wir zu einem wesentlichen Teil aus der jeweiligen Auslegung der misogynen Philosophenanekdoten des Theophrastfragments bei Hieronymus, die Ph. Delhaye in einem berühmt gewor-denen Aufsatz analysiert hat (Delhaye 1951).[16]

Die Argumentationsform Exemplum stellt eine doppelte Synekdoche dar (von Moos 1987: 172f.; Lausberg 1960: Nr. 572f.): Für das Ganze einer Idee steht eine Person, und die ganze Biographie dieser Person wird auf eine durch blosse Nennung abrufbare Anekdote reduziert. Urtyp: Alexander vor dem Fass des Diogenes als Sieg der Philosophie über die Macht. Berühmtester Fundort für Exempla war im Mittelalter neben der Bibel das Handbuch des Valerius Maximus, der im Unterschied zum Chronisten und *polyhistor* als der 'selektive' Historiker 'par excellence' galt, weil er aus der Vielfalt des Geschehenen nicht alles, sondern gezielt nur die *memorabilia, notabilia, digna, utilia*, also nur das Reprä-sentative, das Lehrreiche, eben die funktionalisierbaren, kategorisierbaren Exem-pla berichtete und in einer die Inventio und thematische Zuordnung erleichtern-den Systematik arrangierte.[17]

Was lehren nun die antike und die mittelalterliche Rhetorik über das Exem-plum? Die Stillehre der *elocutio* gibt Aufschluss über bestimmte Tropen und Figuren, die sich als verkürzte Erzählungen oder Ereignisvermerke definieren lassen. *Exemplum* heisst hier die einfache Nennung einer historischen Person als metaphorische Chiffre für eine bestimmte Anekdote oder ein Apophthegma. Curtius (1948: 69) bezeichnete dies glücklich als 'Beispielfigur', unglücklich jedoch als *imago*.[18] Daneben gibt est die Antonomasie oder Anspielung ganz ohne Nennung (*ille qui*), die metonymische und synekdochische Katachrese im Singular ('eine Messalina', 'ein Goliath', 'ein Nero' für Gestalten des jeweiligen Charakters) oder im Plural (*Croesi, Catones* für Männer wie Croesus und Cato); deren Sonderfall, die sogenannte Vossianische Antonomasie der Ineinssetzung von Vergleichendem und Verglichenem (*mea Venus, alter Achilles*); der Mediävist kann hier oft adäquater von typologischen Kurzformen sprechen (wie *novus David, alter Jonas*). All diese Kürzel und Wortfiguren im Bereich von Vergleich, Metapher und Metonymie haben den Charakter einer historischen Analogie.[19] Sie beziehen sich auf denselben anerkannten Bildungsfundus des obligaten Geschichtswissens, der ihre Verständigungsfunktion begründet. Diese Arten der 'Beispielfigur' zeigen kaum etwas spezifisch Mittelalterliches. Der Historiker Paul Kirn schrieb hierzu (1955: 68): 'Der Vergleich mit typischen Figuren ist noch heute unentbehrlich. Nennen wir jemand eine Hamlet-Natur oder einen zweiten Napoleon, eine Kleopatra oder eine Frau Pompadour, so ersparen wir uns lange Ausführungen. Dementsprechend verfuhren schon die alten und mittelalterlichen Geschichtsschreiber. Nach Thomas Beckets Ermordung wird Heinrich II. von England ein Nero, Herodes, Julian und Judas genannnt ...'

Verlassen wir das Niveau der Tropen, Figuren und *colores rhetorici* und betrachten wir dasselbe historische Analogieverfahren auf der höheren Stufe der Argumentationstheorie, so stossen wir auf ein Hauptstück der antiken (und im Grunde auch der allgemeinen) Rhetorik: auf die Lehre von der Induktion, vom beweiskräftigen Vergleich. Der Unterschied zwischen dem stilistischen und dem argumentativen, dem illustrierenden und dem induktiven Vergleich geht allein schon aus der getrennten Behandlung beider Arten in der Theorie der Antike hervor.[20] Insbesondere bei Aristoteles und in der aristotelischen Tradition erscheint das *paradeigma/exemplum* im Rahmen der Beweisgründe, der schmückende Vergleich (*eikon/similitudo*) jedoch unabhängig davon in der Stil- oder *ornatus*-Lehre.[21] Quintilian macht sogar ausdrücklich auf die Mehrdeutigkeit des lateinischen Wortes *similitudo* - Beispiel, Gleichnis, Vergleich, Ähnlichkeit - aufmerksam und schliesst es darum als Übersetzung von griechisch *paradeigma* aus der Argumentationslehre des 5. Buchs seiner *Institutio* aus, während er es allein im Rahmen der 'Verschönerungstechniken' im 8. Buch über den *ornatus* zulässt.[22]

Bei Cicero und in der *Rhetorica ad Herennium* wird der Unterschied zwischen stilistischem und argumentativem Vergleich allerdings durch eine generelle Figurenlehre verwischt, weil mehr der semantische als der intentionale Aspekt interessiert. Der *Auctor ad Herennium* zum Beispiel versteht unter *similitudo* offenbar 'beweisender Vergleich' und 'übertragene Rede' zugleich, da er die Intentionen *ornandi causa, probandi causa, apertius dicendi causa, ante oculos ponendi causa* hintereinander aufzählt, als gäbe es keinen grundsätzlichen Unterschied zwischen 'Beweisen' und 'Verdeutlichen'.[23]

Diese primär stilistisch orientierte Vergleichslehre und überdies die spätantike Vermengung der rhetorischen mit der grammatikalischen Tropenlehre haben die Tradition[24] der mittelalterlichen Rhetorik-Handbücher zweifellos stärker geprägt als die aristotelische Paradeigma-Theorie. Diese ganz von der Logik beherrschte

Beispiellehre ist jedoch (von Anfang an durch Boethius verbreitet) vornehmlich Bestandteil der mittelalterlichen Dialektik geworden.[25] Die antike innerrhetorische Unterscheidung von *exornatio* und *probatio* wurde somit - *cum grano salis* gesprochen - zu einem Unterscheidungskriterium für die zwei Disziplinen des Triviums, Rhetorik und Dialektik. Man darf diese Differenz jedoch nicht überbewerten, da alle mit der Sprache befassten 'Künste', die *artes* des *logos* (im Doppelsinn von *ratio et oratio*), im Mittelalter als eine unauflösliche Einheit galten. Seit dem 12. Jahrhundert wurden diese *artes sermocinales* gelegentlich einfach *logica* oder auch *eloquentia* genannt und durch Klassifikationen unterteilt, in denen die Rhetorik bald ein eigenständiges Fach bildete, bald als Kunst der *exornatio* zur Grammatik, das heisst zur *ratio loquendi*, bald als *probatio* zur Dialektik oder *ratio disserendi* gerechnet wurde.[26] Die einseitige Festlegung mittelalterlicher Rhetorik auf die primär elocutionellen und darum nahtlos in die Poetik übergehenden Traktate etwa eines Matthäus von Vendôme oder eines Galfred von Vinsauf und anderer wäre abwegig, schon wegen der hochentwickelten rhetorisch-dialektischen Argumentations**praxis** des Mittelalters. Sie passt zu der Simplifizierung, dass es nur in der Antike Beredsamkeit und ein Bedürfnis nach Rednerausbildung gegeben habe, mittelalterliche Rhetorik hingegen zu einer 'Kolorierkosmetik' verkommen sei. Übersehen werden dabei die vielfältigen Verwendungsmöglichkeiten rhetorisch-dialektischer Beweislogik - auch ohne eigentliches 'Forum' - für die verschiedensten administrativen Aufgaben vom Brief- und Notariatswesen zum juristischen Prozessverfahren sowie für die wissenschaftliche Darstellung und intellektuelle Kommunikation überhaupt. Diese Anwendungsarten folgten seit der Frühscholastik mehr oder weniger alle dem Modell der philosophisch-theologischen Disputation, ganz zu schweigen von der (quasiforensischen) Predigt oder Kanzelrede, deren spezielle Kunstlehre, die *ars praedicandi* zahlreiche *praecepta* gerade auch aus der Dialektik übernahm.

Die mittelalterliche Argumentationstheorie zum Exemplum geht direkt oder indirekt auf Aristoteles zurück. Am bekanntesten war stets (auch schon vor der Wiederentdeckung des ganzen Organon im 12. Jahrhundert) die ganz abstrakte, für die Definition von Dialektik und Rhetorik grundlegende Lehre von der logischen Form des Beispiels in der *Analytica priora*[27]: Während der stringente, voll ausgeführte dialektische Beweis immer entweder aus dem Syllogismus oder aus der Induktion besteht, ist der rhetorische Beweis eine Kurzform von Syllogismus oder Induktion, das heisst ein Enthymem oder ein Paradeigma. Wie aus dem Syllogismus durch Auslassung einer Prämisse der verkürzte Schluss oder das Enthymem entsteht, so wird der volle Induktionsbeweis durch Übergehen eines logischen Schrittes (nämlich der Verallgemeinerung oder Regelgewinnung aus hinreichend vielen Einzeldaten) zu einer verkürzten Induktion oder einem Beispiel. Im Unterschied zum induktiven Aufstieg von erschöpfend repräsentierten Einzelfällen zum Allgemeinen ist das Beispiel ein Schluss 'vom Einzelnen auf Einzelnes' unter der stillen Voraussetzung eines Schlusses 'vom Einzelnen zum Ganzen und zurück zum Einzelnen'. Diese Theorie wird mit folgendem (im Mittelalter wohlbekannten) logischen Musterfall illustriert:[28] Wenn es schlecht ist, dass die Athener gegen die Thebaner Krieg führen, so ist es auch schlecht, dass die Thebaner die benachbarten Phocier bekriegen. Das implizite 'Tertium' zwischen den Sätzen heisst: Kriegführen gegen Nachbarn ist schlecht. Im ersten Buch der 'Rhetorik' (I 2, 1356b, 1357b) wird dasselbe unter dem Aspekt der persuasiven Wirkung erörtert: Das Beispiel müsse dem gleichen Ganzen, beziehungsweise dem gleichen Stoffgebiet (*genos*) entstammen wie der vorliegende Fall. Die Zuhörer kennen den Ausgang des Paradeigmas. Darum kann der Redner einen quasi-prognostischen Schluss auf den gegenwärtigen Problemfall ziehen. Er weiss zum Beispiel dass Peisistratos, nachdem er sich eine Leibgarde zugelegt hatte, zum Tyrannen wurde. Wenn nun auch Dionysios eine Leibgarde fordert, so wird den Zuhörern glaubhaft, dass Dionysios ebenfalls nach der Tyrannis strebe.[29]

Die speziellere, das Stoffgebiet des Beispiels betreffende Theorie findet zich im 2. Buch der 'Rhetorik'.[30] Aristoteles teilt hier das *paradeigma* als Oberbegriff ein in a) schon vorhandene, tatsächlich geschehene oder vorgefundene Beispiele und b) in selbst erstellte, erfundene, nicht wirkliche Beispiele. Das massgebliche Kriterium ist dabei offenbar die Wirklichkeitsnähe der Vergleichsobjekte. Das schon vorgegebene *paradeigma* ist der sachdienliche Präzedenzfall, das historische Beispiel. Es heisst ebenfalls *paradeigma*, aber im engeren Sinn. Die doppelte, weite und enge Bedeutung von *paradeigma*, die Quintilian später ausdrücklich auch für das lateinische Äquivalent *exemplum* übernimmt, lässt sich daraus erklären, dass das historische Beispiel in der antiken Rhetorik als Beschreibungsmodell für alle Vergleichsargumente diente und so etwas wie das Vergleichsargument *per antonomasiam* darstellte. Aristoteles illustriert das eigentliche, historische Paradeigma mit Darius und Xerxes (*Rhet.* II 20, 1393 a-b), zwei persischen Herrschern, die Europa erst angegriffen haben, nachdem sie Ägypten erobert hatten. Diese Geschehnisse erlauben dem Redner den Schluss, dass auch der gegenwärtige Perserkönig, wenn er Ägypten erobert, nach Europa ziehen werde; weshalb man ihn daran hindern müsse, Ägypten zu erobern.
Die Kategorie der selbst erstellten Beispiele besteht aus den Argumentationsformen Parabel und Fabel. Die Parabel - 'wie Sokrates sie brauchte' - steht dem historischen Beispiel näher, da eine hypothetische Geschichtswirklichkeit (die A. Demandt [1984] 'ungeschehene Geschichte' nennt), ein 'Als ob' oder 'Was wäre, wenn ...' dem Beweise dient. Aristoteles führt zur Illustration das berühmte platonische Steuermannsgleichnis an:[31] die absurde Hypothese, dass der Steuermann aus der Schiffsmannschaft durch das Los bestimmt wird (ein Argument gegen die demokratische Staatsform, in der Ämter durch Zufall statt nach Fähigkeiten verteilt werden). Das zweite selbst erstellte Beispiel ist der *logos* oder die in bestimmten historischen Situationen erfolgreich angewandte Tierfabel Äsopischer Art.[32] Historisches *paradeigma*, Parabel und Fabel stehen hinsichtlich der Überzeugungskraft in absteigender Rangfolge hintereinander: Aristoteles betont, die historischen Beispiele seien 'schwerer zu finden', aber beweiskräftiger, die selbst erstellten seien leichter zu finden, aber weniger beweiskräftig (*Rhet.* II 20, 1394a). Besonders der Fabel, die sich für Reden vor dem geschichtenhungrigen Volk eignet, fehlt nach einem Wort von H.R. Jauss (1975: 311) bei aller 'ästhetischen Evidenz des Anschaulichen' doch 'die höhere Kraft des Faktischen'. Obwohl die Kategorie der Fabel von einigen späteren Theoretikern nach dem Muster des Aristoteles in die rhetorische Exemplum-Theorie übernom-

men wurde, galt die Fabel in der literarischen Praxis der Antike nicht nur nicht als Exemplum, sondern, wie Nøjgaard hervorhebt,[33] geradezu als der wichtigste Gegensatzbegriff zu dem wesentlich historischen, nicht-fiktionalen Exemplum. Auch die mittelalterlichen Exemplum-Theorien sämtlicher Trivium-Fächer beziehen sich vorwiegend auf historische oder quasi-historische Beispiele, was den berühmten altlateinischen Definitionen entspricht, etwa derjenigen Quintilians (V 11.6): ... *rei gestae aut ut gestae utilis ad persuadendum id quod intenderis commemoratio*; oder derjenigen der *Rhetorica ad Herennium* (IV 49.62)[34]: [...] *alicuius facti aut dicti praeteriti cum certi auctoris nomine propositio*. Traditionell blieb die Abgrenzung dieses als 'vergangenes Ereignis' definierten Exemplums von andern Arten des Vergleichs, insbesondere vom Naturvergleich, der *rei similitudo* (was hier nicht weiter ausgeführt werden kann).[35] Ein unscheinbares Zeugnis aus dem 12. Jahrhundert mag punktartig beleuchten, wie stark der historische Charakter des Exemplums im Mittelalter bewusst blieb: Petrus Comestor stellt in seiner bibelhermeneutischen *Historia scholastica* (103 *PL* 198: 1589-90) fest, dass das Gleichnis Jesu vom reichen Prasser und vom armen Lazarus korrekterweise nicht *parabola*, sondern *exemplum* heissen müsse, weil Lazarus wirklich gelebt habe und die Geschichte sich tatsächlich zugetragen habe.

Es kann hier nicht darum gehen, die theoriegeschichtlichen Spuren quellenphilologisch zu sichern, sofern Aristoteles wesentliche anthropologisch-strukturelle Aspekte einer Theorie des Beispiels aller Zeiten formuliert hat, wie dies etwa Chaim Perelman in seinem Kapittel über den 'cas particulier' voraussetzt und mit Belegen aus Antike und Neuzeit überzeugend illustriert (1977: 119-26). Wie immer man sich zur These einer 'allgemeinen Rhetorik' oder gar allgemeinen 'pragmatischen Linguistik' stellt,[36] die methodischen Parallelen etwa zwischen den erwähnten prognostischen Beispielen aus der griechischen Kriegsgeschichte und der mittelalterlichen Nutzung von Präzedenzien und Präjudizien in deliberativen Situationen sind evident und brauchen hier nicht illustriert zu werden. Die polemische Literatur zum hoch-und spätmittelalterlichen Kirchenkampf seit dem Investiturstreit besteht zu einem substantiellen Teil aus solchen Exempla, wie die Arbeiten von Gerhard Ladner, Ludwig Buisson, Jürgen Ziese, Hans-Werner Goetz und andere hinreichend gezeigt haben. Auf diese Selbstverständlichkeit hinzuweisen, ist allerdings deshalb nicht ganz müssig, weil der homiletische Exemplumbegriff den engen Gattungsrahmen, in dem er zur Not berechtigt sein mag, mittlerweile kulturgeschichtlich expansiv zu verlassen droht und gelegentlich bereits zu einer Art Schlüsselbegriff für ein bestimmtes Mittelalterbild geworden ist, in dem die finsteren Töne - Dogmatismus, Indoktrination, Denkverbot - wieder dominieren. Das andere, aristotelische und eigentlich rhetorische Exemplum ist umgekehrt ein strategisches Mittel scharfsinnigen Denkens und Redens. Es hat in den geistigen Auseinandersetzungen des hohen und späten Mittelalters eine zentrale, keineswegs nur propagandistische, sondern oft auch problematisierende und ideologiekritische Rolle gespielt.[37]

Eine der ausführlichsten Abhandlungen des Mittelalters über die Beweisführung mit Exempla findet sich in der um 1160 (in Hildesheim) entstandenen *Rhetorica ecclesiastica*, einem Lehrbuch des kanonischen Prozessrechts (beziehungsweise einem *ordo iudiciarius*), dessen allgemeine Beliebtheit zwei spätere Versfassungen (für die Memorierung) bezeugen. Dieses Werk stammt aus der Übergangsperiode zwischen der alten, ganz in der Trivium-Rhetorik integrierten Jurisprudenz und der neuen, seit dem 12. Jahrhundert zur selbständigen Fachlehre aufsteigenden Rechtswissenschaft der Glossatoren und Kanonisten. Darum verbindet es die herkömmliche schulrhetorische Methodik mit den neuentwickelten dialektisch-hermeneutischen Ausgleichstechniken für gegensätzliche Autoritäten nach dem Muster des (im übrigen häufig benützten) *Decretum Gratiani*.[38]

In einer einleitenden Erläuterung der Grundbegriffe des Prozessverfahrens definiert die *Rhetorica ecclesiastica* ihren eigentlichen Gegenstand, die *causa*, mit einem Anklang an die *exemplum*-Definition der *Rhetorica ad Herennium* als *disceptatio de certo dicto vel facto certae personae*.[39] Die etwas später gebotene Definition des Exemplums selbst lautet ähnlich (*Rhet. eccl.*: 39): *Exemplum est dictum vel factum alicuius vel aliquarum personarum introductio simili negotio [...] ut id de quo agitur faciendum vel non faciendum astruatur*. Die *causa* ist somit das *dubium*, der Streitfall; das *exemplum* ist der zum pragmatischen Vergleich herangezogene eindeutige Fall, das rhetorische *certum*, mit dem der Zweifel beseitigt, Tunlichkeit oder Untunlichkeit erwiesen wird. Beide Begriffe sind nach traditioneller Formel doppelt bestimmt als *dicta* und *facta*, das heisst als zitierbare Aussprüche und erzählbare Ereignisse (Von Moos 1987: 157ff.). In der *causa*-Beschreibung wird die antike Lehre von der Chria oder vom *dictum personale* herangezogen. Die Chria (hier allerdings zum Neutrum *chrion* verunstaltet) ist der in einem konkreten historischen Ereigniszusammenhang entstandene Ausspruch, der - wie jede finite, umstandsbedingte *Hypothesis* in eine infinite, allgemeingültige *Thesis* - in eine zeitlose 'Sentenz' verwandelt werden kann.[40] Dies bedeutet, in Juristensprache übersetzt: Der Richter müsse das debattierte *dictum personale* des Falls in sein eigenes *dictum impersonale*, in die Regel, den rechtskräftigen, generalisierbaren Urteilsspruch (auch *sententia* genannt) überführen. Zu diesem Zweck liefern ihm die zwei Parteien (*oratores*) 'Informationen'; sie 'unterrichten' ihn mit drei Arten von Autoritäten: In absteigender Rangordnung 1. mit dem Gezetz (*lex*), 2. dem Gewohnheitsrecht (*consuetudo*) und 3. den *exempla*.[41]

Aus diesen wenigen Angaben geht schon hervor, dass das juristisch-rhetorische Exemplum des Mittelalters nicht mehr (wie etwa bei Aristoteles) allein auf historischer Faktizität, sondern ebenso auf autoritativer Textualität, auf Worten, nicht nur auf Taten beruht. Da historische Ereignisse überdies nicht vom Medium ihrer Überlieferung abgelöst gedacht werden konnten und auch als eine Art 'Texte' galten, darf man sogar sagen, dass mittelalterliche Exempla entschieden mehr *dicta* als *facta* sind. Jedenfalls gehören sie nicht in den Bereich der Empirie, sondern der Hermeneutik: gleichviel ob Aussprüche oder Taten, Erlasse oder Rechtshandlungen, Apophthegmen oder Anekdoten, sind sie grundsätzlich **lesbar**, interpretierbar, in ihrer Bedeutung diskutierbar. Sie unterliegen dem 'conflit des interprétations'.

Mit Nachdruck hebt die *Rhetorica ecclesiastica* danach den relativen oder subsidiären Charakter der *consuetudo* und des *exemplum* hervor. Sie sind keine unbedingt gültigen Autoritäten wie die *lex*, sondern Hilfs- und Ersatzautoritäten bei Gesetzeslücken und Leerstellen der Theorie (nämlich *pro lege cum lex deficit*).[42] Dies entspricht vordergründig der Justinianischen Rechtsregel für Richter: *legibus, non exemplis iudicandum est*, [43] erinnert jedoch zutiefst an die grundsätzliche christliche Umwertung des römischen Exemplum-Begriffs, wie sie die Kirchenväter in ihrer Kritik der sakrosankten *exempla maiorum* und der *consuetudo* des patriotischen Ahnenkults betrieben haben (von Moos 1987: 81ff.). Deshalb führt die *Rhetorica ecclesiastica* unter dem Stichwort *consuetudo* auch jene berühmte lange Reihe von *canones* an, die das etablierte heilige Alte der Kritik des vernünftigen Neuen unterwerfen. Diese Stellen bilden, wie uns Gerhart Ladner gelehrt hat, eine zentrale Legitimationsgrundlage der gregorianischen Kirchenreform.[44] Sie gipfeln in der von Gregor VII. zur persönlichen Kampfparole auserkorenen patristischen Pointe (Tertullians, Cyprians und Augustins), die später nicht zufällig (ohne Quellenangabe) von Luther wieder aufgegriffen worden ist und seither hauptsächlich als eigener Ausspruch des Reformators bekannt geblieben zu sein scheint:[45] 'Christus hat nicht gesagt: <ich bin die Gewohnheit>, sondern: <ich bin die Wahrheit>. Ist die Wahrheit aber offenbar geworden, so muss ihr die Gewohnheit nachstehen'. Von Augustin stammt eine andere berühmte Maxime der erwähnten *canones*-Kette:[46] 'Wir fragen nicht nach dem, was geschehen ist, sondern nach dem, was zu geschehen hat. Denn die Vernunft ist allen Exempla vorzuziehen.' Die Tunlichkeit (*facienda*) ist so zum Kampfbegriff gegen die 'Fakten' (*facta*), gegen die Macht der Beispiele geworden. Trotz der christlichen Betonung des Neuen, Diskontinierlichen richtet sich diese Kritik am Exemplum, genau genommen, nur gegen dessen spätrömische Verknöcherung und 'Ikonisierung', stellt es jedoch in Wirklichkeit als ein echtes Argument gerade wieder her. Wenn die Entwicklung des römischen Exemplums gegenüber dem argumentativen Paradeigma der griechischen Rhetorik in eine Personalisierung und moralisch heroisierende Erstarrung geführt hat, so kann das christliche, namentlich das kirchenrechtliche Exemplum als Verjüngung des logischen Verfahrens, als Rehabilitierung der ursprünglichen, ganz funktionalen Denkform gelten. Denn die Berufung auf ein rationales Entscheidungsprinzip bei der Applikation von Beispielen (*ratio exemplis anteponenda*), auf das, was Cicero *iudicium* nennt, gehört durchaus zum Wesen des antiken Beispielbeweises. Das Mittelalter hatte keinen Anlass mehr, heidnische Exempla apologetisch zu entwerten, doch Augustins überlieferungskritische Instrumentalisierung des Exemplums zum untergeordneten Überzeugungsmittel der *ratio fidei* sorgte in der Kirchengeschichte immer wieder für Infragestellungen der eigenen Tradition.

Hierzu bietet die *Rhetorica ecclesiastica* interessantes Illustrationsmaterial, was bei einem gewöhnlichen Schulbuch der Fachrhetorik auffallen könnte, jedoch der besonderen Verwendungsart keineswegs widerspricht: Der Traktat legt von vornherein das Hauptgewicht auf die formalen, übungshaften, spielerischen Aspekte, auf das strategische Scharfsinntraining der Schüler. Nicht zufällig proklamiert er seine eigene *utilitas* als die Ausbildung des Anwalts in der Kunst, subtile und schlagfertige Antworten auf jedwedes Problem zu finden, und den Richter zu schnellen, logisch eleganten Entscheidungen zu befähigen.[47]

Das Werk führt nur ein einziges positives Beispiel für das Beispiel an:[48] Das Gesetz schreibe vor, zu Lebzeiten des Bischofs dürfe kein Nachfolger eingesetzt werden. Nun habe aber Augustin zu Lebzeiten des Amtsvorgängers Valerius den Bischofsstuhl von Hippo bestiegen. Dieses Exemplum wird sprachlogisch durch Begriffsdeutung mit dem Gesetz in Einklang gebracht: Augustin sei nicht 'nachgefolgt', sondern als Helfer 'hinzugekommen', *non successit, sed in adiutorium accessit*. Das Exemplum dient somit definitionsgemäss dazu, eine **Ausnahme**, einen in der Regel nicht enthaltenen oder vielleicht nicht vorgesehenen Spezialfall regelkonform zu formulieren und für analoge Fälle das Gezetz zu ergänzen, beziehungsweise verbindlich zu präzisieren.

Könnte man hier den Eindruck gewinnen, das Exemplum sei inhaltlich als fallgerechte *auctoritas* gekennzeichnet, die es in umfassender Kenntnis der Kirchengeschichte nur zu finden und anzuwenden gelte, so zeigen sämtliche weiteren Illustrationen, die allen der Beispielkritik (*examinatio exemplorum*) dienen, dass die Kunst der Zuordnung von bestehenden, aber mehrdeutigen Autoritäten zu bestimmten Aspekten des Falls das zentrale methodische Lernziel darstellt. Was Peter Weimar (1967: 117f.) von der juristischen Logik des Hochmittelalters überhaupt sagt, trifft ganz besonders auf die Exempla zu, dass nämlich nicht die Autorität irgendeiner Stelle von sich aus, sondern nur die *ad hoc* überzeugende Eingrenzung ihrer Geltung ein Problem zu lösen, einen Fall zu entscheiden erlaubte.[49] Diese konsensfähige Fixierung des Geltungsbereichs aber hat ihre eigenen Persuasionsregeln, ihre formale Topik. Die *Rhetorica ecclesiastica* zählt nach dem Schema der rhetorischen Status-Lehre folgende bei der Exempla-Kritik zu beachtenden Gesichtspunkte auf[50]: 1. *tempus*, Zeitaspekt, das heisst der Anachronismus im historischen Beispielvergleich;[51] 2. *causa*, Aspekt der Veranlassung, unvergleichbare historische Situation oder Kontextualität;[52] 3. *voluntas*, Aspekt der Absicht, divergierende Intention bei gleicher Tat in Exemplum und Fall;[53] 4. *differentia personarum*, ausschlaggebender Standesunterschied (nach unserem '*quod licet Iovi non licet bovi*'-Prinzip);[54] 5. *completio prophetiarum*, unterschiedlicher Stellenwert einer historischen Parallelele aufgrund der prophezeiten und sich stufenweise erfüllenden Heilsgeschichte;[55] 6. *expositio*, Sinnkritik, einseitige Auslegung angesichts der Bedeutungsvielfalt ein und desselben Begriffs oder Ereignisses;[56] 7. *interpretatio privilegiorum*, nicht generalisierbare Ausnahmen oder 'Sonderbewilligungen';[57] 8. *exemplorum contra exempla inductio*, Einsatz von Gegenbeispielen.[58]

Widerlegungsregeln gab es schon in der antiken Exemplum-Rhetorik; sie richteten sich hauptsächlich gegen die Unsachgemässheit oder gegen die nichtzustimmungsfähige Ausgefallenheit von Beispielen und empfahlen ebenfalls Gegenbeispiele.[59] Doch eine so ausführliche Systematik mit so reichem Übungsmaterial wie die *Rhetorica ecclesiastica* und verwandte Texte sie vorführen, ist erst seit dem Hochmittelalter möglich; sie bildet das Ergebnis jener seit dem 11. Jahrhundert, spätestens seit Abaelards *Sic et non* sich allgemein durchsetzenden Wissenschaftsreform, die hervorging aus der methodischen Kombination rhetorisch-dialektischer *exercitationes* des herkömmlichen Triviums mit bibelexegetisch-textkritischen Verfahren der Patristik zur Erklärung widersprüchlicher *auctoritates* in Kirchenrecht und Theologie.[60] Hier jedoch dient die neue Methodik nicht der hermeneutischen Problemlösung und *concordantia discordantium canonum*, sondern der Kampfausbildung zur rednerischen Versatilität.

Ich greife wahlweise einige Beispiele heraus: Gegen die Patriarchen-Exempla Abraham, Jakob, David als Argumente für Vielweiberei richtet sich die Widerlegung *ex tempore*:[61] Was vor dem Evangelium erlaubt war, ist unter der vollkommenen Lehre Christi verboten. Ein weniger konventionelles Beispiel beleuchtet die *responsio ex causa*: Will ein spitzfindiger Anwalt einen Räuber mit dem Raub ägyptischer Wertsachen durch die Juden verteidigen, so könne entgegnet werden, dies sei aus anderem Grund geschehen, einzig deshalb nämlich, weil die Christen - nach offizieller Allegorese der *spolia Aegyptiorum*[62] - heidnische Literaturwerke für geistliche Zwecke ausbeuten dürfen. Man sieht hier, wie selbstverständlich der *sensus spiritualis* (die Beute der Juden als Erlaubnis der Dichterlektüre) geworden ist, da er sich so leicht dazu einsetzen liess, die literale, 'historische', für uns naheliegende Bedeutung als perverse Konstruktion zur Diebstahlrechtfertigung beiseite zu schieben. Das historische Ereignis, das seit Aristoteles das Exemplum begründet, ist nicht objektiv für sich geschehen, sondern es 'geschah' schon im Zeitpunkt des Geschehens providentiell als ein 'Text' für uns, zum Zweck einer besonderen späteren Nutzanwendung, über die sich dann allerdings ein hermeneutischer Streit entzünden konnte (von Moos 1987: 538f). Das Gesinnungsargument *ex voluntate* wird mit Beispielen der Gewalttätigkeit und des Totschlags illustriert: Abraham, Moses, Samuel, Petrus und Paulus, sie alle wurden tätlich - aber aus 'Eifer für die Gerechtigkeit', nicht aus Missgunst oder Rachegefühlen, wie dies ein sophistischer *orator* glauben machen könnte.[63] Der Beweis aus der *completio prophetiarum* wird mit einem heute nicht unplausiblen Beispiel veranschaulicht:[64] Jesus hat niemanden zum Glauben gezwungen, folglich sei gewaltsame Mission nicht rechtens. Dagegen wird jedoch eine heute bedenkliche *refutatio* empfohlen: Erst nach Kaiser Konstantin habe sich das Psalmwort (71.11) 'und alle Völker werden Ihn anbeten' ganz 'erfüllt'; die Errichtung der Reichskirche habe also das heilsgeschichtlich-typologische Recht zur Zwangsbekehrung begründet. Die gegnerische Legitimation der Notlüge oder gar der Erbschleicherei durch Beispiele wie Abraham, der seine Gattin als seine Schwester ausgab, beziehungsweise wie Jakob, der sich selbst dem sterbenden Vater als der erstgeborene Esau vorstellte, wird *per expositionem* widerlegt:[65] altjüdische Verwandtschaftsbezeichnungen hätten einen weiten Sinn gehabt, so dass Sara als Abrahams Base auch Abrahams Schwester heissen konnte, und Jakob nannte sich Erstgeborener, nicht weil er zuerst geboren wurde, sondern weil er das Erstgeburtsrecht beanspruchen durfte. Ähnlich habe Jesus die Juden 'Söhne des Teufels' genannt, obwohl sie bekanntlich von Abraham, nicht vom Teufel abstammen.

Eine praktische Anwendung mehrerer Widerlegungsregeln bietet die *Rhetorica ecclesiastica* im Zusammenhang mit der 'Idoneität' oder Qualifikation von Richtern: Für die These, ein Verbrecher dürfe nicht Richter sein, steht das Beispiel Jesu mit dem *dictum* vor der Ehebrecherin: 'Wer ohne Schuld ist, werfe den ersten Stein!' und dem *factum* des stummen Zeichnens im Sand, das die persönliche Gewissenserforschung lehrt. *Sed obicitur*; folgende *exempla contraria* seien zu gewärtigen: Saul habe trotz seiner Missetat, David trotz seines Ehebruchs und Verrats, Salomo trotz seines Götzendienstes das Volk gerichtet. Dagegen wird hinwiederum eine *obiectio exemplorum* empfohlen: 1. *talis populus, talis propheta*; das sündige Israel habe sündige Richter verdient (das heisst *ex causa diversa*); 2. Die Beispiele bezeugen, was geschehen **durfte**, nicht was geschehen **sollte** (das heisst *ex tempore* oder *ex privilegio*) usw.[66]

Solche bibelexegetischen Subtilitäten gehören zweifellos ganz allgemein zum klerikalen Stil im gelehrten Disput und in der didaktischen Literatur des Mittelalters. Man erinnert sich an Hieronymus, den unentwegt nachgeahmten Musterautor virtuoser Streitschriften. Seine *Libri adversus Jovinianum* sind eine einzige bravouröse Widerlegung der Exempla des ehefreundlichen Gegners durch überraschende, spitzfindige Uminterpretationen, allegorische oder literale 'Ehrenrettungen' der eigenen Ehefeindlichkeit, etwa nach dem Modell:[67] Henoch wurde entzückt, nicht **weil**, sondern **obwohl** er verheiratet war, ausschliesslich wegen seiner Frömmigkeit; Isaak war vermählt, aber einzig als Typus Christi und der Kirche; ebenso sind die Frauen Jakobs ausschliesslich Allegorien für Synagoge und Kirche; David und Salomon waren mehrfach verheirat, weil sie auch sonst Sünder waren; doch zeigt dies klar den Fortschritt vom Alten zum Neuen Bund: hier das Fruchtbarkeitsgebot aus Gen.1.28, da aber das Jungfräulichkeitsgebot; Zacharias und Elisabeth waren darum verheiratet, weil sie noch nicht zum Neuen Bund gehörten usw. usw. Was die *Rhetorica ecclesiastica* rudimentär für die Schulstube zurechtmacht, sehen wir hier in meisterhafter Perfektion.[68]

Die angeführten Beispiele zeigen hinsichtlich der rhetorischen Kontroversstrategie ein methodisches Hauptprinzip: den (oft verfremdenden) semantischen Dimensionswechsel, die überraschende Umdeutung der gegnerischen Sinngebung im eigenen Parteiinteresse. Nicht nur die Exempla-Autoritäten selbst, sondern auch die Deutungskriterien werden nach Bedarf hin- und hergewendet. Braucht der Gegner Exempla, um die Verbreitung eines Phänomens mit Parallelen abzusichern, so werden sie als minderwertige Zeugnisse der sogenannten 'verbreiteten Unsitten', als blosse *consuetudo* fern aller *ratio* abgelehnt. Seltene, aussergewöhnliche Exempla werden umgekehrt als nicht repräsentativ, weil nicht genügend verbreitet, entwertet. Dies geht im Extrem bis zum spezifischen *argumentum e silentio*: 'Nirgends lese ich darüber.., ich finde kein einziges Beispiel..' (gemeint ist: in der Bibel und kanonischen Literatur).[69] Ein Exemplum wird im Literalsinn, das andere in irgendeinem übertragenen Sinn vorgebracht, beziehungsweise widerlegt. Die eigenen Exempla folgen grundsätzlich der dem gegnerischen Verfahren hermeneutisch entgegengesetzten Methode, so dass man sich nie auf der gleichen Bedeutungsebene trifft. Denn das Exemplum wird nicht wegen irgendeines in ihm selbst liegenden, denotativ unzweideutigen Inhalts - und schon gar nicht um der historischen Information willen - angeführt, sondern stets funktional und situativ, als ein nur aus seinen Konnotationen verständliches Beweismittel. Es steht jenseits von Gut und Böse; einzig das Beweisziel, dem es dient, macht es bewertbar (von Moos 1987: 325ff.)

Das für uns vielleicht Eigenartigste ist das auffällige Desinteresse an der historischen Realität oder Faktizität der Exempla. In der wahrhaft ausführlichen Widerlegungslehre der *Rhetorica ecclesiastica* fehlt gänzlich das für uns so naheliegende Gegenargument gegen einen Präzedenzfall: dass er sich nämlich gar nicht oder ganz anders ereignet hat, als der Gegner vorgibt. Man stritt im Mittelalter weniger über Fakten als über Bedeutungen. Was heute 'semiotisches'

Denken heisst, war (für Intellektuelle) keine Kunst oder Geheimlehre, sondern Naturanlage und Mentalität.[70]

Die hermeneutische und rhetorische Abzweckung der Exempla hatte eine nicht nur literarische oder gelehrte, sondern durchaus auch eine praktische, politische Bedeutung, die ein wenig im Schatten des üblichen Mittelalterverständnisses stehen dürfte. Gerade weil Vergangenheit nicht als Vergangenheit etwas galt, sondern nur als zeichenhaftes Exemplum, und weil andererseits die meisten Argumentationen mit Vergangenheitszeugnissen geführt wurden, war paradoxerweise nicht irgendein Traditionalismus die Folge, sondern eine fast spielerischaleatorische Auslegungsfreiheit gegenüber fester, verbindlicher Tradition. Der Autoritätsglaube erzeugte sozusagen aus sich selbst heraus das Gegengift: die hermeneutische und rhetorische Immunität gegen das reine, das heisst plumpe *argumentum ab auctoritate*, das nach einer jedem mittelalterlichen Dialektikschüler bekannten Grundregel des Boethius das schwächste aller Argumente ist (*locus ab auctoritate est infirmissimus*).[71] Mit anderen Worten, in dem berühmten Satz Alans von Lille, der schon zum Motto für die sogenannte 'Renaissance des 12. Jahrhunderts' ausersehen wurde, heisst dies:[72] 'Doch da die Autorität eine wächserne Nase hat und mithin nach verschiedenen Richtungen umgebogen werden kann, muss sie mit Vernunftgründen gestützt werden.'


ANMERKUNGEN

* Für eine kürzere italienische Fassung dieses Beitrags cf. Von Moos (1987).

1.  *Quidem si ad doctrinam, ut oportet, loqui volumus, magis eorum usus quam proprietas sermonis aemulandus est, sicut et ipse grammaticae princeps et locutionum instructor Priscianus edocet* [*Inst.* VII 28].

2.  Vgl. auch Le Goff (1988), Bremond-Le Goff (1982) und Berlioz-David (1980). Eine ausführliche Auseinandersetzung mit diesem Exemplum-Begriff siehe in: Von Moos (1987: 113f.).

3.  Vgl. Von Moos (1987: Anm. 108, 317, 353).

4.  Vgl. Von Moos (1987: Anm. 106, 287, 364).

5.  Iohannes de Sancto Geminiano, *Summa de exemplis et similitudinibus rerum*, Venetiis MCCCLXXXXVI, Torino, Bibl. Naz. XV VIII 128, c. 1vA, zitiert nach Vitale Brovarone (1980: 97): *Non autem visum est mihi de exemplis historialibus aliquid in hoc opere ponere ex eo quod tam de historia Biblie quam etiam de vitis sanctorum et insuper de factis gentilium diversa per diversos opera facta sunt satis sufficienter.*

6.  Vgl. Lausberg (1960: Nr. 810ff.).

7.   Augustinus, *De civ. Dei* IV 4; Johann von Salisbury, *Policraticus* III 14 (Webb 1909, I: 225); vgl. Cary (1956: 95ff.) und Von Moos (1987: Anm. 481).

8.   Vgl. Barwick (1928: 261-86) zu Cicero *De Inv.* I 27; *Rhet. ad Herennium* I 7.12-11.19; Von Moos (1987: Exkurs III; Anm. 147, 1206).

9.   Von Moos 1987; vgl. auch Battaglia (1965: 447-86; 487-548), Buisson (1958: passim; 1966: 1-175; 1968: 458-76); Caplan (1927: 284-95); David (1980: 67-86); Daxelmüller (1983: 627-59); Friedrich (1942); Gebien (1969); Goetz (1987); Honstetter (1977); Jennings (1974: 215-33); Kessler (1978); Knape (1984); Lang (1940: 1-97); Lumpe (1966: 1229-57); Michel (1987); Von Moos (1972: s.v. *exemplum*; 1984: 207-61); Schenda (1969: 69-85); Schon (1954); Smalley (1980); Studer (1957: 87-141); Verweyen (1970); Ziese (1972).

10.  Quintilian V II.15-16 (*commemoratio*); Lausberg (1960: Nr. 414-8); Von Moos (1987: Par. 19f.); David (1980: 72f.); Gebien (1969: 70f.).

11.  Vgl. Johann von Salisbury, *Policraticus* VIII 9 (Webb 1909: II, 129): Odysseus; ebd. IV II (II, 272-4): Brutus.

12.  Curtius (1948: Kap. V 1, 90ff.); Von Moos (1972: III, Nr. 552-62): *exempla mortalitatis*.

13.  Von Moos (1972: III, Nr. 1345-96).

14.  Von Moos (1972: III, Nr. 454-505; I/II, Nr. 726ff., 812ff.; Zink (1978: 33ff.): Bernhard.

15.  Vgl. oben Anm. 10 und zum Beispiel Ruberg (1978: 93ff.); Hempel (1970: 198ff.); Anton (1968: 419ff.); Eberhardt (1977: 442f., 472, 604f., 616, 628); Dronke (1970: Kap IV: 'Peter Abelard: Planctus und Satire'); Ohly (1976): Judas.

16.  Vgl. auch infra.

17.  Vgl. Ps.-Robert Grosseteste, *Summa Philosophiae*, cap. XIV (*De historiographis*), ed. Baur (1912: 289, 18ff.): *Valerius Maximus, qui accidentia tantum notabilia diversorum temporum conscripsit*. Zu Valerius Maximus als 'Geschichtsschreiber' der römischen Geschichte vgl. Guenée (1980: 70, 108, 116f., 250, 274, 307, 315ff.); Von Moos (1987: Anm. 299, 395, 698).

18.  Von Moos (1987) Exkurs II: '*Imago*': ein Phantom der Exemplaforschung.

19.    Von Moos (1987: 61ff.); Lausberg (1960), Nr. 416: Antonomasie, Nr. 581ff.: *significatio*, 'Vossianische Antonomasie'.

20.    Vgl. McCall (1970: 187ff., 257ff. u. passim); Von Moos (1987: 48ff., Anm. 145, IIIff.).

21.    *Rhet.* II 20, 1393a-b (*paradeigma*); III 4, 11, 1406b-1407b, 1412b-1413a (eikon); vgl. McCall (1970: 24ff., 50ff., 192).

22.    Quint. V 11-31 (*exemplum*); V 11.5: *Similitudo adsumitur interim et ad orationis ornatus. Sed illa cum res exiget; nunc ea quae ad probationem pertinent, exsequar.* Damit wird verwiesen auf Kap. VIII 2.72-81 (*Similitudo*). Vgl. McCall (1970: 178ff., 187ff., 192ff.; Lausberg (1960: Nr. 422).

23.    *Rhet. ad Her.* IV 45.59-49.62 (zu den 4 *causae dicendi* der *similitudo*); ebd. II 29.46 (*exornatio*); IV 49.62 (*exemplum*); Cic., *De orat.* 2.169; 3.205-6; *Inv.* 1.30.49 (Vergleichsarten). Vgl. McCall (1970: 57ff., 76ff., 87ff.; Von Moos (1987: 54ff.).

24.    Von Moos (1987: Anm. 58ff.); Holtz (1981: 201ff.); ders. (1979: 207-20).

25.    Aristot., *Rhet.* I 2, 1356b-1357a-b; II 20, 1393a; *Top. I* 1, 156b-157a und vor allem *Anal.pr.* II 24, 68b-69a, in der Boethius-Übersetzung (Minio-Paluello, *Aristoteles latinus* III 1-4: 134f.); vgl. Benoit (1980: 182-92); Von Moos (1987: 188).

26.    Vgl. Garfagnini (1971: 915-54); Brasa Diez (1981: 357-67); Gerl (1981: 306-27); Murphy (1961: 194-204; 1978: 198-230, bes. 203ff.); De Rijk (1962: 97ff.; 1967: 77ff.); Michaud-Quantin (1969: 855-72); Otte (1971: 92ff.); Weisheipl (1965: 54-90, bes. 65 ff.); Von Moos (1987); Köhn (1986: 203-84, bes. 269ff.); Lewry (1983: 45-63).

27.    II 24 68b-69a, interpr. Boethius (Minio-Paluello 134-5): *Exemplum autem est quando medio extremum inesse ostenditur per id quod est simile tertio [...] Eodem autem modo et si per plura similia fides fiat medii ad extremum. Manifestum igitur quoniam exemplum est neque ut pars ad totum neque ut totum ad partem, quando ambo quidem insunt sub eodem, evidens autem alterum. Et differt inductione quoniam haec quidem ex omnibus individuis extremum ostendebat inesse medio et ad extremum non copulabat syllogismum, hoc autem copulat et non ex omnibus ostendit.* Aristot., *Top.* VIII 1-2, 155a-156b, 157a; *Rhet.* II 20, 1303a; I 2, 1356a; Boeth., *In topica Ciceronis* (PL 64) 1050 zur Theorie des Exemplums als verkürzter Induktion und des Enthymems als verkürztem Syllogismus. Vgl. Benoit (1980: 184ff.); Von Moos (1987: 188ff.).

28. *Anal. priora* a.a.O. (Anm. 28). Diese Exemplum-Definition findet sich mit demselben Illustrationsbeispiel im *Catholicon* des Johannes Balbi (Mainz 1460), repr. 1971 s.v. *exemplum*; vgl. Bremond-Le Goff (1982: 30) ohne Erwähnung der aristotelischen Quelle.

29. Das Beispiel des Tyrannen bietet auch Julius Victor in seiner *Ars rhetorica*, VI 3 (*Rhet.lat.min.*, ed. Halm) 399: *Si custodes corporis Dionysio dederitis, idem faciet quod Pisistratus, qui quum a suis civibus custodes corpori postulasset, tyrannidem occupavit. Hoc enim manifestum est de Pisistrato, dubium autem erat de Dionysio.*

30. *Rhet.* II 20, 1393a-b; Quint. V 11.1; vergleiche McCall (1970: 24ff., 187ff.); Benoit (1980: 189ff.); Dornseiff (1924-5: 206-28, bes. 215ff.).

31. Ebd. 1393b: vgl. Quint. V 11.3; McCall (1970: 27); Von Moos (1987: Anm. 126).

32. *Rhet.* II 20, 1393b-1394a; vgl. Von Moos (1986: 48 ff.).

33. Nøjgaard (1964: 82); vgl. Alewell (1913: 18ff.); Schmidt (1979: 77ff.); Von Moos (1987: 54ff.).

34. Zur Verbreitung dieser Definitionen im Mittelalter vgl. Von Moos (1987: 57ff., 158ff.).

35. Von Moos (1987: 48ff.).

36. Zu den anthropologischen Möglichkeiten des Beispielsgebrauchs vgl. Von Moos (1987: 22ff.). Gegen verfrühte (vornehmlich linguistische) Versuche einer 'Allgemeinen Rhetorik' - im Unterschied zu den bestehenden Theorien von der Antike zur Neuzeit versteht sie sich als 'neue Rhetorik' oder 'Metarhetorik' - vgl. Fumaroli (1980: 12ff.) und dessen Lob auf Heinrich Lausbergs vorbildliche 'rhétorique des rhétoriques historiques'.

37. Dies ist die Hauptthese meiner Arbeit, *Geschichte als Topik* (1987).

38. Vgl. Wahrmund (1905: 1962); Ott (1892); Lang (1940: 97ff.); Stelzer (1982: 59, 192ff.) und zu Entstehungsort und - zeit Fowler - Magerl (1984: 45-56). Das Werk dürfte danach einer Niederschrift von Vorträgen für Kanoniker des Prämonstratenserordens entstammen, was damit zusammenhängen könnte, dass die Prämonstratenser ihre Seelsorge auch auf juristischen Beistand vor Gericht ausgedehnt haben. Zu den Versfassungen von Eilhard von Bremen in Sachsen nach 1192 (ed. Wahrmund a.a.O.I. 5, 1906/1962) und von Altman von St. Florian vermutlich in Passau 1204/5 vergleiche ebd. 122-124.

39. *Rhet. eccl.* 3; vergleiche *Rhet. Her.* IV 49.62 oben S. 61 angeführt. Zu einer ähnlichen Definition der *causa* bei Radulf von Longchamp vgl. Von Moos (1987: Anm. 554).

40. Vgl. Von Moos (1987: 161ff., 251ff.); Priscian, *Praeexercit. (Rhet. lat.min.,* ed. C. Halm) 552; Jul. Rufin. (ebd.) 44f.; Quint. I. 9.3ff.; VIII 5.3; Isid., *Etym.* 2. 11.1-2; vgl. Lausberg (1960: Nr. 1118) - *Rhet. eccl.* 3: *Causa est origo vel seminarium totius actionis vel ratio, unde sententia nascitur. Est autem sententia, ut dicit Isidorus, dictum impersonale ut: 'veritas odium parit, obsequium amicos'. Impersonale dicitur ad differentiam personalis, qui est crion.*

41. *Rhet. eccl.* 6f.: *Quoniam autem suum est iudicis, lectione et meditatione se instruere, nostrum autem est, praeceptione eum erudire; tripliciter instruemus eum auctoritatibus: legibus, exemplis, praeterea ratione et consuetudine, de quibus postea suo loco dicetur. Quoniam autem inter haec lex dignior est, de ipsa primitus agendo assignemus, quid sit lex...* Trotz der Unklarheit dieser Inhaltsangabe ist der nachfolgende Text klar in die drei Sektionen gegliedert: *de legibus* (7-35), *de consuetudinibus* (35-38), *de exemplis* (39-50). Allerdings findet sich 32 auch folgende Einteilung: *quatuor diximus esse necessaria iudici ad officium suum peragendum: consuetudines, auctoritates, exempla, rationes.* Die Widersprüchlichkeit entsteht durch die Nebeneinanderstellung der Begriffe *ratio* und *auctoritates*, obwohl die *ratio* die anderen Autoritätsarten überragt und leitet. (Im übrigen könnte es sich auch um Protokollierungsfehler handeln; siehe oben Anm. 39). Spätestens im 13. Jh. sind die 3 Argumentationsklassen *lex, ratio, exemplum* jedenfalls eine fest etablierte juristische Begriffsordnung aufgrund der boethianischen Topik der *modi arguendi*; dazu Horn (1978: 265ff.). Zum Verhältnis von *ratio* und *auctoritas* vgl. auch unten S. 65.

42. *Rhet. eccl.* 35; vgl. Gratian D 9 c. 7, XII c. 6 mit Isidor, *Etym.* II 10,2.

43. *Codex Iustiniani* 7, 14, 13.

44. *Rhet. eccl.* 10, 36; Gratian D 8 c. 5-9; D 9 c. 6-7, 11. Zum Problemkreis des Gegensatzpaars *exemplum/consuetudo - ratio/veritas/reformatio in melius* vgl. Ladner (1966: 266ff.; 1959: 319ff.; 1952: 36ff.; 1982: 1-33); Buisson (1958: 26ff.; 1966: 102ff.); Ziese (1972: 77ff.); Olsen (1969: 62, 78ff.); Kuttner 1982: 299ff.; Smalley (1975: 104ff.); Gilchrist (1973: 35-82; 1980: 192-229).

45. Tert., *De virginibus velandis* I 1 (Corpus Christianorum s.lat. 2) 1209: *Sed Dominus noster Christus veritatem se, non consuetudinem cognominavit.* Cyprian, *Ep.* 74.9 (CSEL 3) 806; *Sententiae LXXIV episcoporum* (Soden 1909: 262f.) Nr. 30 (Konzil von Karthago 256): *In evangelio Domi-*

*nus: 'Ego sum, inquit, 'veritas', non dixit: Ego sum consuetudo.* Aus
Augustinus, *De baptismo* III 5-6 (CSEL 51) 303, dort gefolgt von der
Erklärung: *Itaque veritate manifesta cedat consuetudo veritati.* Zur
Tradition dieser Stelle im Mittelalter und zu weiteren *auctoritates* des
Hauptvermittlers: *Decretum Gratiani* D 8 c. 5 (in der *Rhet. eccl.* 10, 36).
Vgl. Von Moos (1987: 86ff.). - Martin Luther, *Trost der Christen zu
Halle* (Weimarer Ausgabe 23) 414f.: '...hat nicht gesagt: ich bin Gewohn-
heit und Brauch, sondern: ich bin die Wahrheit. [...] wenn die Wahrheit
offenbar wird, soll Gewohnheit weichen.' Dies wird vom Erforscher des
abendländischen Gewohnheitsbegriffs Gerhard Funke (1974: 610; 1961:
187f.) ausschliesslich Luther zugeschrieben.

46. Aug., *Civ.* I 22 (Corpus Christianorum s. lat. 47) 24. 26ff.: *Non modo
    quaerimus utrum sit factum, sed utrum fuerit faciendum. Sane quippe
    ratio exemplis anteponenda est, cui quidem et exempla concordant, sed
    illa, quae tanto digniora sunt imitatione quanto excellentiora pietate* (=
    Gratian D 9 c. 11). Zur Tradition dieser *auctoritas* im Mittelalter vgl.
    Von Moos (1987: Anm. 211, 214).

47. *Rhet. eccl.* 2: *Materia huius lectionis est ecclesiasticae censurae discep-
    tatio. Utilis eius canonum cognitio, in ecclesiasticis negotiis circumspecta
    discretio, [...] propositis quaestionibus subtilis et acuta responsio, omnium
    controversiarum facilis et rationabilis terminatio. Intentio eius est,
    instruere personas in iudicio constituendas, partim secundum normam
    canonum, partim secundum artificiosam doctrinam rhetorum.*

48. Ebd. 39 unmittelbar nach der oben S. 64 angeführten Definition.

49. Vgl. auch Von Moos (1987: 251ff.) und infra.

50. *Rhet. eccl.* (wie Anm. 39) 40: *Amodo superest ostendere, quae et quot
    sint, quibus in exemplorum obiectione possimus respondere. Sunt autem:
    tempus, causa, voluntas, personarum diversa qualitas, prophetiae comple-
    tio (in examinatione) exemplorum, circumspecta interpretatio privilegio-
    rum, specialis honor, prius licitorum postmodum facta prohibitio, exem-
    plorum contra exempla inductio. Haec omnia in exemplo introducto debe-
    mus attendere et exemplum secundum hoc examinare.* (In den ebd. 40-50
    folgenden Abschnitten kommen nur die 8 erwähnten Punkte zur Sprache,
    so dass *specialis honor ... bis ... facta prohibitio* als Apposition zu Punkt
    7 zu verstehen ist.) Zur Status-Lehre vergleiche Lang (1940: 74ff.);
    Gründel (1963: 16ff.); Meyer (1951: 43ff.); Von Moos (1987: Reg. s.l. *status*).

51. *Rhet. eccl.* 40f.: *Ex tempore sic possumus occurrere....*

52. Ebd. 41: *... respondere possumus ex causa, quod...*

53. Ebd. 42: *Ex voluntate quoque examinari potest factum...*

54. Ebd. 42f.: *Differentia quoque personarum in factis, quae pro exemplo inducuntur, diligenter est pensanda.*

55. Ebd. 43f.: *Completio prophetiarum in examinatione exemplorum nihilominus est attendenda.*

56. Ebd. 44f.: *Per expositionem quoque exemplum cessare potest.*

57. Ebd. 46f.: *Honor quoque quorundam privilegiatorum specialis est nec ab aliis potest in exemplum sumi ... Possumus etiam ex prius licitis exemplorum cassare obiectionem...* (Entspricht sachlich auch der *responio ex tempore*.)

58. Ebd. 48f.: *Per aliorum quoque exemplorum inductionem ... possumus respondere.*

59. Honstetter (1977: 191ff.); McCall (1970: 181); Martin (1974: 119); s.z. B. Ps.-Aristoteles = Anaximenes, *Rhet. ad Alexandrum* 1403a; Quint. V 13.23-4.

60. Kuttner (1982: 300ff.); Weimar (1973: 129ff.); Von Moos (1987: 238-285): '*Verba auctorum* und das neue Denken in Alternativen' mit einer Analyse des *Sic et non*-Prologs von Abaelard; Kluxen (1981: 273-93).

61. *Rhet. eccl.* 40f.: *Contra haec sic ratione temporis respondere poterimus quod videlicet, antequam evangelium claresceret multa permittebantur, quae tempore perfectioris doctrinae eliminantur.* Vgl. auch Anm. 65 und 58; Lang (1940: 77ff.); Gründel (1963: 16ff.); Borst (1969: 12ff., 21ff.) zu diesem Anachronismusaspekt.

62. *Rhet. eccl.* 41: *Item si probetur rapinam licere exercere exemplo Israelitarum, qui a vicinis Aegyptiis accomodatis sibi preciosis eorum abierunt. Hoc enim ad hoc illis fuit permissum, ut aliud in ecclesia significaret agendum, paginas videlicet philosophorum quasi quosdam domos Aegyptiorum spoliandas exemplis et sententiis ibi quaesitis et quodam ornatu verborum illius paginae quasi spoliis quibusdam deo construendum tabernaculum, ut ipse apostolus et Augustinus et Hieronymus fecerunt. Causa vero alia est significationis, alia infirmitatis.* Zur Tradition des Motivs *spolia Aegyptiorum*; vgl. Gnilka (1980: 71ff.); De Lubac (I 1959: 300ff.); bes. Aug. *Doctr. Christ.* II 40, 60.

63. *Rhet. eccl.* 42: *...Ab his inquam omnibus, si exempla proferuntur, a voluntate possumus respondere; voluntas enim alia est cum zelo iustitiae [...] alia cum livore vindictae.*

64.    *Rhet. eccl.* 43f.: *si contendat haereticus, neminem invitum esse ad fidem trahendum, [...] quod nec in evangelicis scriptis nec in apostolicis reperiatur exemplum, quo demonstretur aliquem ad fidem coactum esse, possumus respondere, quod nondum impleta erant, quae propheta dicit: adorabunt eum omnes reges terrae et timebunt gentes nomen tuum et omnes reges terrae gloriam tuam. Qua completa ius maioris potestatis ecclesiae permissum est quam prius [...] Obicientibus ergo, quod in evangelio nemo invitus legitur ad fidem conversus, expletionem prophetiae obicere possumus. Tempore Christi et evangelistarum praedicta prophetia nondum erat impleta, sed postquam Constantinus et alii imperatores fidem Christi susceperant [...] exinde omnes gentes quamvis nolentes ad fidem Christi erant trahendae et cogendae exemplo Christi, qui Paulum [...] postestate prostravit64. ...*

65.    *Rhet. eccl.* 45f.: *Item si adversarius mentiri licere contendat [...] vel si astruat idem exemplo Abrahae, qui Aegyptum ingrediens ait uxori suae: novi quod pulchra sis; timeo quod occidant me Aegyptii propter te; dic ergo obsecro, quod soror mea sis, ut bene sit mihi propter te* [Gen. 12]. *Vel sumpto exemplo a Iacob, qui respondens patri suo ait: ego sum Esau primogenitus tuus* [Gen. 27...] *Si, inquam, contendat adversarius horum exemplorum obiectione, fas esse mentiri, facile singula ventilare possumus, si diligenter, quod dicitur, exponere sciamus. [...] Item Abraham uxori suae non persuasit mentiri, sed quod uxorem esse se taceret et sororem esse diceret, quod tamen erat, quia tunc temporis non solum de eodem patre vel eadem matre vel eodem utroque fratres aut sorores dicebantur, sed et filii fratrum [...] Item quod Iacob primogenetum se dicebat, dictum est non nascendo, sed ius primogenitorum ritu venditionis adeundo. Iuxta quem modum et Dominus loquens [...] ad Iudaeos: vos ex patre diabolo estis et desideria patris vestri facere vultis* [Jo. 8.44]; *licet de Abraham essent quantum ad generationem.*

66.    Ebd. 4: *Ad hoc breviter respondere possumus: talis populus talem meretur prophetam et propter peccata populi permittit deus ypocritam regnare. Vel quod his exemplis non ostenditur, quid fieri licuerit, sed quid in vindictam excessuum illius populi dominus fieri permiserit.*

67.    Hieronymus, *Lb. adv Iovinianum* I 17ff. (PL 23); vgl. Opelt (1973: 43ff., 191).

68.    Ein nicht minder virtuoses Zeugnis einer mittelalterlichen *refutatio exemplorum* bietet Johann von Salisbury, *Policraticus* (VII 19, Bd II, 1909: 175-8). Vgl. Von Moos (1987: S. 238ff.), eine sprühende parodistische Satire gegen den skrupellosen Umgang mit heiligen Präzedenzfällen: Ein ehrgeiziger Anwärter auf den Bischofsstuhl wird vorgeführt, der mit unglaublichem Einfallsreichtum seine Qualifikation nachweisen möchte und zu diesem Zweck gegen jeden nur denkbaren Einwand ein biblisches

oder hagiographisches Exemplum anzuführen versteht. Fast fünfzig Patriarchen und Heilige werden herbeizitiert, die alle demonstrieren, wie leicht aus jedem Fehler ein Vorzug gemacht werden kann (z.B. 'er ist minderjährig, doch auch Daniel war ein Knabe, als er die Greise wegen Susanna zurechtwies').

69.     Vgl. Von Moos (1987: 333ff., Anm. 464, 654; oben Anm. 65).

70.     Vgl. Von Moos (1987: 512ff.) zum mittelalterlichen Wirklichkeitsbegriff.

71.     Boeth., *Comment. in top. Ciceronis* 6; id. *De diff. topicis* 3 (PL 64: 1166 C, 1174); vgl. auch Horn (1978: 261ff.) und Makdisi et al. (1982).

72.     Alanus ab Insulis, *De fide catholica* IV (PL 210) 333 A: *Sed quia auctoritas cereum habet nasum, id est in diversum potest flecti sensum, rationibus roborandum est.* Vgl. Zimmermann (1981: 87-105), auch zu der nicht weniger berühmten Halfter-Metaphor für die Autorität bei Adalhard von Bath; Chenu (1967: 155ff., 361ff.).

# BIBLIOGRAPHIE

ALEWELL 1913
Alewell, K., *Das rhetorische Paradeigma, Theorie, Beispielsammlungen, Verwendung in der römischen Literatur der Kaiserzeit*. Leipzig 1913.

ANTON 1978
Anton, H.H., *Fürstenspiegel und Herrscherethos in der Karolingerzeit*. Bonn 1968.

BARWICK 1928
Barwick, K., Die Gliederung der Narratio in der rhetorischen Theorie und ihre Bedeutung für die Geschichte des antiken Romans. In: *Hermes* 63 (1928) 261-86.

BATTAGLIA 1965
Battaglia, S., L'esempio medievale. In: *La coscienza letteraria del medioevo*. Napoli 1965: 447-86.

BATTAGLIA 1965b
Battaglia, S., Dall'esempio alla novella. In: *La coscienza letteraria del medioevo*. Napoli 1965.

BAUR 1912
Baur, L. (ed.), *Ps. Robert Grosseteste, summa philosophia*. Münster 1912.

BENOIT 1980
Benoit, W.L., Aristotle's Example: The Rhetorical Induction. In: *Quarterly Journal of Speech* 56 (1980):

BERLIOZ-DAVID 1980
Berlioz, J., David, J.M., Rhétorique et histoire, L'exemplum et le modèle de comportement dans le discours antique et médiéval. In: *Mélanges de lÉcole française de Rome 92.1* (1980): 1-9.

BORST 1969
Borst, A., *Geschichte an mittelalterlichen Universitäten*. Konstanz 1969.

BOYER-McKEON 1976
Boyer, B.B., McKeon, R., *Prologus Petri Abaelardi in sic et non*. Chicago-London 1976.

BRASA DIEZ 1981
Brasa Diez, M., Tres clases de logica en Juan de Salisbury. In: *Sprache und Erkenntnis im Mittelalter*. Berlin 1981: 357-67.

BREMOND-LE GOFF 1982
Bremond, Cl., Le Goff, J., Schmitt, J.Cl., *L'exemplum*. Turnhout 1982.

BUISSON 1958
Buisson, L., *Potestas und Caritas. Die päpstliche Gewalt im Spätmittelalter*. Köln-Graz 1958.

BUISSON 1966
Buisson, L., Die Entstehung des Kirchenrechts. In: *ZRG Kan* 52 (1966): 1-175.

BUISSON 1968
Buisson, L., Exempla und Tradition bei Innocenz III. In: *Adel und Kirche. Festschrift G. Tellenbach*. Freiburg 1968: 458-76.

CAPLAN 1927

Caplan, H., Rhetorical invention in Some Medieval Tractates of Preaching. In: *Speculum* 2 (1927): 284-95.

CARY 1956

Cary, G., *The Medieval Alexander*. Cambridge 1956.

CHARLAND 1936

Charland, Th.M., *Forma praedicandi*. Paris-Ottawa 1936.

CHENU 1967

Chenu, M.-D., *La théologie au douzième siècle*. Paris 1967.

CURTIUS 1948

Curtius, E.R., *Europäische Literatur und Lateinisches Mittelalter*. Bern 1948.

DAVID 1980

David, J.M., Maiorum exempla sequi: L'*exemplum* historique dans les discours judiciaires de Cicéron. In: Berlioz, J., David, J.M. (eds) 1980, 67-86.

DAXELMÜLLER 1983

Daxelmüller, Chr., Exemplum. In: *Enzyklopädie des Märchens*, 1983: 627-59.

DELHAYE 1951

Delhaye, P., Le dossier anti-matrimonial de l'Adversus Jovinianum et son influence sur quelques écrits latins du XII s. In: *Medieval Studies* 13 (1951):

DE LUBAC 1959

De Lubac, H., *Exégèse médiévale. Les quatre sens de l'Écriture*. I Paris 1959.

DEMANDT 1984

Demandt, A., *Ungeschehene Geschichte. Ein Traktat über die Frage: Was wäre geschenen, wenn ...?* Göttingen 1984.

DE RIJK 1962-67

De Rijk, L.M., *Logica modernorum. A Contribution to the History of Early Terminist Logic*. Assen I 1962, II 1967.

DORNSEIFF 1924-5

Dornseiff, *Literarische Verwendungen des Beispiels*. Warburg 1924-5.

DRONKE 1970

Dronke, P., *Poetic Individuality in the Middle Ages*. Oxford 1970.

EBERHARDT 1977

Eberhardt, O., *Via Regia, Der Fürstenspiegel Smaragds von St. Mihiel u. seine literarische Gattung*. München 1977.

FOWLER-MAGERL 1984

Fowler-Magerl, L., *Ordo iudiciorum vel ordo iudiciarius*. Frankfurt-am-Main 1984.

FRIEDRICH 1942

Friedrich, H., *Die Rechtsmetaphysik der Göttlichen Komödie, Francesca da Rimini*. Frankfurt-am-Main 1942.

FUMAROLLI 1980

Fumarolli, M., *L'âge de l'éloquence. Rhétorique et res literaria de la Renaissance au seuil de l'époque classique*. Genève-Paris 1980.

FUNKE 1958

Funke, G., *Gewohnheit*. Bonn 1958 (Göttingen 1961).

FUNKE 1974

Funke, G., Art. Gewohnheit. In: *Historisches Wörterbuch der Philosophie III*

(1974):

GARFAGNINI 1971
Garfagnini, G.C., Ratio disserendi e rationandi via: il Metalogicon di Giovanni di Salisbury. In: *Studi Medievali* 12 (1971): 915-54.

GEBIEN 1969
Gebien, K., *Die Geschichte in Senecas philosophischen Schriften.* Konstanz 1969.

GERL 1981
Gerl, H.B., Zum Spannungsfield von Logik, Dialektik und Rhetorik. Die Programmatik des Metalogicon von Johannes von Salisbury. In: *Tijdschrift voor philosophie* 43 (1981): 306-27.

GILCHRIST 1973, 1980
Gilchrist, J., The Reception of Pope Gregory VII into Canon Law. In: *Zeitschrift der Savigny Stiftung für Rechtsgeschichte Kanonische Abteilung* 90 (1973): 35-82, 97 (1980): 192-229.

GNILKA 1980
Gnilka, Chr., Usus iustus, ein Grundbegriff der Kirchenväter im Umgang mit der antiken Kultur. In: *Archiv für Begriffsgeschichte* 14 (1980): 34-76.

GRÜNDEL 1963
Gründel, J., *Die Lehre von den Umständen der menschlichen Handlung im Mittelalter.* Münster 1963.

GUENÉE 1980
Guenée, B., *Histoire et culture historique dans l'Occident médiéval.* Paris 1980.

HALM 1863
HALM, C., *Rhetores Latini Minores.* Leipzig 1863.

HEMPEL 1970
Hempel, W., *'Übermuot diu alte' ... Der superbia-Gedanke und seine Rolle in der deutschen Literatur des Mittelalters.* Bonn 1970.

HOLTZ 1979
Holtz, L., Grammairiens et rhéteurs romains en concurrence pour l'enseignement des figures de rhétorique. In: *La Rhétorique à Rome, Caesardonum* 14 bis, (1979).

HOLTZ 1981
Holtz, L., *Donat et la tradition de l'enseignement grammatical,* Paris 1981.

HONSTETTER 1977
Honstetter, R., *Exemplum zwischen Rhetorik und Literatur. Zur gattungstheoretischen Sonderstellung von Valerius Maximus und Augustinus.* Konstanz 1977.

HORN 1978
Horn, N., Argumentum ab auctoritate in der legistischen Argumentationstheorie. In: Behoreends, O. (ed.), *Festschrift F. Wieacker.* Göttingen 1978: 261-72.

JAUSS 1975
Jauss, H.R., Negativität und Identifikation. In: *Position der Negativität.* München 1975.

JENNINGS 1974
Jennings, M., Lucan's Medieval Popularity: The Exemplum Tradition. In: *Rivista*

*di cultura classica e medievale* 16 (1974): 215-33.

KESSLER 1978
Kessler, E. *Petrarca und die Geschichte*. München 1978.

KIRN 1955
Kirn, P., *Das Bild des Menschen in der Geschichtsschreibung von Polybius bis Ranke*. Göttingen 1955 (1968).

KLUXEN 1981
Kluxen, W., Der Begriff der Wissenschaft. In: Weimar, P. (ed.), *Die Renaissance der Wissenschaften 12. Jahrhundert*. Zürich 1981: 273-293.

KNAPE 1984
Knape, J., *'Historie' in Mittelalter und früher Neuzeit, Begriffs- und Gattungsgeschichtliche Untersuchungen im interdisziplinären Kontext*. Baden-Baden 1984.

KNAPP 1975
Knapp, F.P., *Similitudo. Stil- und Erzählfunktion von Vergleich und Exempel in dem lateinische, französischen und deutschen Grossepik des Hochmittelalters*. Wien 1975.

KÖHN 1986
Köhn, R., Schulbildung und Trivium im Lateinischen Hochmittelalter. In: Fried, J. (ed.), *Schulen und Studium im sozialen Wandel des hohen und späten Mittelalters*. Sigmaringen 1986.

KUTTNER 1982
Kuttner, S., The Revival of Jurisprudence. In: Benson, R.L., Constable, G. (eds), *Renaissance and Renewal in the Twelfth Century*. Oxford 1982: 299-323.

LADNER 1952
Ladner, G.B., Die mittelalterliche Reform-Idee und ihr Verhältnis zum Idee der Renaissance. In: *MIÖG 60 (1952): 31, 59, 36 ff.*

LADNER 1959
Ladner, G.B., *The Idea of Reform*. Cambridge Mass. 1959.

LADNER 1966
Ladner, G.B., Art. Erneuerung. In: *Reallexikon für Antike und Christentum* VI (1966): 240-75, 266 ff.

LADNER 1982
Ladner, G.B., Terms and Ideas of Renewal. In: Benson, R.L., Constable, G. (eds), *Renaissance and Renewal in the Twelfth Century*. Oxford 1982: 1-33.

LANG 1940
Lang, A., Rhetorische Einflüsse auf die Behandlung des Prozesses in der Kanonistik des 12. Jahrhunderts. In: *Festschrift E. Eichmann*. Paderborn 1940: 1-97.

LAUSBERG 1960
Lausberg, H., *Handbuch dem Literarischen Rhetorik*. München 1960.

LE GOFF 1986/7
Le Goff, J., L'exemplum et la rhétorique de la prédication aux XIIIe-XIVe siècle. In: Leonardi, Cl. (ed.), *Atti del Convegno internazionale di studi dall' A.M.U.L.* Soleto 1986/7. Im Druck.

LEWRY 1983
Lewry, O., Rhetoric at Paris and Oxford in the Mid-thirteenth Century. In: *Rhetorica* 1 1983): 45-63.

LUMPE 1966
Lumpe, A., Exemplum. In: *Reallexikon für Antike und Christentum* 6 (1966): 1229-57.

MacCALL 1970
McCall, M.H., *Ancient Rhetorical Theory of Simile and Comparison*. Cambridge, Mass. 1970.

MAKDISI et al. 1972
Makdisi, G., et al., (ed.), *Islam, Byzance, Occident, Colloque international de la Napoule*. Paris 1982.

MARTIN 1974
Martin, J., *Antike Rhetorik*. München 1974.

MEYER 1951
Meyer, E., Die Quaestiones der Rhetorik und die Anfänge juristischer Methodenlehre. In: *Zeitschrift der Savigny Stiftung für Rechtsgeschichte, Roman. Abteilung* 67 (1951): 30-73.

MICHAUD-QUANTIN 1969
Michaud-Quantin, P., L'emploi des termes *logica* et *dialectica* au moyen âge. In: *Arts libéraux et philosophie au moyen age*. Montreal-Paris 1969: 855-72.

MINIO-PALUELLO 1969
Minio-Paluello, L. (ed.), *Aristoteles latinus*. Brugge 1969.

MURPHY 1961
Murphy, J.J., The Arts of Discourse 1050-1400. In: *Medieval Studies* 23 (1963): 194-204.

MURPHY 1978
Murphy, J.J., Rhetoric and Dialectic in 'The Owl and the Nightingale'. In: Murphy, J.J. (ed.), *Medieval Eloquence*. Berkeley-Los Angeles-London 1978: 198-230.

NØJGAARD 1964
Nøjgaard, M., *La fable antique*. Copenhague 1964.

OESTERLY 1872
Oesterly, H. (ed), *Gesta Romanorum*. Berlin 1872.

OHLY 1976
Ohly, F., *Der Verfluchte und der Erwählte. Vom Leben mit der Schuld*. Opladen 1976.

OLSEN 1969
Olsen, G., The Idea of the Ecclesia primitiva in the Writings of the Twelfth Century Canonists. In: *Traditio* 25 (1969): 61-86.

OPELT 1973
Opelt, I., *Hieronymus' Streitschriften*. Heidelberg 1973.

OTT 1892
Ott, E., *Die Rhetorica ecclesiastica*. Wien 1892.

OTTE 1971
Otte, G., *Dialektik und Jurisprudenz*. Frankfurt-am-Main 1971.

OWST 1933

Owst, G.R., *Literature and Pulpit in Medieval England. A Neglected Chapter in the History of English Letters and of the English People.* Cambridge 1933 (Oxford 1961).

PERELMAN 1977

Perelman, Ch., *L'empire rhétorique. Rhétorique et argumentation.* Paris 1977.

RUBERG 1978

Ruberg, U., Beredtes Schweigen ... In: *Münsternsche Mittelalterschriften* XXXII München 1978.

SCHENDA 1969

Schenda, R., Stand und Aufgaben der Exemplaforschung. In: *Fabula* 10 (1969): 69-85.

SCHMIDT 1979

Schmidt, P.L., Politische Argumentation und moralischer Appell: Zur Historizät der antiken Fabel im frühkaiserzeitlichen Rom. In: *Deutschunterricht* 31/6 (1979): 74-89.

SCHON 1954

Schon, P.M., *Vorformen des Essays in Antike und Humanismus, Ein Beitrag zur Entstehungsgeschichte der 'Essais' von Montaigne.* Wiesbaden 1954.

SMALLEY 1975

Smalley, B., Ecclesiastical Attitude to Novelty c. 1100 - c. 1250.. In: Baker, D. (ed.), *Church, Society and Politics.* Oxford 1975: 113-31.

SMALLEY 1980

Smalley, B., *English Friars and Antiquity in the Early Fourteenth Century.* Oxford 1980.

STELZER 1982

Stelzer, W., *Gelehrtes Recht in Österreich, Von den Anfängen bis zum 14. Jahrhundert.* Wien 1982.

STUDER 1957

Studer, B., Sacramentum et exemplum chez Saint Augustin. In: *Recherches Augustiniennes* 10 (1957): 87-141.

VERWEYEN 1970

Verweyen, T., *Apophthegma und Scherzrede, Die Geschichte einer einfachen Gattungsform und ihre Entfaltung im 17. Jahrhundert.* Bad Homburg 1970.

VITALE BROVARONE 1980

Vitale Brovarone, A., L'exemplum tra due retoriche. In: Berlioz, J., David, J.M. (eds), *Rhétorique et histoire...*, 1980: 87-112.

VON MOOS 1972

Von Moos, P., *Consolatio. Studien zur mittellateinischen Trostliteratur.* 4 Vol. München 1972.

VON MOOS 1984

Von Moos, P., The Use of Exempla in the Policraticus of John of Salisbury. In: Wilks, M. (ed.), *The World of John of Salisbury.* Oxford 1984: 207-61.

VON MOOS 1986

Von Moos, P., *Geschichte als Topik, Das Rhetorische Exemplum von dem Antike zur Neuzeit und die historiae im Policraticus des Johann von Salisbu-*

*ry*. Hildesheim-New York 1986.

VON MOOS 1986/7
Von Moos, P., Retorica e poetica tra XII e XIV secolo. In: *Atti del 2 Convegno internazionale di studi dall' A.M.U.L.* Spoleto 1986/7. Im Druck.

VON SODEN 1909
Von Soden, H., *Sententiae LXXIV episcoporum*. Göttingen 1909.

WAHRMUND 1905
Wahrmund, L. (ed.), *Rhetorica ecclesiastica (Inc.: Tam veteri quam novi)*. Innsbruck 1905 (Achen 1962).

WEBB 1909
Webb, C.C.J. (ed.), *John of Salisbury Policratici sive de nugis curialium et vestigiis philosophorum Libri VIII*, Oxford 1909.

WEIMAR 1967
Weimar, P., Argumenta brocardica. In: *Collectanea S. Knutter IV* 1967: 89-124.

WEIMAR 1967
Weimar, P., Die legistische Literatur der Glossatorenzeit. In: Coing, H., *Handbuch der Quellen und Literatur der neueren europäischen Privatrechtsgeschichte* I. München 1973.

WEISHEIPL 1965
Weisheipl, J.A., Classification of the Sciences in Medieval Thought. In: *Medieval Studies* 27 (1965: 54-90).

WELTER 1927
Welter, J.Th., *L'exemplum dans la littérature religieuse et didactique du moyen âge*. Paris-Toulouse 1927 (Genève 1973).

ZIESE 1972
Ziese, J., *Historische Beweisführung in den Streitschriften des Investiturstreits*. München 1972.

ZIMMERMANN 1981
Zimmermann, A., Die Theologie und die Wissenschaften. In: Weimar, P. (ed.), *Die Renaissance der Wissenschaften 12. Jahrhundert*. Zürich 1981.

ZINK 1978
Zink, M., Joinville ne pleure pas, mas il rêve. In: *Poétique* 23 (1978).

A.M. Mulder-Bakker

# A Pantheon full of examples. The World chronicle of Godfrey of Viterbo

Godfrey of Viterbo, *notarius* and chaplain of Frederich Barbarossa and his son Henry VI, was a busy man.[1] He prided himself on how as chaplain of the emperor he had been in the thick of the continual tumult at court by day and by night, saying Mass, reading the hours, dealing with lawsuits, drafting letters, looking out daily for new lodgings and obtaining stipends for himself and his people; he had also gone on legations to all parts of the world, twice to Sicily, three times to Provence, once to Spain, frequently to France and forty times to Rome. And if this had not been enough he had written a mirror for princes and a world chronicle in 20 and more books. He had written them in corners in the crowded palace, underway on horseback or in the shadow of trees and in the danger of battle. He had never known the tranquillity of hermitage or monastery and had to complete his work in the turmoil of battle and the uproar at court (W: 105, 24).

*Life at court*

According to Bremond-Le Goff (1982:43) and Schmitt (1985: 9-10) the medieval example had taken definite shape at the beginning of the 13th century. That is in the period when clerics tried to strengthen their hold on the great mass of believers; when they tried to impress on them a moral life of christian stamp and a christian system of values (in the period therefore when lay people were for the first time taken seriously). Bremond and his colleagues draw special attention to the lay people in the towns and to the rôle of Friars and Preachers in instructing them.These mendicants were the real discoverers of the medieval *exemplum*. If I understand them rightly, they are of the opinion that the phenomenon fits into the large movement of inner christianisation that Vauchez and Duby traced out.[2]

They disregard similar developments however, that took place in other circles of lay people some decades earlier. I mean the developments at the courts of lay princes and nobles in Western Europe. Thanks to the studies of Bumke (1979), Keen (1984) and others we have learnt, that there, at the courts, great centres of culture were created that had a stimulating effect on others. Princes interested in literature and scholarship, though not lettered (*literati*) in the traditional sense themselves, commissioned clerics to produce for them all kinds of literature and learning. The scholar and translator Burgundio of Pisa, wrote to Frederick Barbarossa: 'Since I noticed in my conversations with you, illustrious emperor, that your majesty is interested in learning the nature of things and their origins, I have decided to dedicate the Latin translation of this book (*De Natura hominis* by Nemesius of Emesa) to you.'[3] Works of theological and historical art, epics and love poems, but also saints lives of a special kind were the results. Many of these princes and their surroundings had access for the first time to written culture and the tenets of the christian faith. Men such as Godfrey, chaplains and notaries at the courts, were confronted with their questions and desires. They tried to respond to them in their writings (Guénee 1980: 65-9). At the court of Frederick Barbarossa e.g. men like Henry of Veldeke, Hugh of Honau and Godfrey can be found, as well as bishops such as Anselm of Havelsberg and Otto of Freising (Mulder-Bakker 1983: 164-7). They came across people there who only now for the first time were consciously getting to know the content of the christian message. The people in this group had, of course, belonged to the community of the faithful since time out of mind and had taken part in the rites and practices, but they had never had time and attention for the tenets of the doctrine; they had never actually been confronted with the doctrine of the Trinity, the idea of Christ as God and man, the virgin birth. Now they came to learn of them, we can imagine, that all these dogmas seemed rather unnatural ideas, wonderful, surpassing reason. People like Godfrey saw it as their task to make the content of orthodox belief, with all its incomprehensibility and (at first sight) repulsiveness, comprehensible and acceptable for the ordinary faithful. They did this by presenting Bible knowledge and important dogmas without scholarly pretensions; they also did it by drawing attention to examples from the past of faithful princes who were rewarded and unbelieving kings who were punished, and by depicting in detail a life pleasing to God in former times (Mulder-Bakker 1983: 205-9).

It seems of interest, therefore, to scrutinize their texts and not to forget the historical works; all the more so because the historians of that circle produced a new kind of historical writing. As we know, previous historians had considered themselves in the first place as compilers and collectors of old and traditional material (Sigebert of Gembloux is a good example of this). They tried to summarize tradition into a short and condensed form to hand it down to posterity. They paid not much attention to writing an attractive story. Now from the twelfth century onwards they set themselves the task of delighting and captivating the reader more than they had done before. Men such as Geoffrey of Monmouth, the author of the *Kaiserchronik* and Godfrey of Viterbo tried hard to write attractive stories. Since they were, as their predecessors, convinced that history was the mistress of life, *historia magistra vitae*, and a good vehicle for conveying their instruction, they were inclined to retail witty anecdotes or absorbing episodes in their histories in order to put their message across. Elaborating upon old and familiar material they built up an historical narrative, which delighted and at the same time educated, which taught and also conveyed a point of view. This did not apply to every historical writer, but certainly did to those who addressed themselves to the new exponents of culture. We come across many of these historical writers in the entourage of new, up-and-coming princely courts. Around the Anglo-Norman house of Plantagenet, around the Sicilian kings and around the Hohenstaufen we encounter scholars who recorded the history of the recent dynasty, the new empire, but also more distant history which would give the new dynasty a background and a place in history. This background could go as far back as Charlemagne, Alexander or the Creation (Guénee 1980: 58-65).

Their historical products bore the marks of this. They sometimes resembled storehouses of anecdotes or, as Smalley (1974: 22) said, enormous boxes of chocolates: 'You dip into the collection as though it were a chocolate box'. They resemble, indeed, in one way or another, the collections of *exempla* of later times. Therefore, the courts and the texts circulating there in comparison with the towns and the mendicant preachers is my first point of interest. As we shall see later on, the importance of history will be my second point.

*The Pantheon of Godfrey of Viterbo*

Living at the German imperial court, Godfrey adopted this new form of historical writing and wrote a world chronicle to supply the new demand. The *Pantheon* in its definitive form, and written in both prose and verse, explicitly intended to instruct the young king Henry VI and the lay princes around him who were destined for important government duties and could well use the wisdom and knowledge of their forebears. According to Godfrey they had to acquire a good knowledge of *philosophia*, or, more precisely, of the *antiquorum regum vitae et gesta atque historiae* (P: 2, 14) on the one hand and the *scripturarum dogmata* (P: 2, 4) on the other; so as to draw conclusions about their own dealings. Only when they had this 'philosophical' insight would they be able to acquit themselves of their tasks in government in a fitting manner. Only then could they give a good example to their subjects and resist the temptation to disregard the law, although, as princes they were not bound by the law. A king who was ignorant of philosophical wisdom, seemed to roam (*errare*) more than to reign (*regnare*) (P: 2, 6).

So Godfrey wanted to impress two subjects upon the minds of his pupils. First, the history and the great deeds of the kings of the past, in order to extract instructions for the present and the future. Secondly, christian doctrine, also in its historical context and beginning from the Creation. 'I am frequently asked', Godfrey said, 'where was God at that time? In what world? ... and how can He be three and one at the same time?' (P: 2, 23). He wanted to go into this in simple language. He derived his material from Peter Comestor, but all exegetical or dogmatic discussion, a fundamental element in the *Historia Scho-*

*lastica*, he omitted. As we shall see later on, he also chose a specific form for these parts of his chronicle.

## *A Pantheon full of examples*

In search of Godfrey's handling of *exempla* and examples I have put myself two questions. First I tried to get an idea of Godfrey's handling of *exemplum* and examples as illustrative stories in general, and then I studied this more in detail in the Alexander-passage.[4]

Godfrey apparently knew the Ciceronian definition of example. Dealing with the Punic Wars and the rôle of Atilius Regulus in these, he quoted the well-known words of Cicero and concluded: *Hec autem dicta, modernis ad exemplum sunt reseruata* ('these words should be held in mind as an example by people in our days') (P: 238, 53 v). In the course of his work he makes use of at least four further kinds of *exempla*. On the one hand *exemplum* can be used as an equivalent of *similitudo* in the sense of a graphic illustration of something theoretical: in his sections on christian dogmas he compares the virgin birth to sunbeams falling through the window. He does so under the headings *exemplum* or *similitudo*.[5] On the other hand Godfrey makes use of the term *exemplum* when the fate of one historical king or emperor influences the conduct of another: Galienus saw the miserable end of his co-emperor and changed his ways (W: 171, 19).

The third and fourth categories of examples are of more interest to us. *Exemplum* can be used more or less as an equivalent of the Latin *exemplar*, to indicate the exemplary significance of an historical figure within a certain tradition. Cain was the first human being in history to plunder and to murder. So he became the prototype of all murderers and plunderers (P: 75, 43). We shall see that Alexander could be considered as his most brilliant pupil (P: 230, 36). Historical figures thus passed into proverbial stereotypes. Nebuchadnezar stood for all bad rulers in historiography (P: 187, 51) and Ninus for a heathen worshipper (P: 102, 20). Especially the heroes of the distant past could expect to become proverbial prototypes. Authorities writing in former generations had shifted the disparate data out and moulded these figures into types and ideals. For later historians these types had taken definite shape and could be handled as such. As far as Alexander is concerned, we can follow this process in the world chronicles I have seen from Frutolf of Michelsberg in the 11th century onwards (see appendix). When Godfrey comes to deal with him, he brings these typical elements into play to explain his own intentions. After depicting the historical events, he could turn to the reader (*'o lector'*) and drive home the moral lesson. Sometimes he did so explicitly under the heading *Author reddit rationem* (P: 228, 2), sometimes more implicitly by concluding an episode with some moralistic remarks: *Quod miraculum aut ideo fuit, quia Alexander erat magnus Dei cultor, aut quia per eum Deus superbiam Persarum fuerat puniturus* (P: 224, 52). In respect of the content and the purport of these histories they function as examples for the reader. It must be emphasized though, that these examples derive their authority, their value not from the author of the chronicle, nor from previous authors, but from the prince to whom these stories were attached.

The last category of *exempla* are short stories with a message in themselves used to illustrate a certain point. In the eyes of later generations the emperor Henry IV, at the end of the 11th century, had been a bad ruler. Swayed by envy and a despotic ferocity he bullied his people. Godfrey demonstrated this by telling a short story about an, unnamed, knight who could fight a lion and was murdered by Henry IV; no specific date was given. He introduced this digression with the words: *Inuidia fertur nimia potuisse notari / Et nimia feritate sua nequam reputari, / De quibus exempla pagina pauca dabit* (P: 500, 3-26).

Especially in the section on the German emperors, the forefathers of Frederick and Henry, it is remarkable that short summaries of the historical facts are followed by relatively long *historiae* in verse about one or two rather unimportant events. These events are usually not representative of the emperors in question, whereas they are revealing indeed for the conduct of emperors in general. For example, the great deeds of Otto III, the emperor who wanted to revive the universal Roman Empire and did not live long enough to marry, was treated in only 17 lines of prose, followed by a long poem of 85 lines on a queen (whose queen?) who seduced a count whose guest she was (P: 481, 10). The emperor's behaviour is described in detail, Frederick and his son may have learnt a lot from it, but the event as such was not characteristic for Otto's reign, nor was it for the long march of events. Similar examples could be told about other emperors.

Godfrey wanted to captivate as well as to instruct his lay princes. He did so by dealing with two different kinds of subject. He wanted to impress on his readers both the main points of the christian faith and the great deeds of the kings in the past. If one turns over the leaves of his chronicle, one notices that Godfrey treated the christian faith in an almost scholastic manner. Short treatises, completely in prose - for Jews and heretics might attach less weight to verses - are inserted at turning-points in history, at the Creation and at the birth of Christ (P: 31, 1-69, 13; 275, 30-322, 55). These parts of the chronicle are entirely without illustrative examples or anecdotes. Godfrey admits that he knew many fine stories about Christ and the apostles or wonderful miracles on the saints, but he passed them by (P: 343, 28). In his history he treated *historiae*, charming stories, usually written in verse to please the reader and meant to teach lay princes how to conduct themselves and how to rule. As we have seen, kings needed such philosophical wisdom, for they were not, as normal beings, bound by the law. They had to decide on their own attitude and had to account for that before God. These *historiae* thus contributed, like the sections on the christian faith, to their salvation.[6]

All things considered, these *historiae* were not illustrative digressions within a historical discourse, they were not second rate tales, but indeed the kernel of the whole chronicle. Those little poems served to envelop the philosophical lessons. The historiographical discourse as such served as their chronological framework. It anchored, as it were, the disconnected poems in history. In earlier drafts of his world chronicle Godfrey had strung together long series of poems without any connecting text in prose. Only a number of *isagoge* had introduced large complexes of material (Schulz 1926: 86-131). In the final version Godfrey had cut these former *isagoge* up into short introductions to the different reigns and emperors. They were now meant to introduce the material by giving the large historical context, and to summarize the story for pupils who were not capable of understanding the verses. The alternation of prose and verse was meant to stimulate the reader to further reading (P: 2, 19).

I would not, however, go so far as to assert that the chronological framework was unimportant. It was an essential part, actually. The many different tales were anchored in history and given authority by it. Disconnected stories were of no value, *historiae* within their chronological context, about the kings of the past were.

A second point is that history served to locate figures in time and in terms of salvation. Kings of the pre-christian era were of a different kind from christian rulers. They lent themselves to other stories than medieval kings. They were normally unbelieving, heathen worshippers who refused to listen to the Word of God, spoken by the Old Testament-prophets. They lent themselves to stories which denounced this, and demonstrated that emperors were expected to be faithful adherents of the Christian (papal) Church. The emperors of the Middle Ages were considered to be 'Christians at heart'; in their case matters of peace and justice, a righteous government, were appropriate subjects to deal with.

As far as I can see, Godfrey had a certain kind of historical consciousness; he had an eye for historical evolution. He saw the necessity of calling up the past in its chronological context. Kings and events were to him not scattered examples from the past, as they were to John of Salisbury to be handled at will, stripped of all historical idiosyncracies and to be reproduced and multiplied at will.[7]

But more can be said. Godfrey felt that people stood consciously in a long tradition. Kings belonged to a renowned dynasty and felt it as their duty to keep that tradition up, both by having the praises of their forefathers sung, *and* by performing equally glorious deeds. They had the history of their dynasty written down, the saints of the family venerated, and the praises of the ancestral warriors sung. According to Hauck and others the epic poetry of the *Dietrich-Epik* for example, the sagas and songs of the Goths, can be considered as the praises of the forebears of the medieval German aristocracy (Hauck 1954). Kings clung to this tradition. Historians such as Godfrey and Frutolf of Michelsberg before him adhered to tradition as well -and thought it proper- but preferred a different past; they sought their prototypes in a different, a more peaceful and, in their eyes, more salutary history. They thought it was harmful for the well-being of the christian community when kings in admiration of the valiant heroes, brave in war, proud and angry, driven into battle by a personal sense of honour, clung to that tradition and turned their own hands to enmity and war. That is why humanistically minded clerics opposed this hero-cult and were urged to offer an alternative. They sought and found good examples in the classical past and in the Bible. By bringing these heroes into play, they tried to persuade their princes to follow the ideal of a just and peaceful ruler, governing by law-giving and doing justice instead of feuding and fighting. And thanks to this strongly felt tradition they were to a certain degree successful. To conclude with a quotation from Keen's fine book on *Chivalry* (1984: 6) 'Without clerical learning in the background, chivalry could scarcely have progressed far beyond a kind of hereditary military professionalism, occasionally heroic but essentially crude'.

After all, I wonder if history, the historical tradition, the fact that examples were supposed to have happened in the past, is not of more importance than Bremond and others believe, notwithstanding their emphasis on the historical veracity of the *exemplum*. The fact that events had taken place in the past, was essential for people in the Middle Ages, it was, as we could say, a matter of life and death, because it was a matter of salvation. Christianity and salvation were a matter of history. It was essential to the christian faith that the gospel was dealt with, not so much in a systematic doctrine as in historical narratives, in the histories of the Old and the New Testament and in the history of the Church. Historical narratives in general are, therefore, of essential, of salutary importance.

*Alexander as an exemplum*

To illustrate all this: 'I'd like to tell you, among other wonderful stories, the miraculous and exceptional deeds, so delightful and charming to hear, of Alexander'. This is how medieval historians - in this case Frutolf of Michelsberg (Waitz 1843: 70) - introduced the Alexander romance to their readers. In many a medieval world chronicle Alexander is thus a key-figure. He is that at least, in Godfrey's chronicle and in the other two medieval world chronicles with which I wish to compare Godfrey's, namely those of Frutolf of Michelsberg and Jans Enikel. Frutolf of Michelsberg wrote a *Liber cronicorum* (Waitz 1843) at the end of the 11th century. He was the first to incorporate the classical Alexander romance into historiography. The second is Jans Enikel, who wrote a world chronicle in German at the end of the 13th century, not for kings but for an urban public.

Frutolf lived in Bamberg, a town where the Salian emperors enjoyed staying. He incorporated a long *Excursus de Vita Alexandri* into his chronicle, apparently to entertain his readers *and* to insert an ideal portrait of an emperor along his own lines (Schmale-Schmale-Ott 1972; Mulder-Bakker 1983: 57-111): However, he never makes his aims explicit. At first glance the *Vita Alexandri* looks like a mere compilation of old and traditional material. It is a scholarly rearrangement of disparate passages which he found in his sources. But it adds up to a coherent portrait, a long and continuous discourse of the great deeds of Alexander and the *miracula* he met, without digressions - the whole *vita* as such is a digression - and interruptions. It is a portrait of a brave and righteous king, who showed courage, leadership and loyalty to his relatives and followers, who was self-confident but also conscious that he was a mortal man, guided by a higher hand. In short he was the paragon of all kingly virtues except at the end of his life before his cruel death. The abundance of motives Frutolf employed can be seen in the appendix.

Jans Enikel, on the other hand, wrote his *Weltchronik* (Strauch 1900) in the last quarter of the 13th century (Kugler 1982: 216-52; Liebertz-Grün 1984: 74-101). He belonged to the knightly class of burghers in Vienna and wrote a world chronicle in German, a voluminous work in both prose and verse. Unlike that of Frutolf, his chronicle is a rather loose string of independent tales, 'witzige Histörchen' told with undeniable pleasure (Kugler 1982: 235). Writing for the Viennese aristocracy, people who now had access to written culture and had a strong belief in all that was written, he could not fall back on the traditional schemes. His chronicle lacked Frutolf's and Godfrey's typological schemes, it also lacked the clear chronological framework. These things meant nothing to his readers. Even the stereotyped great kings and emperors were sometimes lacking. The heroes of the past were often pushed into the background to clear the way for anonymous men and unknown events, instead. As Kugler (1982: 238) remarked: 'anonymen "Helden"... mit geringen Mitteln, mit Witz und einer gehörigen Portion gesunden Menschenverstandes'. The different tales all tell a story of their own and within the empirical world of the Viennese burgher they were thought to be self-evident. An explicit moralisation is also lacking here.

Out of the abundant Alexander material Jans chose only three charming tales, not characteristic for Alexander, not characteristic for his universal empire, but illustrating general human vices: pride, strife for gain and the unreliability of women.

Between the two is Godfrey (P: 221-231, 55). He knew of the chronological coherence and of the worldwide importance of Alexander. In his view Alexander was the first universal ruler who visited Jerusalem and honoured God, by bowing for the high priest and entering the temple. He was the first emperor who had the right attitude towards God and was therefore the prototype of all universal rulers until the End of Time, when the Last Emperor, the *Rex Romanorum*, would enter Jerusalem again and would place his crown on Christ's Grave to return his power to God from whom all rulers had received their power. This universal ruler Alexander was of the utmost suitability to Godfrey to emphasize both the worldwide authority of the medieval German Empire *and* the desired moral conduct of each individual emperor. Henry VI, a descendant of the old Roman Emperors himself and an exponent of that imposing tradition, was, as it were, to follow in their steps.

After summarizing the memorable deeds of Alexander in prose and praising them in verse, Godfrey therefore selected several single episodes to make his ideas explicit. By shaping these into more or less self-contained poems under separate headings, he made the typological significance of Alexander explicit and illustrated his moral conduct. Under the heading *Tres processiones principales* he dealt with Alexander's visit to Jerusalem (P: 226, 9-31); under the heading *Planctus Alexandri super Darium* he gave the pathetic story of Alexander's confrontation with the dying Darius, deserted by his followers by the roadside (P: 226, 40-227, 23). Darius admonishes him there: 'see how I have to die a miserable death: *talibus exemplis cautior esto tibi* (P: 227, 8); fortune pushes one up and pushes one down; she gives empires and she takes them away. Do not pride yourself on your success, it is not yours'.

On his journey through the Far East Alexander met the ignominous races of Goth and Magoth and also the innocent savages, the Brahmins. He enclosed Goth and Magoth behind the Caspian Gates: *ne ferat exemplum vita nefanda malum* (P: 228, 12-229, 4). This tour de force was not his achievement either, for he prayed to God to move the mountains at exactly the moment when God had already determined to move them. These races of Goth and Magoth were the same as those which would confront the Last Emperor on his journey to Jerusalem, so Godfrey had the opportunity to refer to this Emperor who would wear the *aurea lamina* on his forehead, the same as was worn by the high priest before whom Alexander bowed.

In a last section *De disputatione inter Alexandrum et regem Brachmanorum* (P: 229, 5-231, 39), Godfrey dealt with the 'legal Roman structure' of the world empire and the moral conduct of Alexander and Dyndimus.[8] Alexander boasted of being descended from Jupiter and ruling over a highly civilized, wealthy empire, conquered by his own brave fighting. Dyndimus stood up to this bravado and insisted on Alexander's personal disdain for the law. Was he not a robber who condemned a plunderer? Referring to Cain, the first robber of mankind, he wrote: *Ejus ad exemplum rapuit post turba malorum, / ex quibus (o tu rex) stas summus in orbe latronum ...* (P: 230, 36).

All the characteristics of Godfrey's chronicle can be seen here in a nutshell. The whole history was considered to be a mistress of life; the deeds of the kings of the past served to inform the present king about the honourable tradition in which he stood and had to give him good examples of how to behave. At the end of his chronicle Godfrey would address himself to Henry in person and would underline: *Regibus antiquis, Henrice monarce, coheres,/ tu diadema feres, Romani culminis heres* (W 269, 2). And he was to warn him:[9]

> If your majesty will not respect the rights and duties of prince and subjects, what right have you to call yourself a king? If you cannot be your own guide, still less shall you be mine. Alexander the Great's tutor instilled bad habits into his prince; the king learned this as a child, he regretted it as an adult. Alexander conquered Darius and also Babylon, but he could not overcome the instilled habits...

Out of solicitude for his well-being and his eternal salvation, he lectured the king. The king who was not bound by the laws should bind himself, and he should take the life of Alexander as a warning. In Godfrey's opinion Alexander was a good example for later generations - is he a good *exemplum* too?

NOTES

1.  On Godfrey of Viterbo: Baaken (1978) and Mulder-Bakker (1983: 183-241).
    The Pantheon was edited by Pistorius (1613) and reedited by Pistorius-
    Struve (1726). A partial edition was published by Waitz (1872).
    The edition of Pistorius is referred to as: P. and Waitz' as: W.

2.  Vauchez (1981: 154), who quotes Duby (1976: 261): 'après 1200 ... la
    religion chrétienne avait finalement cessé d'être affaire de rites et
    affaire de prêtres. Au XIVe siècle, elle tendait à devenir adhésion des
    masses'.

3.  Classen (1974: 28, note 30). This sentence seems to me more than a
    formal politeness.

4.  Chesnutt (1984: 593) also draws attention to Godfrey's *Pantheon* as a
    possible source of *exempla*.

5.  *Similitudines de partu virginis* (P: 335, 25); *Exemplum trinitatis et simili-
    tudo de sole* (P: 10, 3).

6.  *Quum ergo Reges, non in leges, sed in Deum peccent, et Dei solius,
    vestroque examini* (= pope Urbanus III) *reseruentur: antiquorum regum
    vitam et gesta atque historias oportet eos cognoscere: ut causae prece-
    dentium, fiant eis in posterum cautio futurorum* (P: 2, 12-15).

7.  *Policraticus, Prologue* (Webb 1909: I, 12, 17); Book I, iv (Webb, I 29, 22)
    e.a. Elaborate factual details concerning the important figures and events
    prove Godfrey's point of view, see e.g. his introduction of Alexander:
    *Annis ab Adam 5888, a diluvio 1638: a diuisione linguarum 1537: ab
    imperio Nini 1371: a destructione Troiae 772: anno ab Urbe condita 427:
    mortuo rege Graecorum Philippo, Alexander filius eius, in regnum succes-
    sit...* (P: 221, 23-30).

8.  Alexander asked Dyndimus: *scribite quas leges, quod opus, quae jura
    tenetis* (P:229, 11) and explained himself: *Omnia castigo, tanquam Deus,
    ordine divo,/ omnia solvo, ligo, summo diademate vivo* (P: 230, 9) and
    *Jura damus populis, sed nos non lege tenemur,/ unde nec ex factis
    aliquid peccasse videmur./ Quod mihi complacuit, lex mihi semper erit* (P:
    231, 8-11).

9.  *Si tibi non fueris, nec mihi rector eris/ doctor Alexandri Magni pravos
    sibi mores/ finxit et incessus inhonestos absque decore;/ rex puer hec
    didicit, set didicisse dolet./ Vicit Alexander Darium simul et Babilonem;/
    set nequit inpressum sibimet devincere morem...* (W: 270,9).

## ALEXANDER THE GREAT IN EXEMPLA

Checklist: Tubach (1969)

A = Frutolf
B = Godfrey
C = Jans Enikel

| | | A | B | C |
|---|---|---|---|---|
| 90. | A. advised by Parmenyon | (x) | | |
| 91. | affected by vice of Leonidas | | | |
| 92. | and Amazons | x | x | |
| 93. | and Anaximenes | | | |
| 94. | and Aristotle | x | | |
| 95. | and battle | x | | |
| 96. | and Bucephalos | x | | |
| 97. | and candle | | | |
| 98. | and Cassander | (x) | | |
| 99. | and father's friend | | | |
| 100. | and gift | | | |
| 101. | and habits | (x) | | |
| 102. | and heir | | | |
| 103. | and high priest | x | xx | |
| 104. | and immortality | x | | |
| 105. | and Lampsacus | | | |
| 106. | and mother's adultery | x | | |
| 107. | and philosopher | | | |
| 108. | and slayers | x | xx | |
| 109 | and wonders of India | x | x | |
| 110. | army of Alexander plagued | x | x | |
| 111. | water parts for army of A. | | x | |
| 112. | as guest of Porus (F.:Darius) | x | | |
| 113. | as pirate | | x | |
| 114. | attempt to kill A. | x | | |
| 115. | buying friends | | | |
| 116. | conquests of A. | x | x | x |
| 117. | death of A. predicted | x | | |
| 118. | defeats King Porus | x | | |
| 119. | father of A. revenged | | | |
| 120. | forces father to renounce 2nd wife | x | | |
| 121. | funeral oration of A. | | | |
| 122. | gait of A. | | | |
| 123. | glass diving vessel of A. | | | |
| 124. | illegitimate birth of A. | x | x | |
| 125. | in air and ocean | x | x | |
| 126. | in paradise | | | x |

| | | | | |
|---|---|---|---|---|
| 127. | jousts with princes | (x) | | |
| 128. | kills friends | | | |
| 129. | kills Nectanabus | x | | |
| 130. | like tree | | | |
| 131. | meets ass first | | | |
| 132. | mother of A. tricked by sorcerer | x | | |
| 133. | not divine | | | |
| 134. | physician of A. accused | x | | |
| 135. | poisoned | x | x | |
| 136. | received in Jerusalem | x | xx | |
| 137. | receives gifts from Darius | (x) | | |
| 138. | restores captive girl | | | |
| 139. | saves city | | | |
| 140. | sends peppercorns | x | | |
| 141. | stone of A. | | | x |
| 142. | summons castles to surrender | | | |
| 143. | takes manners of Persians | | | |
| 144. | three bad qualities of A. | | | |
| 145. | three questions of A. | | | |
| 146. | troops of A. demoralized | x | | |
| 147. | walls in Jews | | xx | |
| 148. | warned about greatness | | x | |
| 149. | wounded | | | |
| 327. | Aristotle advises A. | | | |
| 328. | Aristotle warns A. | | | |
| 750. | offers Brahmins a gift | | | |
| 1122. | watches a burning coal on boy | | | |
| 3289. | and a miller | | | |
| 3596. | wishes to go to paradise | | | |
| 3751. | philosophers at A.'s grave | | | |
| 3821. | and Plato | | | |
| 3830. | and Queen of the south | | | |
| 1673. | and Diogenes | | | |

# BIBLIOGRAPHY

BAAKEN 1978
Baaken, G., Zur Beurteilung Gottfrieds von Viterbo. In: Hauck, K., Mordek, H. (eds), *Geschichtsschreibung und geistiges Leben im Mittelalter. Festschrift für H. Löwe*, Köln-Wien 1978, 373-96.

BUMKE 1979
Bumke, J., *Mäzene im Mittelalter. Die Gönner und Auftraggeber der höfischen Literatur in Deutschland (1150-1300)*. München 1979.

CLASSEN 1974
Classen, P., *Burgundio von Pisa. Richter, Gesandte, Übersetzer*. Heidelberg 1974.

CHESNUTT 1984
Chesnut, M., Exempelsammlungen im Mittelalter. In: *Enzyklopädie des Märchens*, IV. 1984: 593-604.

DUBY 1976
Duby, G., *Le temps des chathédrales. L'art et la société*. Paris 1976.

GUENÉE 1980
Guenée, B., *Histoire et culture historique dans l'Occident médiéval*. Paris 1980.

HAUCK 1954
Hauck, K., Haus- und Sippengebundene Literatur mittelalterliches Adelsgeschlechtes von Adelssatiren des 11. und 12. Jahrhunderts aus erläutert. In: *Mitteilungen des Instituts für Österreichische Geschichtsforschung* 62 (1954): 121-45.

KEEN 1984
Keen, M., *Chivalry*. New Haven-London 1984.

KUGLER 1982
Kugler, J., Jans Enikel und die Weltchronistik im späten Mittelalter. In: *Einführung in die deutsche Literatur des 12.-16. Jahrhunderts*, II. Opladen 1982.

LIEBERTZ-GRÜN 1984
Liebertz-Grün, U., *Das andere Mittelalter. Erzählte Geschichte und Geschichtserkenntnis um 1300*. München 1984.

MULDER-BAKKER 1983
Mulder-Bakker, A.B., *Vorstenschool. Vier geschiedschrijvers over Alexander en hun visie op het keizerschap*. Groningen 1983.

PISTORIUS 1613
Pistorius, J. (ed.), *Gottfried von Viterbo. Pantheon*. Frankfurt 1613.

PISTORIUS-STRUVE 1726
Pistorius, J., Struve, B.G. (eds), *Gottfried von Viterbo. Pantheon. Rerum Germanicarum scriptores... II*, Regensburg 1726.

SCHMALE-SCHMALE-OTT 1972
Schmale, F.J., Schmale-Ott, J. (eds), *Frutolf und Ekkehards Chroniken und die anonyme Kaiserchronik*. Darmstadt 1972.

SCHULZ 1926
Schulz, G., Die Entstehungsgeschichte der Werke Gottfrieds von Viterbo. In: *Neues Archiv der Gesellschaft für ältere deutsche Geschichtskunde*, 46 (1926):

86-131.

SMALLEY 1974

Smalley, B., *Historians in the Middle Ages*. London 1974.

STRAUCH 1900

Strauch, P. (ed.), *Jans Enikel, Weltchronik*. MGH Deutsche Chroniken, III, 1900.

TUBACH 1969

Tubach, F.C., *Index Exemplorum. A Handbook of Medieval Religious Tales*. Helsinki 1969.

VAUCHEZ 1981

Vauchez, A., *La Sainteté en Occident aux derniers siècles du Moyen Age d'après les procès de canonisation et les documents hagiographiques*. Rome 1981.

WAITZ 1872

Waitz, G. (ed.), *Frutolf of Michelsberg. Liber Chronicorum: Ekkehardi Uraniensis Chronica*. MGH ss, VI. 1843.

WAITZ 1843

Waitz, G. (ed.), *Gottfried von Viterbo. Pantheon*. MGH ss, XXII. 1872.

WEBB 1909

Webb, C.C.J. (ed.), *John of Salisbury Policratici sive de nugis curialium et vestigiis philosophorum Libri VIII*. Oxford 1909.

F.P. Knapp

# Antike und moderne Beispielfiguren in Wolframs 'Parzival' als Stilphänomene und Intertextualitätssignale

In meinem Buch *Similitudo* habe ich folgende Definition des Exempels gegeben: Das Exempel 'ist eine einer besonderen (dem vorliegenden Darstellungszusammenhang angehörenden) Grundvorstellung des (zwischen)menschlichen Bereichs in (zumindest) innerer Vergleichsform direkt oder indirekt gegenübergestellte Vergleichsvorstellung des (im weitesten Sinne) historisch fixierten Menschenlebens. Selbstverständlich kann Exempel auch das gesamte Gebilde und auch den Vorgang der Gegenüberstellung meinen' (1975: 181).

Ausgeschlossen bleiben dabei das Beispiel im engeren Sinne beziehungsweise die daraus entwickelte Beispielerzählung, die an einem konkreten Einzelfall eine allgemeine, meist sentenzartige Aussage exemplifiziert, ebenso wie Fabel und Parabel, wo ein Bildteil einem (bisweilen bis auf Null reduzierten, aber auch unausgesprochen als Bezugspunkt vorhandenen) Auslegungsteil gegenübersteht, desgleichen auch das *Exemplum dictum* der antiken Rhetorik, das eine Sentenz mit der Angabe dessen, der sie (angeblich oder tatsächlich) geprägt hat, verbindet, und schliesslich selbstverständlich alle historischen Angaben eines Textes, die in keinerlei Vergleichsbeziehung zur dargestellten Grundvorstellung stehen.

Wie bereits der Titel meiner Untersuchung zeigt, ist hier von Exempeln die Rede, welche in einen epischen Gesamtzusammenhang eingeordnet sind. Als diesen habe ich den Versroman *Parzival* Wolframs von Eschenbach (Lachmann-Hartl 1952), entstanden im ersten Jahrzehnt des 13. Jahrhunderts, gewählt, dies unter anderem deshalb, weil mir dafür bereits eine eigene Studie zur logischen und grammatischen Struktur des bildhaften Vergleichs als Ausgangspunkt zur Verfügung steht (1979a: 59-86).[1]

In die dort erstellten Kategorien gilt es vorerst die rund dreissig Exempla einzuordnen, was selbstverständlich nicht ganz gelingen kann, da dem Exempel das sprachlogische Element der Bildhaftigkeit ja gerade fehlt. Dennoch lässt die analoge Sphärenduplizität von Grund- und Vergleichsbereich eine zumindest ähnliche Kategorisierung auf textlinguistischer Ebene zu. Es muss aber vorab betont werden, dass das schmale Textkorpus eine Verallgemeinerung auf die poetische Praxis der klassischen mittelhochdeutschen Epik nicht erlaubt.

Der Gruppe IA, dem partiellen Vergleich, bei dem der Vergleichsbereich kein satzwertiges Satzglied umfasst, sind erwartungsgemäss keine Exempla unseres Korpus eindeutig zuzuordnen.
Ihr nahe stehen folgende Fälle:
187,14 *Jeschûten, Enîten,*
       *und Cunnewâren de Lâlant,*
       *und swâ man lobes die besten vant,*
       *dâ man vrouwen schoene gewuoc,*
       *ir ( = Condwîrâmûrs) glastes schîn vast under sluoc*
       *und bêder Isalden.*

     (Nr. 9-10: 'Der Glanz von C.s Schönheit übertraf bei weitem den der J., E., C. de L. und der hervorragendsten, wo immer man sie fand, da man von der Schönheit der Damen sprach, und auch der beiden Isolden.')

Der Fall kann als Transformation der Phrase 'a war grösser als b' (I A 1.2) aufgefasst werden.
Dasselbe gilt von
796,7 *Parzivâls schoene was nu ein wint,*
       *und Absalôn Dâvîdes kint,*
       *von Ascalûn Vergulaht,*
       *und al den schoene was geslaht,*
       *und des man Gahmurete jach,*
       *...*
       *ir deheins schoene was der gelîch,*
       *die Anfortas ûz siecheit truòc.*

     (Nr. 32: 'P.s Schönheit war nun ein Nichts. Und A., Davids Sohn, V. von A., und was man G. zusprach ... - die Schönheit keines von ihnen war der gleich, die A. nach Überwindung seiner Krankheit an sich hatte.')

Nach der Oberflächenstruktur liegt allerdings ein negierter totaler Vergleich (Typ II - s.u. Nr. 15) vor.
   Bereits der Gruppe I B, dem partiellen Vergleich, bei dem der Vergleichsbereich einen Gliedsatz umfasst, sind folgende Fälle einzufügen:
289,17 *der minne er ( = Parzivâl) muose ir siges jehen,*
       *diu Salmônen ouch betwanc.*

     (Nr. 31: 'P. musste der Minne ihren Sieg zugestehen, die auch Salomon bezwungen hatte.')

Hier liegt die Transformation eines Vergleichssatzes in einen Relativsatz mit *ouch* vor. Die beiden Subjekte sind ident, die Prädikate semantisch eng verwandt.

Ebenfalls in Form eines Relativsatzes tritt der Vergleichsbereich auf in
795,30 *der durch sant Silvestern einen stier*
    *von tôde lebendec dan hiez gên,*
    *unt der Lazarum bat ûf stên,*
    *der selbe half daz Anfortas*
    *wart gesunt unt wol genas.*

(Nr. 33-34: 'Der um St. Silvesters willen einen toten Stier lebendig
weggehen liess und L. gebot aufzustehen, derselbe bewirkte, dass A.
gesund und ganz geheilt wurde.')

Die Vergleichsbeziehung wird nur durch das *selbe* angedeutet. Sie erscheint
stark gelockert. Das Exempel für die Wunderkraft Gottes steht an der Grenze
zum Beispiel im oben definierten Sinne.

Die Vergleichsform ist dagegen nicht nur erhalten, sondern noch durch den
Einsatz von *tuon* als Prädikat 2 verstärkt (Typ I B 1.2) in
420,25 *wurdet ir mirs nimmer holt,*
    *ich taete ê als Rumolt,*
    *der künec Gunthêre riet,*
    *do er von Wormz gein Hiunen schiet:*
    *er bat in lange sniten baen*
    *und inme kezzel umbe draen.*

(Nr. 25: 'Selbst wenn ihr mir deshalb für immer böse seid, wollte ich es
lieber wie R. machen, der König G. einen Rat gab, da dieser von W. zu
den Hunnen abreiste: Er bat ihn, grosse Brotschnitten zu rösten und im
Sossenkessel umzudrehen.')

Gegenüber dem Normaltypus sind die Prädikate aber vertauscht (Ich wollte euch
raten, wie es R. bei G. tat). Die Ausweitung des Vergleichsbereichs (= VB)
geschieht, wie häufig, mittels eines Gliedsatzes und eines selbständigen Satzes.

Liegt hier eine Gleichsetzung (*Adaequatio*) vor, so in weiteren Fällen eine
Steigerung (*Comparatio*):
387,1 *Des kom Melijacanz in nôt,*
    *daz im der werde Lanzilôt*
    *nie so vaste zuo getrat,*
    *do er von der swertbrücke pfat*
    *kom und dâ nâch mit im streit.*
    *im was gevancnusse leit,*
    *die vrou Ginovêr dolte,*
    *die er dâ mit strîte holte.*

(Nr. 7: 'Davon (= von der Begegnung mit Gâwân) kam M. so in Bedrängnis, dass ihm der treffliche L. nie so sehr zu Leibe gerückt war, als er
vom Weg der Schwertbrücke kam und hernach mit ihm kämpfte. Ihn

hatte die Gefangenschaft bedrückt, welche Madame G. erduldete, die er im Kampf befreite.')

Ein modal-konsekutiver Satz formt den Vergleich ('mehr als jemals') um. Derselbe Typ (I B 1.3.1) ist zu finden in

399,11 *disiu burc (= Ascalun) was gehêret sô,*
    *daz Enêas Kartâgô*
    *nie sô hêrrenlîche vant,*
    *dâ vrovn Dîdôn tôt was minnen pfant.*

(Nr. 16: 'Diese Burg war so geschmückt, dass E. Karthago niemals so herrlich vorfand, wo Madame Didos Tod der Minne verpfändet wurde.')

Der Vergleichssatz bewahrt ist dagegen in

401,5 *hie kom Gâwân zuo geriten.*
    *âvoy nu wart dâ niht vermiten,*
    *erne wurde baz empfangen*
    *dan ze Karidoel waere ergangen*
    *Ereckes empfâhen*
    *dô er begunde nâhen*
    *Artûs nâch sîme strîte,*
    *unt dô vrou Enîte*
    *sîner vröude was ein condewier,*
    *sît im Maliclisier*
    *daz twerc sîn vel unsanfte brach*
    *mit der geisel da ez Gynovêr sach,*
    *unt dô ze Tulmein ein strît*
    *ergienc in dem creize wît*
    *umbe den spärwaere.*
    *Idêr fil Noyt der maere*
    *im sîne sicherheit dâ bôt:*
    *er muose im bieten vür den tôt.*

(Nr. 11: 'Hier kam G. herbeigeritten. Hei, nun versäumte man hier nicht, ihn besser zu empfangen, als der Empfang Ereks ausgefallen war, da dieser nach seinem Kampf A. aufsuchte und da E. seine Freude leitete, seitdem der Zwerg M. ihm, wobei G. zusah, brutal die Haut mit der Geissel verletzt und in Tulmein in einem weiten Kampfring um den Sperber ein Kampf stattgefunden hatte. Der berühmte Sohn N.s, I., schwor ihm da den Unterwerfungseid. Er musste ihn anbieten, um den Tod zu vermeiden.')

Es ist dies der am stärksten erweiterte VB in unserem Korpus. Aber alles ist aus der genannten Kernstruktur entwickelt: 'G. wurde besser als E. empfangen'. Prädikat 2 ist nur eine nominale Periphrase von Prädikat 1.

Das vorletzte Exempel 399,11 (Nr. 16) enthielt das Prädikat 1 *was gehêret,* das auch als nominaler Ausdruck aufgefasst werden kann, wie er dann eindeutig vorliegt in

589,5 *dar ûffe stuont ein clariu sûl*

*...*

*si was lieht unde starc*
*sô grôz, vroun Camillen sarc*
*waer drûffe wol gestanden.*

(Nr. 18: 'Darauf stand eine glänzende Säule ... Sie war leuchtend und breit, so gross, dass der Sarg von Madame Camilla gut darauf hätte stehen können.)

Hier liegt wiederum eine Gleichsetzung vor, allerdings eine hypothetisch formulierte, welche die Vergleichssphäre im Irrealis mit der Grundsphäre verschmilzt. Noch deutlicher geschieht dies in

768,1 *Ich vüere sô creftigez her,*
*Troyaere lantwer*
*unt jene die si besâzen*
*müesen rûmen mir die strâzen*
*ob si beidenthalp noch lebten*
*unt strîtes gein mir strebten,*
*si möhten siges niht erholn,*
*si müesen schumpfentiure doln*
*von mir und von den mînen.*

(Nr. 19: 'Ich führe ein so gewaltiges Heer an, dass die trojanischen Landesverteidiger und diejenigen, welche sie belagerten, mir den Weg freimachen müssten, wenn sie auf beiden Seiten noch lebten und mit mir kämpfen wollten. Sie könnten den Sieg nicht erringen, müssten vielmehr eine Niederlage von mir und den meinen hinnehmen.')

Dieselbe grammatische Struktur dient hier zum Ausdruck einer Steigerung ('mein Heer ist gewaltiger als das von...').
 Noch weit häufiger als in Form eines Gliedsatzes tritt der Vergleichsbereich eines Exempels in Form eines selbständigen Satzes auf. Die Steigerung 'Gawan ertrug grössere Bedrängnis als XYZ zusammen' wird folgendermassen ausgedrückt:

583,4 *nâch der aventiure urkünde*
*hete er ( = Gâwân) sich gearbeitet,*
*gehoehet und gebreitet*
*sînen prîs mit grôzer nôt.*
*swaz der werde Lanzilôt*
*ûf der swertbrücke erleit*
*unt sît mit Meljacanze streit,*
*daz was gein dirre nôt ein niht,*
*unt des man Gârelle giht,*
*dem stolzen künege rîche,*

*der alsô ritterlîche*
*den lewen von dem palas*
*warf, der dâ ze Nantes was.*
*Gârel ouch daz mezzer holte,*
*dâ von er kumber dolte*
*in der marmelînen sûl.*
...

583,25 *Li gweiz prelljus, der vurt*
*und Erec der Schoydelakurt*
*erstreit ab Mabonagrîn,*
*der newederz gab sô hôhen pîn,*
*noch dô der stolze Iwân*
*sînen guz niht wolde lân*
*Uf der aventiure stein.*
*solten dise kumber sîn al ein,*
*Gâwâns kumber slüege vür,*
*waege iemen ungemaches kür.*

(Nr. 1-4: 'Gemäss dem Zeugnis der Aventüre hatte er sich abgemüht, seinen Ruhm in schwerer Bedrängnis erhöht und verbreitet. Was immer der treffliche L. auf der Schwertbrücke und hernach im Kampf mit M. erlitt, das war gegen diese Bedrängnis ein Nichts, und auch, was man von G., dem stolzen, mächtigen König, erzählt, der so rittergemäss den Löwen von dem Palast, den es dort in Nantes gab, warf. G. holte auch das Messer in der Marmorsäule, wovon er Leid erduldete ... *Li gués perillos* (die gefährliche Furt), die Furt, und E., der *joi de la court* (die Freude des Hofes) von M. erkämpfte - keines von beiden verursachte solch heftige Bedrängnis, noch (jenes), als der stolze Iwein nicht davon abstehen wollte, den Stein der Aventüre zu begiessen. Wenn all diese Bedrängnisse eins wären, G.s Leid überwöge sie, wenn jemand die Art der Not abwägen wollte.')

Es scheint hier so, als ob der Grundbereich (= GB) den VB umschlösse. Doch dürfte hier der Autor den Zuhörer beziehungsweise Leser bewusst in die Irre führen. Die erste *nôt* 583,7 ist tatsächlich die Bedrängnis im Kampf, insbesondere auf dem Wunderbett in Klinschors Zauberschloss. Mit ihr lässt sich auch die *nôt* 583,11 identifizieren. Nach der zitierten Partie aber heisst es: *welhen kumber mein ich nû?* (584,5), und der Erzähler gibt die Antwort, es handle sich um das Minneleid, das Gawan um Orgeluses willen erduldet. Obwohl es sich in allen Fällen um ritterliche Abenteuer, vier fremde und ein eigenes, noch zu bestehendes, handelt, hat sich der GB unversehens gewandelt. Ja, es scheint fraglich, ob er nicht im nachhinein auch die *nôt* 583,7/11 affiziert, indem der Erzähler gleichsam einen eigenen Fehler korrigiert. Mit solchen freien Assoziationsketten ist bei Wolfram stets zu rechnen. Wie dem auch sei, die Comparatio (Typ I C 1) ist jedesmal deutlich verbalisiert, einmal durch ein Prädikativ + Vergleichspartikel *gein*, einmal durch ein attributives Adjektiv + Vergleichspartikel *sô* (beide-

male im Vergleichssatz), einmal durch ein Verb des Überbietens im Grundbe-
reichssatz (vergleiche 187,14: Nr. 9-10).

Den einfachsten Fall einer direkten Gleichsetzung im selbständigen Satz
(Adaequatio realis, Typ I C 2.1) bietet
712,5   *ôwê, liebiu niftel mîn,*
        *daz dîn jugent sô hôher minne schîn*
        *tuot! daz muoz dir werden sûr.*
        *als tet dîn swester Sûrdamûr*
        *durch der Kriechen lampriure.*

> (Nr. 6: 'Ach, meine liebe Nichte, dass du in deiner Jugend die An-
> zeichen so starker Liebe aufweist! Das muss bitter für dich werden.
> Ebenso erging es deiner Schwester S. wegen des griechischen Kaisers.')

Wie in 420,25 (Nr. 24) fungiert hier *tuon* als Prädikat 2, das offenbar beide
vorhergehende Prädikate ersetzt. Deshalb ist wohl der Punkt nach *sûr* zu billi-
gen, obschon der letzte Satz auch als Gliedsatz aufgefasst werden könnte.

Die Gleichsetzung kann auch durch das hinweisende Pronominaladjektiv *solh*
ausgedrückt werden. In dem betreffenden Fall ist allerdings die Vergleichsform
durch die Wahl von Prädikat 2 stark verschleiert:
321,10  *ime gruoze er ( = Gâwân) mînen herren sluoc.*
        *ein kus, den Jûdas teilte,*
        *im solhen willen veilte,*

> (Nr. 29: 'Bei der Begrüssung erschlug er meinen Herren. Der Kuss, den
> J. gab, stellte ihm eine solche Gesinnung zur Verfügung.')

Weniger kompliziert liegt der Fall in 582,26, wo die Vergleichspartikel durch
*ouch* ersetzt ist:
587,22  *diu junge werde Itonjê*
        *truoc nâch roys Gramoflanz*
        *mit triuwen staete minne ganz:*
        *daz was Gâwâns swester clâr.*
        *vrou Minne, ir teilt ouch iuwern vâr*
        *Sûrdamûr durch Alexandern.*

> (Nr. 5: 'Die junge, edle I. hegte treue, beständige, vollkommene Liebe
> für König G. Das war G.s wunderschöne Schwester. Madame Minne, ihr
> liesset eure Nachstellung auch S. durch Alexander zuteil werden.')

Nur scheinbar demselben Typus gehört folgender Fall an:
253,9   *dô natzten diu ougen ir ( = Sigûne) die wât.*
        *ouch was vroun Lunêten rât*
        *ninder dâ bî ir gewesen.*
        *diu riet ir vrouwen 'lât genesen*
        *disen man, der den iuwern sluoc:*

*er mac ergetzen iuch genuoc.'*
*Sigûne gerte ergetzen niht,*
*als wîp die man bî wanke siht*
*manege, der ich wil gedagen.*

(Nr. 13: 'Da benetzten die Augen ihr die Kleidung. Auch war Madame Lunetes Rat keineswegs dort bei ihr gewesen. Diese hatte ihrer Herrin geraten: 'Lasst diesen Mann, der den euren erschlug, am Leben. Er kann euch hinreichend entschädigen.' S. begehrte keine Entschädigung, wie viele Frauen, die man als wankelmütig erkennt und von denen ich nicht reden will.')

Das *ouch* dient hier zur Anfügung einer freien Assoziation. Die Vergleichssituation wird erst im nachhinein auf Umwegen hergestellt, einerseits durch die Wiederaufnahme des Verbs *ergetzen*, andererseits durch den Vergleich mit wankelmütigen Frauen, für welche Lunetes Herrin, Laudine, als Paradebeispiel dient. Wollte man die zugrundeliegende Struktur rekonstruieren, so ergäbe sich statt einer Gleichsetzung eine Steigerung: 'S. war weit treuer als Laudine'.
Inhaltlich und formal verwandt ist das Exempel

436,1   *Durch minne diu an im erstarp,*
        *daz si der vürste niht erwarp,*
        *si minnete sînen tôten lîp.*
        *ob si worden waer sîn wîp,*
        *dâ hete sich vrou Lûnete*
        *gesûmet an sô gaeher bete*
        *als si riet ir selber vrouwen.*
        *man mac noch dicke schouwen*
        *vroun Lûneten rîten zuo*
        *etslîchem râte gar ze vruo.*

(Nr. 14: 'Um der Liebe willen, die mit ihm gestorben war, da der Fürst sie nicht hatte geniessen können, liebte sie den Toten. Wenn sie seine Gemahlin geworden wäre, hätte sich Madame Lunete bei ihr einen so vorschnellen Vorschlag, wie sie ihn ihrer eigenen Herrin gemacht hatte, überlegt. Man sieht auch heute häufig Madame Lunete herbeireiten, um viel zu früh etliche Ratschläge zu erteilen.')

Der Vergleichspunkt liegt hier wiederum im Mass weiblicher Treue. Die anvisierte, aber unausgesprochene Beispielfigur ist Laudine, Lunetes Herrin. Der Rest der Vergleichsform ist in dem *âals* 436,7 erhalten ('L. hätte S. weniger rasch als Laudine einen solchen Rat gegeben'). Bei diesem wie dem vorangehenden Exempel wird hypothetisch die Beispielfigur mit der Person des Grundbereichs identifiziert und die Irrealität im ersten Fall durch die Negation, im zweiten durch den Konjunktiv bezeichnet.
  Eine Comparatio irrealis mit deutlicher erkennbarer Vergleichsform wird vorgenommen in

773,15 *si prîsten al gemeine*
*die tiuren edeln steine*
*die dran verwieret lâgen.*
*niemen darf mich vrâgen*
*von ir arde, wie die waeren,*
*die liehten unt die swaeren:*
*iuch hete baz bescheiden des*
*Eraclîus oder Ercules*
*und der Krieche Alexander,*
*und dennoch ein ander,*
*der wîse Pictagoras,*
*der ein astronomierre was,*
*und sô wîse âne strît,*
*niemen sît Adâmes zît*
*möhte im glîchen sin getragen.*
*der kunde wol von steinen sagen.*

(Nr. 20-22: 'Man lobte allgemein die wertvollen Edelsteine, die darin (dem Helm) eingelegt lagen. Niemand soll mich fragen, von welcher Beschaffenheit sie waren, die leichten und die schweren. Euch hätte darüber Eraklius oder Ercules besser Auskunft geben können und der Grieche Alexander (der Grosse) und noch ein anderer, der weise Pythagoras, der ein Astronom war und unbestritten so weise, dass niemand seit Adams Zeit vergleichbare Weisheit besessen haben kann. Der konnte trefflich von Steinen berichten.')

Die ausgesparte Grundbereichsfigur in diesem typischen Bescheidenheitstopos ist das Erzähler-Ich (das aber nur hinter längst verstorbenen 'Kapazitäten' zurückstehen will). Von dem Vergleich 'Besser als ich hätten XYZ Bescheid geben können' ist immerhin Teil II als selbständiger Satz erhalten geblieben.

Nur in implizierter Vergleichsform treten zwei Fälle von Adaequatio irrealis (I C 2.2) auf.

219,23 *Condwîr âmûrs vrumt mich grâ.*
*Pilâtus von Ponciâ,*
*und der arme Jûdas,*
*der bî eime kusse was*
*an der triuwelôsen vart*
*dâ Jêsus verrâten wart,*
*swie daz ir schepfaere raeche,*
*die nôt ich niht verspraeche,*
*daz Brôbarzaere vrouwen lîp*
*mit ir hulden waer mîn wîp,*
*sô daz ich sie umbevienge,*
*swie ez mir dar nâch ergienge.*

(Nr. 27-28: 'C. liess mich ergrauen. P. von Pontia und der arme J., der mit einem Kuss bei der treulosen Unternehmung beteiligt war, bei der J. verraten wurde, - wie immer ihr Schöpfer das (= ihr Verhalten) auch rächen mochte, ich wollte die Pein auf mich nehmen, vorausgesetzt dass die Herrin von B. mit Zuneigung meine Gattin wäre, so dass ich sie umarmen dürfte.')

504,25  *ob ez halt vrou Kamille waere,*
*diu mit ritterlîchem maere*
*vor Laurente prîs erstreit,*
*waer si gesunt als si dort reit,*
*ez wurde iedoch versuocht an sie,*
*ob si mir strîten büte alhie.*

(Nr. 17: 'Selbst wenn es Madame Camilla wäre, die zum Ruhm ihres Rittertums vor Laurentium Anerkennung erkämpfte, und wenn sie gesund wäre, wie sie dort ritt, so würde ich (= Gawan) doch mein Glück gegen sie versuchen, wenn sie sich mir zum Kampf stellte.')

Zugrunde liegt im ersten Fall der Vergleich 'Ich würde die Höllenqual wie XY erdulden wollen', im zweiten Fall 'Ich würde gegen jene Unbekannte wie gegen X kämpfen wollen'.

Da hier in der Oberflächenstruktur das Kategoriensignal fehlt und auch bei den Nummern 13 (253,9) und 14 (436,1) nur undeutlich zu erkennen ist, könnten wir alle vier Fälle ebensogut der Gruppe zuweisen, die ich in Anlehnung an einen mittelalterlichen Ausdruck als Similitudo inexpressa bezeichnet habe (1975: 69). Diese erfreut sich in der mittellateinischen Poetik besonderer Wertschätzung, da sie der manieristischen Tendenz des dunklen Stils entgegenkommt. Da Wolfram auf seine, durchaus eigenständige Weise demselben Stilideal frönt, würde man die Verwendung solcher Exempla noch häufiger erwarten, als sie tatsächlich gebraucht werden.

Aus dem logischen Zusammenhang ergibt sich der Vergleich von selbst in 421,20  *Segramors enbin ich niht,*
*den man durch vehten binden muoz:*
*ich erwirbe sus wol küneges gruoz.*
*Sibche nie swert erzôch,*
*er was ie bî dâ man vlôch:*
*doch muose man in vlêhen,*
*grôz gebe und starkiu lêhen*
*empfieng er von Ermrîche genuoc:*
*nie swert er doch durch helm gesluoc.*

(Nr. 26: 'S. bin ich nicht, den man zur Verhinderung eines Kampfes fesseln muss. Ich erringe auch so vorzüglich die Gunst des Königs. Sibich zog nie das Schwert, er war stets dabei, wo man floh. Dennoch musste man um sein Wohlwollen betteln. Grosse Gaben und reiche Lehen erhielt er von Ermanrich genug, und doch schlug er nie ein Schwert durch einen

Helm.')

Hier besteht kein Zweifel, dass der feige Herzog Liddamus sich zuerst von dem Artusritter, einem Akteur des *Parzival*-Romans, abhebt und hierauf mit dem feigen, aber einflussreichen Günstling des Königs Ermanrich vergleicht.
Komplizierter liegt der Fall bei

826,25 *durch waz verlôs daz guote wîp*
*werdes vriundes minneclîchen lîp?*
*er ( = Loherangrîn) widerriet ir vrâgen ê,*
*do er vür si gienc vome sê.*
*hie solte Ereck nu sprechen:*
*der kunde mit rede sich rechen.*

(Nr. 12: 'Wodurch verlor die treffliche Frau ihren vornehmen, liebenswerten Geliebten? Er hatte sie zuvor gewarnt zu fragen, als er vom Meer zu ihr hingegangen war. Hier sollte nun Erek reden - der konnte mit Worten Rache nehmen.')

Das hat fast die Form eines Rätsels. Die Grundvorstellung, Loherangrins unerbittliche Haltung ist gänzlich ausgespart, die Vergleichsvorstellung, die Nachgiebigkeit Ereks, der seiner Gattin die Übertretung des Redeverbots letztlich verziehen hat, verschlüsselt. Die Methode des Erzählers, eine Beispielfigur hypothetisch in die Handlung des Romans hineinzuziehen, kennen wir bereits (vergleiche Nr. 17 und andere).
  Liegt hier eine Comparatio inexpressa vor, so in 143,21 eine Aequatio inexpressa. Der Vergleich 'Wenn der Artushof über Parzival spotten sollte, werde ich Enite ebenso verspotten' ist dabei aber nur mühsam zu erschliessen.

143,21 *mîn hêr Hartman von Ouwe,*
*vrou Ginovêr iuwer vrouwe*
*und iuwer hêrre der künec Artûs,*
*den kumt ein mîn gast ze hûs.*
*bitet hüeten sîn vor spotte.*
*ern ist gîge noch diu rotte:*
*si suln ein ander gampel nemen*
*des lâzen sich durch zuht gezemen,*
*anders iuwer vrouwe Enîde*
*unt ir muoter Karsnafîde*
*werdent durch die mûl gezücket*
*unde ir lop gebrücket.*

(Nr. 8: 'Herr H. v. Aue, Madame G., Eurer Herrin, und Eurem Herrn, dem König A., denen kommt ein Gast von mir ins Haus. Bittet darum, dass man ihn vor Spott behütet. Er ist weder Geige noch Rotte. Sie sollen sich ein anderes Spielzeug nehmen. Das mögen sie sich aus Anstand angelegen sein lassen, sonst werden Eure Herrin E. und ihre Mutter K. durch die Mühle gedreht und ihr Ansehen zerbröckelt.')

Die Gruppe der partiellen Vergleiche (= Typ I) ist damit abgeschlossen.

Einen einzigen totalen Vergleich (= Typ II) enthält unser Korpus, allerdings in negierter Form, so dass im Grunde wiederum eine Überbietung dahinter steht (vergleiche auch oben Nr. 32):
573,13 *aller sin tet im ( = Gâwân) entwîch.*

> *sîn wanküssen ungelîch*
> *was dem daz Gymêle*
> *von Monte Rybêle,*
> *diu süeze und diu wîse,*
> *legete Kahenîse,*
> *dar ûffe er sînen prîs verslief.*
> *der prîs gein disem manne lief.*

(Nr. 15: 'Alles Bewusstsein verliess ihn. Sein Kopfkissen war demjenigen ungleich, dass G. von M.R., die liebliche und kluge, K. unterlegte, auf dem er seine Ehre verschlief. Zu diesem Manne hier eilte der Ruhm.')

An der Oberflächengleichung der beiden Kopfkissen ist der tieferliegende Vergleich des Ruhms der beiden Männer aufgehängt.

Zwei der letzten drei Exempla treten in der Form der sogenannten Vossianischen Antonomasie auf, das heisst in der Form eines das entsprechende Appellativum ersetzenden Eigennamens, also einer Art Namenmetapher, bei der der berühmte Namensträger für die durch ihn in hervorragender Weise repräsentierte Eigenschaft steht.[2] In der Regel wird im Falle einer substituierenden Metapher ein Adjektiv wie 'zweiter, anderer, neuer, unser' zu dem Namen (zum Beispiel Paris oder Achill) hinzugefügt. Bei der identifizierenden Metapher[3] ist dies nicht erforderlich. Dieser Gruppe gehören unsere Exempla an:
419,12 *welt irz sîn hêr Turnus,*
> *sô lât mich sîn hêr Tranzes ...*

(Nr. 23: 'Wollt ihr Herr R. sein, so lasset mich Herr T. sein.' Angesprochen ist Kingrimursel, Sprecher ist Liddamus.)

420,22 *Waz Wolfhartes solte ich sîn?*

(Nr. 25: 'Was für ein W. sollte ich sein?' Sprecher ist Liddamus.)

In beiden Fällen geht es um die Verkörperung von Kühnheit beziehungsweise Feigheit, und in beiden Fällen wird die Identifikation als Möglichkeit angesprochen. Die Formulierung des zweiten Exempels stellt es in die Nähe eines totalen Vergleichs ('wie Wolfhart').

Der Vossianischen Antonomasie benachbart, aber der 'echten' identifizierenden Metapher enger verwandt ist schliesslich das letzte Exempel unseres Korpus:
634,17 *Orgelûsen ich ( = Itonjê) geküsset hân,*
> *diu sînen ( = Gramoflanzes) tôt werben kan.*

*daz was ein kus den Judas truoc,*
*dâ von man sprichet noch genuoc.*

(Nr. 30: 'Ich habe O. geküsst, die seinen Tod herbeizuführen versteht.
Das war der Kuss, den J. zu vergeben hatte, von dem man noch häufig
genug spricht.')

Statistisch lassen sich die Ergebnisse der eben vorgenommenen textlinguistischen
Analyse nur mangelhaft auswerten, da die Gesamtzahl der Fälle zu gering und
die Gruppenzuweisung häufig nicht eindeutig ist. Hervorzuheben gilt es jedoch
die erstaunliche Vielfalt der sprachlichen Formulierungen weniger Grundmuster.
Mehr als dreimal kehrt keine von ihnen auch nur annähernd wieder, obwohl im
Grunde nur eine Gleichwertigkeit oder Ungleichwertigkeit zweier personenbezo-
gener Sachverhalte auszudrücken war, und zwar annähernd zu gleichen Teilen
(14mal gegen 12mal). Die Ausdrucksskala der - nach zu vergleichenden Grundvorstellungen gezählten - 26 Exempla reicht vom partiellen Vergleich mit dem
Vergleichsbereich als nicht satzwertigem Satzglied (2mal) über den mit dem
Vergleichsbereich als Gliedsatz (8mal) und den mit dem Vergleichsbereich als
selbständigem Satz (12mal) bis zum totalen Vergleich (einmal) und zur identifizierenden Metapher (3mal). Der Vergleichsbereich als selbständiger Satz ohne
Kategoriensignal (Similitudo inexpressa) ist mehrfach (drei- bis siebenmal), aber
nicht exzeptionell häufig vertreten. Der Vergleich in seiner einfachsten Form
wird jedoch sichtlich gemieden. Wo der Vergleichsbereich stark, ja sogar bis auf
einen Namen reduziert erscheint, dort wird die Vossianische Antonomasie gewählt. Wo Grund- und Vergleichsbereich in einem Satzgefüge beisammenstehen,
löst sich dieser bisweilen daraus durch Anakoluthie (zum Beispiel Nr. 1-4)
und/oder durch Fortsetzung mit einem selbständigen Satz. Eine Systematisierung
der Exempla nach der sprachlichen Ausdehnung des Vergleichsbereichs wird,
abgesehen von dem Problem der Abgrenzung, durch die Tatsache erschwert, dass
mehrfach auf eine Grundvorstellung mehrere Beispielfiguren bezogen sind, die
ihrerseits mit Akteuren des eigenen Textes, also des *Parzival*, zusammen auftreten, aber auch jeweils einen Mitaktanten, der nicht verglichen wird, mit sich
führen können. In Vereinfachung dieses Sachverhalts habe ich die 'eigentlichen'
Beispielfiguren von 1 bis 34 durchgezählt, wobei dann 1-4, 9-10, 20-22, 27-28
und 33-34 jeweils einer Grundvorstellung zugeordnet sind. Das Quadrupelexempel
Nr. 1-4 kommt so auf 22 Verse. Das ausführlichste Einzelexempel Nr. 11 bringt
es auf 17 Verse.

Der Autor hat also, wie wir gesehen haben, seine ganze Kunst darauf
verwendet, seine Exempel auf stets neue, überraschende Weise in den Erzählfluss
einzubetten. Dabei kommt den Namen schon vom Klang her ein eigener Stilwert
zu. Man würde erwarten, dass der Reim eine gewichtige Rolle bei der Wahl der
Namen gespielt haben könnte. Es stehen jedoch nur die folgenden im Zweitreim:
Lanzilot (Nr. 1 und 7), Surdamur (Nr. 6), Karthago (Nr. 16), Turnus (Nr. 23),
Rumolt (Nr. 25), Pilatus von Poncia (Nr. 27). Beim zuletzt genannten müsste man
annehmen, dass der Beiname die Beispielfigur angezogen hätte. So oder so ist
die Ausbeute insgesamt gering. Die Assoziationen müssen also ganz überwiegend

vom Inhaltlichen gesteuert gewesen sein.

Dem wollen wir uns nun zuwenden. Wir bewegen uns dabei im Grenzbereich von *Stilistik und Erzählanalyse*. Da lässt sich als erstes der an sich banale Befund registrieren, dass das Exempel die Bedeutung des jeweils geschilderten Zustands oder Vorgangs beziehungsweise des betreffenden Handlungsträgers hervorzuheben, ja ins Exemplarische, positiv oder negativ Vorbildhafte zu heben versucht. Dahinter steht auch der latente Hang mittelalterlicher Texte zur Lehrhaftigkeit, die jedoch gerade bei Wolfram vielfach ironisch gebrochen erscheint.

Pointiert hervorgehoben werden mittels Exempla die Schönheit einer Frau (Nr. 9-10), eines von schwerer Krankheit genesenen Mannes (Nr. 32), die Pracht eines Hofempfanges (Nr. 11), eines edelsteinbesetzten Helmes (Nr. 20-22), einer befestigten Stadt (Nr. 16), die Grösse eines Heeres (Nr. 19), einer Wundersäule (Nr. 18), die Wunderkraft Gottes (Nr. 33-34), die Spottlust der höfischen Gesellschaft (Nr. 8), die Unerbittlichkeit der Gralsgesetze (Nr. 12), die Kunst heuchlerischer Verstellung (Nr. 29; 30), die Treue beziehungsweise Untreue der Frauen (Nr. 13; 14), die Lebensgefährlichkeit einer ritterlichen Aventüre (Nr. 1-2; 7), Kühnheit beziehungsweise Feigheit eines Helden (Nr. 15; 17; 23; 24; 25; 26), Macht und Qual der Minne, Generalthemen des Höfischen Romans, die auch unter den Grundvorstellungen der Exempla an erster Stelle stehen. Beachtung verdient allerdings, dass es vornehmlich die negativen Seiten der Liebe sind, die einer besonderen derartigen Akzentuierung im Text für wert befunden werden. Selbst die an sich als vorbildhaft geschilderte Liebe Parzivals zu seiner Gattin Condwiramurs gewinnt infolge ihrer Trennung für den Helden Züge übernatürlicher Sinneslähmung, einer zwanghaften Überfremdung. Deren gewaltiges Ausmass kennzeichnet der Erzähler durch das analoge Bild Salomons, des weisesten Königs des Alten Testaments, der, durch wahre, also von Gott kommende und mit Gott verbindende Weisheit ausgezeichnet, dennoch der 'Torheit' der Liebe verfiel.[4] Was sich hier als paradoxe Ambivalenz äussert, führt bei einem haltlosen Menschen zur völligen ethischen Entwurzelung. Das zeigt der Erzähler an der Gestalt Clamides, der für die Gunst Condwiramurs sogar sein Seelenheil einzutauschen bereit ist. Der nicht seltene Topos aus der Minnelyrik, die Gunst der Geliebten über die Freuden des Paradieses zu stellen, wird hier ins Extrem getrieben. Clamide erklärt sich bereit, die ewigen Höllenqualen der beiden ihres Selbstmordes wegen zwangsläufig und fraglos verdammten Erzsünder Judas und Pilatus zu erdulden (Nr. 27-28). Das vollendet das auch sonst zwielichtig angelegte Porträt der Figur.[5] Zwischen Parzival und Clamide steht sozusagen auf halbem Wege Gawan, dessen bis zur Selbstentäusserung gesteigerte Hingabe an die spröde Herzogin Orgeluse der Übermacht der Frau Minne angelastet und mit der schweren Bedrängnis exemplifiziert wird, in die Erec und Iwein gerieten (Nr. 3-4). Wie Gawan geht es aber seiner ganzen von der Fee Terdelaschoye abstammenden Sippe (585,5ff.), insbesondere seinen Schwestern Itonje und Surdamur, wobei diese letztgenannte zugleich als aus einem fremden Text entnommene Beispielfigur fungiert und als solche einmal ihrer liebeskranken Schwester (Nr. 6), einmal ihrer ganzen minneverfallenen Familie an die Seite gestellt wird (Nr. 5). Gawan ist insgesamt das beliebteste Ziel der Exempla. Während dem

Haupthelden nur zwei Beispielfiguren, beidemale (Nr. 8; 31) nicht eben zu seinem ungetrübten Lob, zur Seite gestellt werden, sind es bei Gawan viermal so viele (Nr. 1-4; 7; 11; 15; 29), davon die Hälfte solche, die seine ritterlichen Qualitäten herausstreichen. Es hat den Anschein, als ob der Erzähler den durch den Handlungsverlauf zu Ungunsten Gawans ausfallenden Vergleich mit Parzival auf diese Weise - und auch durch Erzählerkommentare - etwas zu korrigieren trachtete. Das nach Gawan beliebteste Objekt ist der politisch einflussreiche, aber persönlich feige Herzog Liddamus, der sich selbst mit notorischen Feiglingen vergleicht und von besonders kühnen Recken abhebt (Nr. 23-26). Hier tritt die satirisch-karikierende Funktion des Exempels deutlich in Erscheinung.

Statt die an sich aufschlussreiche Funktionsanalyse fortzusetzen, wenden wir uns nun der Frage der *Intertextualität* zu. Die dazu nötige Vorarbeit, die Feststellung der jeweiligen Quellen, ist im wesentlichen von der älteren Forschung geleistet.[6] Ohne ihre Ergebnisse wären die folgenden Überlegungen natürlich weitgehend haltlos. Eine Einteilung der Exempla nach Quellenbereichen ergibt folgendes Bild: Nr. 1-15 entstammen der *matière de Bretagne*, Nr. 16-23 dem Höfischen Roman mit antiken Stoffen, Nr. 24-26 der Heldenepik und Nr. 27-34 der christlichen Heilsgeschichte, das heisst der Bibel und der Legende. Dieses Bild passt zur Gattungsbestimmung des *Parzival* als eines arthurischen Romans, verweist aber zugleich auf dessen Abhängigkeit von dem vorangehenden *roman antique* und auf die Annäherung des Gralromans an die religiöse Epik. Dass auch die Heldenepik anzitiert wird, widerspricht der Gattung und ist längst als wolframsche 'Spezialität' gewürdigt worden.

Abgesehen von der Erzählfunktion dieser Exempla kann für ihre Einführung also nur der kommunikative Aspekt ausschlaggebend gewesen sein. Wolfram von Eschenbach beschwört zwar nicht wie sein Zeitgenosse Gottfried von Strassburg wortreich eine esoterische Gemeinschaft zwischen dem Autor und seinem auserwählten Publikum, schafft eine solche jedoch indirekt durch literarische Anspielungen, die gewiss nicht allgemein, aber immerhin den 'Literaturkennern' verständlich waren. Ein Gutteil dieser Anspielungen machen eben die Exempla aus. Kaum je breitet der Erzähler sie soweit aus, dass der Hörer oder Leser sie von selbst ohne Kenntnis des literarischen Hintergrundes entschlüsseln könnte. Möglich wäre dies vielleicht bei der gedrängten Nacherzählung des ersten Teils von Hartmanns *Erec* (Nr. 11). Da erfahren wir immerhin, dass ein Zwerg Maliclisier[7] vor den Augen Ginovers Erec einen Geisselschlag versetzt, Erec dann in Tulmein einen Zweikampf mit Ider, dem Sohn Noyts, siegreich bestanden und zusammen mit Enite einen prächtigen Empfang am Artushof erhalten hat (Nr. 11). Doch auf kaum ein anderes Exempel trifft dasselbe zu, am wenigsten selbstverständlich dort, wo es auf den Namen der Beispielfigur reduziert erscheint, wie bei Surdamur (Nr. 5), Enite und Karsnafite (Nr. 8), Enite (Nr. 9), den beiden Isalden (Nr. 10), Eraclius (Nr. 20), Wolfhart (Nr. 25), Pilatus (Nr. 27), Absalon (Nr. 32).

Kaum Verständnisschwierigkeiten konnten die Exempla aus Bibel und Legende bieten. Jedem mittelalterlichen Publikum mussten sowohl der Heilige Silvester mit dem Stier als auch Salomon, Absalon (das alttestamentarische Muster der Schönheit), Lazarus, Pilatus und Judas hinlänglich vertraut sein, wenn nicht anders, so aus bildlichen Darstellungen.

Bei den übrigen Exempla waren jedoch literarische Kenntnisse im engeren Sinne gefragt. Die Entlehnungen aus dem bretonischen Sagenkreis nehmen dabei aber insofern eine Sonderstellung ein, als dessen Akteure potentielle Handlungsträger jedes Artusromans und so auch des *Parzival* sind. Teils werden sie offenkundig auch hier als am Artushof weilend vorgestellt wie Erec und Enite (vergleiche 143,28ff.; 187,14; 401,8ff.), teils treten sie sogar unmittelbar in die Handlung ein, wie Meljacanz. Im III. Buch agiert er noch im Hintergrund. Er ist der Entführer des Fräuleins Imane von Beafontane (125,11ff.), den Karnahkarnanz mit seinen Gefährten verfolgt, da sie dem Knaben Parzival begegnen. Im VII. Buch aber steht er vorne auf der Bühne, wird ausführlich als Sohn des Poydiconjunz, als tapferer Krieger, aber vor allem als unhöfischer Frauenschänder, den man eigentlich töten sollte, beschrieben (343,23ff.; 356,21ff.). Schliesslich trifft er im Kampf auf Gawan und wird vom Pferd gestochen (386,23ff.). Bei dieser Gelegenheit fügt der Erzähler als zu überbietendes Exempel Lanzilot ein. Aus dem Wortlaut ist nur zu entnehmen, dass Lanzilot Meljacanz' Gegner gewesen ist, der zuvor eine Schwertbrücke überwunden und hernach die Königin Ginover aus der Gefangenschaft befreit hat. Dass dies durch den Sieg über Meljacanz gelungen ist, lässt sich erschliessen, vielleicht auch noch die Tatsache der Entführung, da Meljacanz ja bereits das entsprechende Image aufgeprägt erhalten hat. Das Motiv der Schwertbrücke bleibt hier jedoch unerklärt, ebenso 583,8ff., wo es abermals zusammen mit dem Zweikampf zitiert wird (Nr. 1). Es wird, wie auch alle weiteren Umstände von Entführung und Rückgewinnung der Königin nur aus der Kenntnis des *Chevalier de la Charrete* von Chrétien de Troyes klar. Es scheint, als korrigiere Wolfram hier Hartmann von Aue, der die Entführung und den Entführer Meljaganz in seinem *Iwein* ebenfalls erwähnt, Lanzilot (Lancelot) aber nicht nennt, so dass der Eindruck entsteht, Gawein könnte der Retter gewesen sein.[8] Die Kenntnis auch dieses Versromans von Hartmann bei Autor und Publikum wird durch die Anspielung auf Iweins berühmtes Quellenabenteuer (Nr. 4) und vor allem auf Lunetes Rat (Nr. 13; 14) nahegelegt. Beide Allusionen setzen hinreichende Vertrautheit mit der Iweingeschichte voraus. Der *Erec* ist aber als Prätext im *Parzival* ohne Zweifel weit stärker präsent, wie Rüdiger Schnell gezeigt hat. Parzivals und Enites Ankunft am Artushof sind für den Erzähler auch der Anlass, den Dichterkollegen beim Namen zu nennen und spielerisch-scherzhaft seine Rivalität mit ihm anzuzeigen, ein teils ämulatives, teils kritisches Verhältnis, das hier nicht weiter darzustellen ist. In der Handlung des *Parzival* tritt Enite freilich ebensowenig auf wie ihr Gatte, aber dieser wird überraschenderweise entgegen den Quellen zu Jeschutes Bruder gemacht (134,6). Das mag Wolframs 'Tick', möglichst viele Personen miteinander in verwandtschaftliche Beziehungen zu setzen, entsprechen, ist aber zugleich Teil eines literarischen Spieles mit Intertextualität. Das Spiel setzt sich mit der Einführung einer ebenfalls aus einem fremden Text importierten Schwester Gawans fort. In keinem Artusromans Hartmanns taucht diese Schwester auf. Auch Wolframs unmittelbare Vorlage, Chrétiens *Gralroman*, kennt sie nicht. Sie ist Chrétiens *Cligès* entnommen und auch auf diesen beschränkt: Surdamur - Soredamurs. Chrétien etymologisiert den Namen selbst als *sororée d'amors* 'von Liebe übergoldet' (Micha V. 972), was Wolfram vermutlich zu der Bildung des sprechenden Namens von Parzivals Gattin, Condwiramurs, aus *conduire* 'führen, steuern' und *amors* 'Liebe', veranlasst hat. Aus dem Text erfährt man, dass Surdamur unsterblich in den griechischen Kaiser Alexander verliebt war oder noch ist (Nr. 5; 6), nicht mehr - ein Beispiel für die Übermacht der Minne, das ohne Wissen um die näheren Umstände dieser Liebesbeziehung ins Leere stösst.

Zu Wolframs Spiel mit der Intertextualität gehört es auch, wenn Beispielfiguren aus fremden Texten und solche aus dem eigenen Text, also 'eigentliche' und 'uneigentliche', bunt gemischt zum Vergleich herangezogen werden. Da wird Gawans Liebespein nicht nur mit Erecs Schoydelakurt- und Iweins Quellen-Aventüre exemplifiziert, sondern auch mit Gawans eigener, noch folgender (!) Furt-Aventüre. Da treten als Schönheitsexempla mit Enite und den beiden Isolden zusammen Jeschute und Cunneware aus dem *Parzival* auf. Besonders liebt es der Erzähler, Exempelfiguren hypothetisch in die Romanhandlung hineinzuziehen. Er setzt den Fall, als ob Lunete Sigune denselben Rat wie ihrer Herrin Laudine gäbe (Nr. 13; 14), als ob die scheinbar gerüstete Dame des Urjans Gawan entgegenreiten könnte wie die Amazone Camilla (Nr. 17), als ob die Heere der Trojaner und Griechen als Gegner von Feirefiz' Heer in Frage kämen (Nr. 19). Dieses Verwirrspiel stellt einerseits nicht geringe Anforderungen an die Aufmerksamkeit, Merkfähigkeit und Literaturkenntnis des Publikums und signalisiert andererseits die freie Verfügbarkeit der diversen literarischen Vorgaben im fiktionalen Raum.

Die von der Forschung ausgemachten Quellen der Exempla sind, abgesehen von Bibel und Legende: *Erec* und *Iwein* Hartmanns von Aue, *Karrenritter* (*Lancelot*) und *Cligès* Chrétiens de Troyes, der *Tristrant* Eilharts von Oberge (für den bretonischen Stoffkreis), die *Eneide* Heinrichs von Veldeke, der *Eraclius* Meister Ottes, das *Alexanderlied* des Pfaffen Lamprecht (für den antiken Stoffkreis), das *Nibelungenlied* (Fassung C) und eine Fassung der (historischen) Dietrichsage (für die Heldenepik). Die Liste kann sich sehen lassen und steht in Kontrast zu Wolframs offen prätendierter Illiteratizität. Ihm war also wohl daran gelegen, seine durchaus laienmässige, lateinischer Buchgelehrsamkeit entgegengesetzte Bildung zur Schau zu stellen. Tatsächlich scheint er hier ja ohne lateinische Quelle auszukommen.[9] Diese Absicht ist der Forschung natürlich längst bekannt, ebenso wie die, sich an den anzitierten Werken zu messen und zu reiben. Neben dem Verhältnis zu Hartmann hat hier vor allem das zu Eilhart[10] und zu dem (wie Hartmann namentlich genannten) Heinrich von Veldeke[11] Beachtung gefunden. Obwohl auf diesem Gebiet noch manches zu tun wäre, sei hier nur noch auf zwei Quellengruppen eingegangen.

Bei den Texten aus der Heldensage scheint sich der etwas paradoxe Befund abzuzeichnen, dass Wolfram einerseits bei seinen Zuhörern/Lesern die Kenntnis der rein schriftlichen C-Bearbeitung des *Nibelungenliedes* (*sniten in öl gebrouwen* C 1497,3), andererseits einer mündlichen Fassung der Ermanrich-Sibich-Geschichte des Dietrichkreises voraussetzt, von der wir erst weit spätere Aufzeichnungen besitzen. Mir scheint die jeweils andere Denkmöglichkeit nicht völlig ausgeschlossen, wenngleich weniger wahrscheinlich - der C-Bearbeiter könnte Rumolts Leckerbissen einer mündlichen Tradition entnommen haben, umgekehrt könnte auch etwas von der Dietrichsage schon um 1200 den Weg aufs Pergament gefunden haben. Wie dem auch sei, wichtiger ist mir der Hinweis darauf, dass im Gegensatz zu den 'westlichen' Dichtern Veldeke, Eilhart, Hartmann, Gottfried ausgerechnet bei Wolfram, der über Beziehungen zum Donauraum verfügte, deutliche Bezüge zur Heldensage feststellbar sind. Im Gegensatz zur verbreiteten Annahme von der Ubiquität der Heldensage im deutschen Sprachraum schliesse ich daraus, dass Heldenepik um 1200 doch eine 'Spezialität' des deutsches Südostens gewesen ist, das heisst nur hier die nötige Prominenz besessen hat, um erfolgreich in das literarische Spiel mit Intertextualität einbezogen zu werden.

Eine vergleichbare Prominenz muss wohl für Wolfram und einen Teil seines Publikums Chrétien de Troyes besessen haben und zwar über seine Stellung als Verfasser der unvollendeten und angeblich auch sonst mangelhaften Vorlage des *Parzival* hinaus. Völlig auszuschliessen ist es freilich nicht, dass Wolfram bei seinen Anspielungen auf den *Cligès* und den *Chevalier de la Charrete* entweder mündlich kursierende, werkenthobene und gleichsam frei schwebende Erzählmotive oder inzwischen verlorene schriftliche deutsche Bearbeitungen der französischen Texte im Auge hatte oder gar uninformierte Hörer/Leser mit esoterischen Wissen beeindrucken und verwirren wollte. Ich vermag jedoch nicht daran zu glauben - ebensowenig wie bei Garel (Nr. 2), für den ich eine verlorene französische Quelle annehmen möchte, auf welche Wolfram sein Publikum bloss flüchtig hinzuweisen brauchte, um die Erinnerung an gemeinsames Wissen wachzurufen.[12] Da uns dieses Wissen fehlt, können wir daraus allerdings keine weiteren Schlüsse ziehen.

Bei Chrétien jedoch können wir es, sofern meine Annahme zutrifft. Danach wäre es legitim, den *Parzival* vor dem Hintergrund nicht nur des *Erec* und *Iwein* (ebenfalls Chrétienscher Texte, wenngleich durch Hartmann vermittelter!), sondern auch des *Karrenritters* und des *Cligès* (genauer des ersten Teils desselben, auf den allein angespielt wird) zu lesen, da der Autor eine solche Lektüre seinem Publikum selbst nahegelegt hätte. Die Konsequenzen vermag ich hier nur anzudeuten. Im ersten Teil des *Cligès* ist das Hauptthema die erwachende und bis zur Qual gesteigerte, weil uneingestandenen Liebe von Alexandre und Soredamors zueinander. Endlose Liebesmonologe prägen das Bild, die merklich in Konkurrenz zu denen der *romans antiques*, etwa des *Roman d'Eneas*, treten. Der *Karrenritter* erzählt von dem auserwählten ritterlichen 'Erlöser', der, getrieben von verzehrender Liebe zu der unerreichbaren Gattin des Königs Artus, diese aus dem mythischen 'Land, von welchem niemand wiederkehrt', befreit, zuvor jedoch auf wunderbare Weise gerade in diesem Land die Erhörung seiner Liebe findet. Wolframs vieldiskutierte Minneauffassung, bisher gemessen an der seiner deutschen Vorgänger und Zeitgenossen, müsste nun auch als Antwort auf diese Konzepte Chrétiens gesehen werden. Insbesondere aber stünden die Erlösergestalten Parzival (Perceval) und Gawan (Gauvain) nicht nur bei Chrétien de Troyes mit Lanzilot (Lancelot) gleichsam in einer Reihe, sondern auch im Erwartungshorizont von Wolframs Publikum. Die im *Parzival* zweimal suggerierte

Analogie Gawan - Lanzilot wäre dann nicht bloss punktuell, sondern auch als Anspielung auf die von der Romanistik natürlich längst entdeckte Motivverwandtschaft der beiden Aventürenwege bei Chrétien zu verstehen. Der Dualität der Protagonisten im *Karrenritter* entspricht eine ebensolche im *Gralroman*, wobei Gauvain jeweils der Part der 'zweiten Geige' zukommt, Perceval somit als gesteigerter Lancelot erscheinen muss. Wie bei Chrétien hätten wir dann auch bei Wolfram die doppelte Zielsetzung des Haupthelden, *minne und des grâles aventiure*, als Überwindung der einseitigen Minneverfallenheit Lancelots durch die religiöse Dimension anzusehen, die allerdings bei dem deutschen Dichter dem anderen Pol weniger krass entgegengestellt, sondern eher harmonisch damit verbunden wird.

Ich breche hier ab. Wie sich gezeigt hat, kann beim *Parzival* von einer ziemlich hohen Intensität von Intertextualität gesprochen werden, sofern man nicht die Massstäbe der insbesondere an der Gegenwartungsdichtung orientierten modernen Intertextualitätsdebatte[13] anlegen will. Man kann resümieren: (1.) Soweit intertextuelle Verweise durch Exempla gegeben werden, erscheinen zwar kaum je wörtliche Zitate, die als solche ausgewiesen werden, aber der Erzähler liefert doch häufig zu den Beispielfiguren den ursprünglichen Kontext andeutungsweise mit. (2.) Sinnvoll ist dies nur, sofern der Autor sich des Bezugs bewusst ist, und den Prätext auch bei einem Teil des Publikums als bekannt voraussetzt. (3.) Seine Abhängigkeit von fremden Texten thematisiert Wolfram mehrfach ausdrücklich, allerdings nur einmal im Zusammenhang mit einem (dem achten) Exemplum. (4.) Die meisten Exempla markieren zwar nur einen punktuellen Bezug, zumindest aber beim *Erec* und wohl auch beim *Karrenritter* darf der Prätext getrost auch als struktureller Vorwurf des *Parzival* angesprochen werden. Dabei ist allerdings das komplizierte Verhältnis der Romane Chrétiens zueinander und das Wolframs zu jedem von ihnen und zu Hartmanns Chrétien-Bearbeitungen in Rechnung zu stellen. (5.) Unverkennbar schliesslich ist insgesamt Wolframs durchaus spannungsreiches Verhältnis zum jeweiligen Prätext ein Dialog, in den der Hörer und Leser immer wieder mit Erfolg einbezogen wird.

ANMERKUNGEN

1. Von dort übernehme ich das Typenregister.

2. Dazu ebenda Knapp (1975: 100ff.).

3. Zu dieser Terminologie ibidem: 122.

4. Dazu vergleiche Reinitzer (1976: 597-639, hier v.a. S. 599ff.).

5. Dazu vergleiche Knapp (1976b: 264ff.).

6. Ein kritisches Resümee der entsprechenden Arbeiten von 1945-1969 findet sich bei Bumke (1970: bes. 198-250); Martin (1903); Singer (1916); Panzer (1940).

7. Hartmann von Aue, *Erec* (Leitzmann-Wolff 1985: V. 1077). Die einzige Handschrift, das Ambraser Heldenbuch, hat hier Maledicur. - Zum Verhältnis des *Parzival* zum *Erec* vergleiche Schnell (1973: 301-32).

8. Dazu vergleiche Haug (1978: 8ff.).

9. Eine Ausnahme könnte Pythagoras (Nr. 22) darstellen. Wie Martin (1903) zu 773,25 anmerkt, stimmt die Schreibung 'Pictagoras' auffällig mit der im Steinbuch des Arnoldus Saxo überein, das die Quelle zu der Edelsteinliste im *Parzival* 791,1ff. gewesen sein dürfte. Im französischen Theben- und Eneas-Roman fehlt der Name, im Troja-Roman bezeichnet er nicht den griechischen Gelehrten.

10. Vergleiche Eggers (1950: 39-51).

11. Vergleiche Poag (1962: 721-35; 1965: 69-76) und Oonk (1976: 19-39).

12. Dasselbe hat schon Martin (1903) zu V. 583,12 angenommen. Ein Garel befindet sich auch unter den Artusrittern, die in Orgeluses Gefangenschaft geraten sind (664,30; 673,4). Da er beidemale zusammen mit einem Gaheriet, Gawans Neffen (*muomen sun* 673,2), auftritt, liegt die Gleichung mit den beiden Brüdern Gauvains in der französischen Artustradition, Guerrehet und Gaheriet (Gahariet, Gueheriet oder ähnlich), nahe, die zusammen in Chrétiens *Conte du Graal* 8141 (im Nominativ) als Gaheriés und Guerrehés (Roach 1959) erscheinen. Die beiden ähnlichen Namen gaben Anlass zur Verwechslung, so dass das Pendant des deutschen Garel nicht sicher zu ermitteln ist. Der Pleier hat die Hauptperson seines Garel-Romans mitsamt seiner Sippenbindung aus Wolframs Angaben übernommen beziehungsweise herausgesponnen - vergleiche Kern (1981: 72f. u. passim). Eine eigene französische Quelle braucht dafür nicht angenommen zu werden. Hingegen setzt der Pleier genauso wie Wolfram die Kenntnis des Karrenritters von Chrétien bei seinem Publikum voraus (ebenda: 71). Kern (ebenda: 254ff.) schliesst sich auch der Ansicht von Gisela Zimmermann (1974: 52,265f.) an, dass Wolframs Bezüge auf die Lancelot-Geschichte kein deutsches Vermittlungsglied benötigen, wie Rosenhagen (1897) vermutet hat. Rosenhagens methodischer Fehler besteht meines Erachtens vor allem in seiner mangelnder Unterscheidung von Allusionen in Exempelform und Übernahmen fremder Stoffe in den eigenen Handlungszusammenhang, wo der Erzähler ziemlich frei verfahren konnte. Seltsam mutet allerdings die Namenform Poydiconjunz für afrz. Baudemagu(s)/Bademagu(s) an. Der erste Teil des Namens hat eine auffallende Ähnlichkeit mit Poydjus und Poydwiz im *Willehalm*, die einem

Baudu(s)/Baudin(s) in der Vorlage entsprechen (vergleiche Knapp 1974: 210f.). Ob im zweiten Teil Verlesung (Martin, Kommentar zu 343,21) oder bewusster Ersatz vorliegt, ist unklar.

13.     Einen guten Forschungsbericht dazu gibt Pfister (Broich - Pfister 1985: 1-30). Ich verwende im folgenden dankbar die von Pfister registrierten Intensitätskriterien, ohne die von ihm geprägten Termini zu übernehmen.

# BIBLIOGRAPHIE

BROICH-PFISTER 1985

Broich, U., Pfister, M., *Untertextualität. Formen, Funktionen, anglistische Fallstudien*. Tübingen 1985: 1-130.

BUMKE 1970

Bumke, J., *Die Wolfram-von-Eschenbach-Forschung seit 1945*. München 1970.

EGGERS 1950

Eggers, H., Literarische Beziehungen des 'Parzival' zum 'Tristrant' Eilharts von Oberg. In: *PBB* 72 (1950): 39-51.

HAUG 1978

Haug, W., *'Das Land, von welchem niemand wiederkehrt'. Mythos, Fiktion und Wahrheit in Chrétiens 'Chevalier de la Charrete' im 'Lanzelet' Ulrichs von Zatzikhoven und im 'Lancelot'-Prosaroman*. Tübingen 1978.

KERN 1981

Kern, P., *Die Artusromane des Pleier*. Berlin 1981.

KNAPP 1974

Knapp, F.P., Der Lautstand der Eigennamen im 'Willehalm' und das Problem von Wolframs Schriftlosigkeit. In: *Wolfram-Studien* II, Berlin 1974: 193-218.

KNAPP 1975

Knapp, F.P., *Similitudo. Stil- und Erzählfunktion von Vergleich und Exempel in dem lateinischen, französischen und deutschen Grossepik des Hochmittelalters*. I Band: Einleitung, Vorstudien, 1, Hauptteil: Lateinische Epiek. Wien-Stuttgart 1975.

KNAPP 1979

Knapp, F.P., Zur logischen und grammatischen Struktur des bildhaften Vergleichs in der Sprache der mittelhochdeutschen und neuhochdeutschen Klassik. In: *Amsterdamer Beiträge zur älteren Germanistik*, 14 (1979): 59-86.

KNAPP 1979B

Knapp, F.P., *Der Selbstmord in der abendländischen Epik des Hochmittelalters*. Heidelberg 1979.

LACHMANN-HARTL 1952

Lachmann, K., Hartl, E., *Wolfram von Eschenbach. Band I: Lieder, Parzival und Titurel*. Berlin 1952[7].

LEITZMANN-WOLFF 1985

Leitzmann, A., Wolff, L., *Hartmann von Aue, Erec*. Tübingen 1985.

MARTIN 1903

Martin, E., *Wolfram von Eschenbach: Parzival und Titurel, 2. Teil: Kommentar*. Halle a.S. 1903.

MICHA 1957

Micha, A., *Chrétien de Troyes, Cligès*, Paris, 1957.

OONK 1976

Oonk, G.J., Eneas, Tristan, Parzival und die Minne. In: *Zeitschrift für deutsche Philologie* 95 (1976): 19-39.

PARZER 1940

Parzer, F., *Gahmuret. Quellenstudien zu Wolframs Parzival*. Heidelberg 1940.

POAG 1962

Poag, J.F., Heinrich von Veldeke's minne; Wolfram von Eschenbach's liebe und triuwe. In: *Journal of English and Germanic Philology* 61 (1962): 721-35.

POAG 1965

Poag, J.F., Wolfram von Eschenbach's Metamorphosis of the Ovidian Tradition. In: *Monatshefte* 57 (1965): 69-76.

REINITZER 1976

Reinitzer, H., 'Über Beispielfiguren im Erec'. In: *DRjs* 50 (1976): 567-639.

ROACH 1959

Roach, W., *Chrétien de Troyes. Le Roman de Perceval ou le Conte du Graal*, Genève, 1959.

ROSENHAGEN 1897

Rosenhagen, G., 'Muntane Cluse (Parzival 382, 14)'. In: *Zeitschrift für deutsche Philologie* 29 (1987): 150-64.

SCHNELL 1973

Schnell, R., 'Literarische Beziehungen zwischen Hartmanns 'Erec' und Wolframs 'Parzival''. In: *PBB*, 95 (1973): 301-32.

SINGER 1916

Singer, S., *Wolframs Stil und der Stoff des Parzival*. Wien 1916.

ZIMMERMANN 1974

Zimmermann, G., *Kommentar zum VII. Buch von Wolframs von Eschenbach 'Parzival'*. Göppingen 1974.

J. Berlioz

# 'Héros' païen et prédication chrétienne: Jules César dans le recueil d'*exempla* du dominicain Etienne de Bourbon (mort v. 1261)

L'emploi des *exempla* tirés de l'Antiquité profane par les rédacteurs des premiers grands recueils de récits exemplaires destinés aux prédicateurs est bien mal connu. Les érudits les ont en règle générale impitoyablement chassés de leurs éditions de texte. C'est ainsi que dans l'édition que le très savant Albert Lecoy de la Marche procura en 1877 du recueil d'Etienne de Bourbon, ne furent retenus que les récits racontés *de visu* ou *de auditu*, mettant en scène des faits contemporains ou des événements antérieurs, authentiques ou légendaires, recueillis oralement. Etaient éliminés sans appel, comme le disait l'éditeur, 'les traits empruntés par lui (Etienne de Bourbon) à d'autres écrivains' (1877:xxvi). De ce fait, il était jusqu'à présent impossible de distinguer chez cet auteur la place réservée aux récits ou aux faits tirés de l'Antiquité, et plus particulièrement de l'Antiquité dite païenne ou profane. La préparation de l'édition intégrale du traité d'Etienne de Bourbon, menée en collaboration, m'a permis de faire un relevé de la matière antique présente dans ce recueil. J'expose ici les premiers résultats de cette recherche, toujours en cours. Je ne saurais toutefois traiter de ce sujet dans toute l'ampleur qu'il mérite. L'abondance des *exempla* (on en compte plus de 260), tous inédits à l'exception de deux seulement, m'oblige à ne retenir qu'un personnage parmi tous ceux qu'Etienne de Bourbon propose aux utilisateurs de son ouvrage. Si la figure de Jules César a été choisie, c'est d'une part que les *exempla* qui le voient intervenir sont relativement nombreux puisque l'on en compte seize, soit 6% environ du total des récits ayant trait à l'Antiquité profane. C'est également que ces *exempla* m'ont paru représenter un échantillon donnant une vision assez claire et représentative des différents types de récits 'antiques' tels qu'on les rencontre dans le traité d'Etienne de Bourbon.

Il sera indispensable dans un premier temps de replacer le personnage de César parmi l'ensemble des figures, des lieux ou des choses appartenant à l'Antiquité païenne, et apparaissant dans le recueil. Les textes intéressant César seront ensuite présentés, regroupés suivant des catégories établies selon la logique de l'*exemplum*. L'étude de leurs sources et de leur modalité de transmission nous conduira à l'analyse du statut pragmatique du 'héros' antique, en l'occurrence Jules César, au sein de la vaste matière exemplaire offerte par le dominicain.

1.    *La galerie des récits 'antiques'*

-    le traité d'Etienne de Bourbon et le *corpus* mis en oeuvre

Quelques précisions pour commencer sur l'oeuvre du dominicain Etienne de Bourbon. Le 'Traité des diverses matières à prêcher' (*Tractatus de diversis materiis predicabilibus*) est le premier en date en même temps que le plus vaste des recueils d'*exempla* puisqu'il comporte, selon l'inventaire dressé par J.-Th. Welter (1973: 215, note 2), 2857 *exempla*, sans compter les nombreuses citations bibliques, les fréquents renvois aux Pères, ainsi que les arguments d'ordre scolastique. Ce traité, destiné à l'usage des prédicateurs, a été composé à Lyon entre les années 1250 et 1261. Etienne de Bourbon l'a rédigé à la fin de sa vie et y a mis, outre son expérience personnelle de prédicateur et d'inquisiteur, toutes ses connaissances accumulées lors de ses missions ou prises dans la bibliothèque des Prêcheurs de Lyon, malheureusement perdue.[1] L'ouvrage, pourtant déjà très vaste, est resté inachevé du fait de la mort de son auteur. Divisé selon les sept dons du Saint-Esprit, il s'arrête au début du cinquième (don de conseil), après avoir été placé successivement sous le signe des dons de crainte, de piété, de science et de force. Malgré cet état d'inachèvement, c'est quasiment l'ensemble de la vie chrétienne qui est abordé puisque le premier don est consacré aux fins dernières, le deuxième au Christ, à la Vierge et à la miséricorde, le troisième à la pénitence et à ses oeuvres, le quatrième aux péchés, et particulièrement aux péchés capitaux, le cinquième aux vertus de prudence, de tempérance et de force. Le sixième don aurait dû être consacré aux dogmes et aux articles de foi, et le septième à l'amour de Dieu, à la paix de l'esprit, au repos de l'âme et à la béatitude éternelle.[2]

Ont été retenus pour la présente étude les *exempla*, issus ou non de sources antiques, mettant en scène des personnages, des lieux ou des choses appartenant à l'Antiquité profane, en dehors de toute référence au christianisme. Les multiples persécutions ou conversions ont donc été écartées.[3]

- la matière antique

L'ensemble des unités retenues s'élève au nombre de 261, ce qui représente, si l'on retient le chiffre déjà cité de 2857 *exempla* (et où sont inclus les *similitudines* issus notamment des bestiaires et des lapidaires), plus de 9% des *exempla* et comparaisons proposés. Ce qui revient à dire que près d'un dixième des récits ou *similitudines* qui doivent dans le traité soutenir la foi chrétienne et fonder un comportement appartiennent au monde profane. L'examen du tableau (voir 00000) des personnages et des thèmes antiques appelle quelques brefs commentaires.

Le monde romain vient en tête avec 42% d'*exempla*. Ce sont les récits mettant en scène des personnages ou des groupes de personnes qui sont les plus nombreux (92 sur 111). Les empereurs romains s'imposent avec 47 *exempla*, ou plutôt avec 63, si Jules César - comme le veulent la tradition médiévale, et Etienne de Bourbon - est compris parmi eux. Le conquérant de la Gaule affiche 16 *exempla*, ce qui le met en tête de tous les personnages romains, suivi de loin par Néron (10 occurrences), puis par Auguste et Titus (7), Tibère (6), Hérode (4), Crassus, Domitien, Adrien, Dioclétien (3), Antonin (2), et Mucius Scaevola, Cincinnatus, Scipion l'Ancien, Pompée, Caligula, Helvius Pertinax, Maximien Hercule, Sévère (1). On remarquera l'absence des légendes virgiliennes.[4]

Le monde grec est représenté par deux groupes d'inégale importance numérique. Les philosophes forment tout d'abord une massive phalange: 35 occurrences, soit près de 14% des *exempla* retenus. Dans quinze cas l'identité des philosophes n'est pas précisée.[5] S'imposent sinon à égalité Aristote, Diogène et Socrate (4 occurrences), suivis de Pythagore (2), puis de Craton, Hippocrate, Lissander, Secundus, Theotistus et Zénon (1). Un second groupe comprend pêle-mème Milon de Crotone (non cité nommément), Périclès et Sophocle, Homère, Lysias et enfin un tyran.

La mythologie grecque et romaine est peu représentée: Hercule, Méduse, Médée, Janus, le géant Tytios (venu par une citation de l'*Enéide*) et la Sibylle. De même qu'Ulysse et les sirènes.

L'Orient en revanche est très présent: les souverains perses, assyriens ou babyloniens ont retenu l'attention du dominicain, souvent par le biais de Paul Orose. L'on compte trente-trois occurrences auxquelles il faut ajouter les cinquante-sept intéressant Alexandre le Grand, qui mobilise ainsi plus du cinquième de la matière antique. Les Brahmanes partagent avec Alexandre trente et un *exempla* et sont les seuls héros pour sept récits.

Jules César s'impose donc parmi les Romains pour ne céder quant au nombre d'occurrences que devant Alexandre le Grand.

2.    *Le dossier*

Seize *exempla* mettent donc en scène Jules César, pour former en tout dix anecdotes différentes, certaines étant répétées une ou plusieurs fois.[6] Pour présenter ces textes, j'ai choisi de les ranger non point suivant la nature de leur information, selon leur contenu historique ou leur valeur morale, mais plutôt conformément à la structure formelle et logique de l'*exemplum* à laquelle ils se rattachent. Trois grands types d'*exemplum* peuvent être dégagés: allégorique, métaphorique et métonymique (Bremond-Le Goff 1982: 113-9).

- l'*exemplum* allégorique

Dans ce type de récit exemplaire, un commentaire reprend pour en fixer le sens un ou plusieurs termes de l'*exemplum*. Le premier exemple de ce type nous est donné sous deux versions. Pour illustrer que le péché entraîne la corrosion de la conscience, Etienne de Bourbon écrit: *'Item*, le pécheur peut dire quand il entre dans sa conscience pour la scruter ce qu'à dit César aux Romains, alors qu'il revenait du siège d'une cité rebelle: 'J'ai trouvé, dit-il, une marmite pleine d'affreux serpents."[7] La parole de César est ici mise en situation et ne peut être abaissée au rang d'une simple citation. Elle apparaît avec d'autant plus de force que César exprime ce que le pécheur doit ressentir face à son âme. L'allégorie se mêle ici de façon complexe à la *similitudo*. Précisons tout d'abord que la comparaison de l'âme à une marmite pleine de serpents ne se comprend qu'à la lumière d'une citation précédente, mise sous le nom de saint Jérôme, et où se voit comparée l'âme rongée par les pensées à la vipère dont les petits lacèrent le sein de l'intérieur.[8] L'élément allégorique intervient, me semble-t-il, de façon plus globale, César et sa sentence devant être interprétés comme l'homme parlant à sa conscience. La parole de César ne précède pas son commentaire allégorique (César représente le pécheur qui ...) mais le suit (le pécheur peut dire ce qu'a dit César ...). Le même récit est employé beaucoup plus loin et sous une forme plus développée, pour souligner que l'homme envieux est - metaphoriquement - plein de vers: *'Item* (l'homme envieux est) semblable à une marmite emplie d'affreux serpents, comme on lit à propos de certains. Jules César qui revenait de légation expliqua son retard par le fait qu'il avait trouvé des marmites pleines d'affreux serpents, c'est dire pleins d'envie et de méchanceté. Ainsi a pu répondre à son père le Christ, alors qu'il était de retour vers lui, quant aux Juifs qui avaient tramé contre lui tout ce qui leur était possible'.[9] Dans cette version la démarche est double. Le pécheur, ici l'homme envieux, se voit comparé à une marmite pleine de serpents. Comparaison rendue explicite et compréhensible par la citation de la sentence de César. Puis ce dernier est pris dans les rets de l'allégorie, étant assimilé au Christ. La personne de César est pourtant ici relativement effacée, l'accent étant mis principalement sur l'image de la marmite pleine de hideux serpents.

Jules César intervient dans un autre *exemplum* allégorisé, de manière plus limpide cette fois, fourni parmi d'autres pour illustrer que la cinquième espèce d'*acedia* est l'insensiblité: *'Item*, on lit que César fit couper la main à des ennemis qui s'étaient rebellés, afin que de leur vivant ils fussent punis d'une longue misère, comme le dit Orose dans son cinquième livre. De même le diable coupe-t-il la main aux coupables de mélancolie (d'*acedia*) pour les rendre inaptes au bien'.[10] César doit donc ici être clairement interprété, par le biais de l'allégorie, comme le diable. Son personnage n'en est pas pour autant jugé négativement, l'accent étant mis sur les coupables et non sur le bourreau.

Ce type de récits est peu fréquent et est utilisé par Etienne de Bourbon surtout à propos des thèmes suivants: animaux (éléphants de Pyrrhus; loups cherchant à faire la paix avec les chiens; gryphons d'Alexandre); objets (sculptures de Rome); groupes (femmes, soldats, esclaves); croyances mythiques (Hercule et Antée).[11]

- *l'exemplum* analogique

L'exemplum de type analogique est introduit généralement par l'adjectif *similis* qui lie fermement le contexte théologico-moral au récit.[12] Pour César, nous en avons deux exemples.

Etienne de Bourbon, voulant montrer que l'avare s'ensevelit lui-même dans ses richesses, écrit: *'Item*, (l'avare est) semblable à Jules César, qui est interprété comme le prince, possédant quasiment le monde entier, et qui lui fit verser tribut en or et en argent, et se vit saisi par lui puisque ses cendres sont conservées à Rome dans une urne d'or.'[13] L'allégorie du prince se lie ici à la stricte comparaison, nous incitant d'ailleurs à ne jamais considérer les catégories comme de rigides carcans, mais plutôt comme de toujours provisoires et commodes instruments de recherche. L'image de César est ici franchement négative, tout comme celles d'Alexandre le Grand ou de Cyrus, héros de récits entourant notre *exemplum*.[14]

Second exemple: *'Item*, l'homme d'Eglise doit être semblable à César qui, dit-on, n'a jamais dit à ses soldats 'Allez', mais 'Venez', en les précédant, comme le Christ qui disait à ses disciples: 'Venez à ma suite.'[15] Il s'agissait pour le dominicain de montrer que l'homme d'Eglise devait entraîner à l'obéissance en faisant montre de sa propre obéissance à Dieu.

Ce type de récit analogique, pouvant être - comme nous l'avons vu - lié à l'allégorie, ne représente que 12% environ de notre *corpus*, soit trente-deux récits. Vingt-sept d'entre eux s'adaptent à des personnages et deux seulement sont positifs: l'*exemplum* que nous venons de citer et un récit mettant en scène la vie exemplaire de Titus.[16] Les *exempla* de type strictement allégorique ou analogique sont de fait peu nombreux dans l'oeuvre d'Etienne de Bourbon. Le type qui s'impose est celui de l'*exemplum* métonymique, ou plus exactement, si nous suivons la terminologie de Claude Bremond (1982: 116) synecdochique.

- l'*exemplum* métonymique ou synecdochique

L'*exemplum* métonymique ou synecdochique illustre la règle générale par une de ses manifestations particulières. Le plus souvent la transition entre la leçon et l'anecdote s'effectue sans formule particulière. Dans le cas de Jules César, nous trouvons dix *exempla* de ce type. Commençons par ceux qui offrent de lui une image positive.

Le récit de Jules César qui encourageait ses soldats en les précédant au combat, déjà rencontré, illustre également ce que doit être le bon exemple.[17] César applique à lui-même ce qu'il commande à ses hommes, tout comme Grégoire de Naziance et Origène reflètent dans leur vie ce qu'ils enseignent à leurs disciples (EdB 337b). Homme de guerre et hommes de Dieu sont mis là sur le même plan. Un deuxième *exemplum* extrait du *Pantheon* de Godefroi de Viterbe montre Jules César demandant à ses soldats de n'emporter en expédition d'autres victuailles que du lard, du pain et du vinaigre, ce afin qu'ils ne perdent pas leurs forces dans les délices.[18] Ce souci n'est cependant pas l'apanage du seul César. Etienne de Bourbon souligne que les anciens Romains, lorsqu'ils étaient en guerre, et afin d'être plus efficaces et plus courageux contre l'ennemi, avaient soin de conserver - bien qu'ils fussent païens - ces deux vertus, la chasteté et la sobriété. Et de citer Isidore de Séville qui faisait dériver *castra* ('les camps') de *casta* ('chastes'), pour proposer ensuite les exemples d'autres grands chefs romains, comme Scipion l'Africain ou Trajan (EdB 236b). Au César sobre et désirant que ses soldats le fussent aussi, s'ajoute le chef maître de lui. Un même récit est utilisé quatre fois dans le recueil pour illustrer et fonder des objets différents: trois fois dans un sens positif et une fois dans un sens néga- tif. C'est la courte anecdote de Jules César, citée sans source précise, qui déclare à quelque vilain qui lui cherchait noise, qu'il ne lui ferait pas l'honneur de sa colère.[19] Les trois récits employés positivement illustrent respectivement: la force qui pousse à mépriser au milieu des périls les choses mesquines; la force qui pousse à supporter d'un esprit égal les maux présents; et enfin la faculté de supporter (*patientia*) qui rend noble. Dans le premier cas Jules César est mis sur le même rang que les lions, David et les martyrs chrétiens, et est étroitement associé à Alexandre le Grand avec qui il partage le goût des vastes combats et le mépris des querelles avec de basses personnes (EdB 655c). Dans le deuxième cas César est encore lié à Alexandre puisqu'à la suite de notre récit est proposée, tirée de la *Gesta Alexandri*, l'anecdote montrant Aristote amenant Alexandre à épargner un homme qui l'avait offensé, le véritable vainqueur étant celui qui triomphait de son propre coeur.[20] Dans le troisième cas enfin l'exem- ple de Jules César précède ceux de deux personnages appartenant également à l'Antiquité: Mucius Scaevola supportant avec courage que sa main fût brûlée, et Socrate refusant de s'évader pour échapper à une mort certaine.[21] Or le même récit est employé pour illustrer un genre de *patientia demeritoria*, la *patientia naturalis*, faculté innée de supporter les épreuves, et qui est celle des gens de guerre qui, bien que non poussés par l'esprit de charité, supportent également les tourments par une certaine probité d'âme naturelle. C'est aussi le cas des lions, pris à leur tour dans un sens négatif. Je reviendrai plus tard sur ce paradoxe. Et j'en viens immédiatement aux *exempla* donnant une image négative de César.

Trois récits, dont l'un est cité deux fois, montrent César sous un jour négatif. Le premier est d'ailleurs moins une anecdote qu'une simple allusion historique. S'agissant de montrer que de l'ambition naissent tous les vices, et plus précisé- ment que les conflits surgissent surtout du fait que l'un veut dominer l'autre, Etienne de Bourbon cite les guerres des Assyriens, des Mèdes, des Grecs, des Romains, et pour finir, des Bretons.[22] Le dominicain n'a que ces paroles pour les Romains: 'Jules César a combattu Pompée son cousin; ils ont livré ces com- bats poussés par le seul désir de dominer le monde.'[23] Toujours dans le même esprit, la carrière mouvementée de César, 'premier monarque et empereur des Romains', et sa fin tragique au bout de trois ans et six mois de pouvoir, four- nissent matière à illustrir que l'honneur dû à l'ambition est fugace et transi- toire.[24] César vient après Ninus, premier roi des Babyloniens, Cyrus, premier roi des Perses et des Mèdes, et Alexandre le Grand, premier monarque des Grecs. Il incarne donc ici le prince romain ambitieux. Le troisième récit, tiré de la *Pharsalia*, est donné deux fois au cours du traité. Il s'agit de la célèbre scène où Jules César fuyant ses troupes révoltées arrive à la cabane du pêcheur Amyclas. Etienne de Bourbon utilise tout d'abord cet épisode pour montrer que l'ambition - nous restons dans le même champ - rend l'homme esclave.[25] Jules

César y apparaît comme un homme tourmenté, craignant toute chose, et louant alors la sécurité et la liberté que procure la pauvreté au pêcheur. Cet *exemplum* suit immédiatement un long récit où un philosophe, en lequel il faut reconnaître Diogène, finit par accuser Alexandre le Grand d'être l'esclave du démon (EdB 365 b-c). Encore une fois le destin 'exemplaire' de César croise celui d'Alexandre. La même anecdote est reprise plus loin, de manière plus développée et serrant de près le texte de Lucain, pour appuyer le fait que la pauvreté soulage l'homme des poids de l'existence, des voleurs et des calomniateurs.[26] Le héros de l'*exemplum* est ici plus Amyclas, nommément cité, que Jules César qui ne sert qu'à le mettre en valeur. Deux récits suivent l'anecdote. Le premier est également tiré de la *Pharsalia*: un roi explore certaines terres dans l'anonymat que lui procure un habit usé; le second montre encore Alexandre rendant visite en secret aux Brahmanes, après avoir déposé son habit royal. Comme César il vivait dans la crainte, surtout de ses propres gardes.[27]

Au sein de ce type d'*exemplum*, qui met en oeuvre une démarche inductive, César apparaît comme un modèle, exemplaire ou répulsif. Et je terminerai sur un cas où le comportement de Jules César est associé au terme d'*exemplum* dans le sens précis d'"exemple'. Pour montrer que les hommes d'Eglise, les *prelati*, doivent être doux et tempérants, Etienne de Bourbon a recours à cinq arguments (*cause*). Sitôt après l'Ecriture Sainte viennent les exemples donnés par les païens: *Ad hanc (mansuetudinem prelati) moventur exemplo gentilium*. L'exemple de Jules César visant à réformer les coutumes romaines pour établir un régime plus clément, avant d'être assassiné par Brutus et Cassius, précède ceux d'Auguste fidèle en amitié et du doux Tibère.[28] Il peut s'agir certes d'un exemple à suivre. J'y verrais plutôt l'expression de l'argument que l'on pourrait dire comme relevant de l'*a fortiori*. Si César faisait montre de clémence, *a fortiori* les prélats ne doivent-ils pas faire de même ... L'argument - Etienne de Bourbon ne parle-t-il pas de *causa* - prend ici l'avantage sur le strict modèle exemplaire. On trouve autre part des récits 'antiques' placés sous le signe de l'*exemplum* ainsi défini. Ainsi à propos de l'adultère, et de sa condamnation: *Item de hystoria gentilium sunt exempla*. Suivent les exemples de Pauline et de Lucrèce.[29]

Sans anticiper sur les quelques remarques que je pourrai faire à partir de ce dossier, tant sur l'image de César que sur le statut du personnage antique dans le recueil d'Etienne de Bourbon, il est à noter immédiatement que les *exempla* dans lesquels apparait César ne relèvent pas d'un même type, mais s'inscrivent sous des catégories logiques différentes, formant un véritable réseau exemplaire.

3.    *La transmission de la matière antique*

Noter que la mention d'origine des *exempla* est en règle générale tout à fait indispensable. Sans revenir sur ce sujet, il suffit de rappeler que l'indication de la source utilisée est pour Etienne de Bourbon un facteur important dans la constitution de l'authenticité du récit exemplaire, de sa crédibilité, et par là de son efficacité potentielle (Bremond-Le Goff 1982: 37). Les mentions de sources ou de canal d'information des *exempla* ayant trait à Jules César, et qui ont été regroupées en tableau appellent un bref commentaire.

Trois auteurs sont cités nommément pour cinq *exempla* représentant quatre anecdotes distinctes. Le premier est Lucain dont la *Pharsalia* fournit l'*exemplum* de César et Amyclas. L'auteur du *De bello civili* est une source peu prisée du dominicain puisque ce dernier ne lui emprunte, outre le récit cité, que l'*exemplum* du roi espion voyageant *incognito*. Ce qui viserait à confirmer la thèse de Margaret Jennings (1974: 218-9) d'un déclin de l'usage du poème de Lucain comme source d'*exempla* à partir du premier quart du XIIIe siècle. Le deuxième auteur est Paul Orose, cité deux fois - la première en association avec des *alia cronica*, dans ses *Historiae adversus paganos*, ouvrage que présente longuement Etienne de Bourbon dans le prologue de son traité.[30] Orose est largement mis à contribution puisqu'il est utilisé cinquante-et-une fois dans notre *corpus*, représentant ainsi la source de près du cinquième des *exempla* de l'Antiquité profane.[31] La précision est poussée jusqu'au livre (*libro . VI.*; . V. *Libro*), comme c'est le cas vingt-et-une fois sur les cinquante-et-une occurrences. Le troisième auteur est Godefroi de Viterbe dont le *Pantheon*, composé entre 1185 et 1187, est utilisé une fois.[32] L'oeuvre de celui que le dominicain appelle Godefroi de Parme, également minutieusement présentée dans le prologue du recueil, est citée vingt fois dans notre *corpus*.[33]

La mention impersonnelle d'une source écrite (*legitur quod*) revient trois fois. La première intervient à propos de la sentence de César sur la ville rebelle, sentence qui dans sa première citation n'avait bénéficié d'aucune mention de source.[34] La deuxième intéresse l'allusion historique empruntée de toute évidence au *Liber exceptionum* de Richard de Saint-Victor, rédigé vers 1153-1160, mais sans doute par le biais du *Speculum historiale* de Vincent de Beauvais.[35] La troisième enfin introduit la seconde des quatre occurrences de l'anecdote de César refusant de s'emporter. La mention de l'écrit soutient donc ici un récit qui n'était introduit, deux folios plus haut, que par la mention imprécise de *fertur quod*, 'on rapporte que'. Les deux occurrences suivantes ne présentent pas de mention de source, Etienne de Bourbon ayant peut-être estimé qu'elle avait été déjà fournie. En tout état de cause on ne peut que remarquer ici le flottement qui existe entre l'appartenance de l'anecdote au domaine de l'écrit ou à celui de ce qui circule par ouï-dire.

La formule *dicitur quod* introduit par deux fois la brève anecdote de César précédant ses troupes au combat; l'anecdote vient peut-être de Suétone.[36] Etienne de Bourbon ne se prononce pas dans ce cas sur son authenticité et ne s'en porte pas garant. Il est à noter que les récits du type *dicitur quod* sont pour notre *corpus* peu nombreux et concernent pour l'essentiel, outre César, les philosophes grecs, Alexandre et la mythologie.[37]

Pour ce qui est des cinq *exempla* privés de citation de source, trois ont été déjà mentionnés. Dans le cas de l'ambition de César et de Pompée, il ne s'agit que d'une simple allusion historique sans constitution réelle de récit. La mention des cendres de César est également fort brève et est sans doute une réminiscence d'un passage des *Otia imperialia* de Gervais de Tilbury qu'Etienne de Bourbon cite comme l'une de ses sources dans son prologue.[38] Si dans le *corpus* utilisé le nombre important d'*exempla* présentés sans mention de source ou même de canal d'information peut surprendre - on en compte 43, soit 14% du totalil faut dire qu'il s'agit surtout d'apophtegmes, de courtes allusions historiques ou de récits dont la source a été précédemment citée.

On aura remarqué qu'Etienne de Bourbon n'a pas utilisé les oeuvres mêmes de César, cependant connues.[39] Quant à Valère Maxime, il n'a pas, semble-t-il, eu accès à son oeuvre.[40] Ce qui frappe c'est bien finalement la diversité de la transmission de la matière antique, malgré le poids compréhensible de l'écrit, s'agissant d'*exempla* historiques, tout autant qua la relative ignorance d'Etienne de Bourbon des sources classiques.

4.    *Du bon usage de César*

Si l'image seule de Jules César dans les *exempla* d'Etienne de Bourbon devait être dressée, elle serait simple et sans surprises. Le vainqueur de Vercingétorix y apparaîtrait comme un personnage dévoré d'ambition, mais bon prince et excellent chef de guerre. On pourrait ajouter que César s'y montrerait autant homme d'action qu'hommes de paroles, puisque ses *facta* se délivrent à deux reprises dans ses *dicta*, à propos de son courage au combat (il précède ses hommes) ou de son sang-froid. On noterait enfin que Jules César ne se voit guère décrit dans ses campagnes, citées, certes, mais sans détails. Au-delà de ce portrait, qu'il resterait à affiner, je voudrais seulement essayer de comprendre comment le personnage de César a pu être retenu à des fins d'édification.

- exemple à suivre ou modèle répulsif?

Une évidence pour commencer. César est un personnage du monde païen qui ne peut en aucune manière être placé au sein d'une anecdote mettant en scène son salut ou la marche vers celui-ci. César est en quelque sorte clos sur son paganisme, dans l'impossibilité absolue d'illustrer ou de représenter métaphoriquement une rédemption ou une damnation.[41] En revanche César est convoqué pour illustrer - de façon statique si l'on peut dire - vices ou vertus, qualités ou défauts. Un seul *exemplum* est utilisé pour les trois premières parties du traité! Il apparaît dans la première, placée sous le don de crainte, dans la section consacrée à la crainte du péché: c'est la parole de César sur la cité rebelle, où précisément la personne du conquérant est peu en cause, l'essentiel reposant dans la métaphore qu'elle fournissait. En revanche César intervient d'abondance, positivement ou négativement, dans la quatrième partie du traité, dans les sections dédiées au mauvais exemple (1), à l'orgueil (3), à l'envie (1), à l'*acedia* (1), à l'avarice (1), à la *gula* (1), ainsi que dans la cinquième partie, sous les vertus de prudence (2), de tempérance (1) et de force (1). César s'impose donc comme un modèle attractif ou répulsif, selon les *exempla* et le contexte théologico-moral, au sein de la stricte définition de la vie morale du chrétien. Cette constatation est par ailleurs applicable, en règle générale, à l'ensemble des *exempla* faisant intervenir des héros païens: 148 anecdotes, soit environ 57% du *corpus*, se trouvent dans la quatrième partie, et pour ne prendre que cet exemple, sont employées dans la section consacrée à l'orgueil; 75 se placent dans la cinquième partie, dont 33 dépendent de la tempérance.

- la force du nom

Les personnages ou groupes de personnes, à l'exception de certains 'philosophes', appartenant à l'Antiquité païenne sont bien déterminés. Contrairement aux
'héros' chrétiens de l'*exemplum*, les 'héros' classiques ne peuvent être n'importe
quels hommes ou n'importe quelles femmes.[42] Le nom du personnage historique
devait sans nul doute, dans l'esprit d'Etienne de Bourbon, frapper l'auditeur. Les
noms de ces personnages ne sont pas interchangeables. Et les confusions de
patronymes restent exceptionelles.[43] Il est probable que que certains noms
propres évoquaient immédiatement et sans ambiguïté, comme par antonomase,
un vice ou une vertu: Néron la luxure, Titus la douceur, Amyclas la pauvreté,
pour ne prendre que ces exemples. Dans le cas de César, la charge morale qu'il
supporte n'est pas univoque, tout comme pour Alexandre le Grand, qui resterait
à étudier. La figure de César, pour le destinataire de ces *exempla*, devait tour à
tour s'incarner dans l'homme de guerre courageux, dans le chef ambitieux ou
dans le prince clément. Confusion redoublée puisque parfois un même récit
pouvait illustrer des messages contradictoires!

- le paradoxe des *exempla* contradictoires

Mettre des personnages païens au service de la morale chrétienne ne va pas
parfois sans paradoxe. Tant que les héros antiques présentent des défauts ou des
vices, la question ne se pose pas: ils sont, tout comme les chrétiens coupables
des mêmes fautes, voués à l'opprobre et présentés comme des modèles répulsifs.
De même, quand leurs qualités sont saisies de façon intrinsèque, sans référence
au christianisme, elles s'imposent sans réserves. Mais il suffit qu'elles soient
confrontées explicitement aux vertus chrétiennes pour qu'elles deviennent défauts.[44] C'est ainsi que le sang - froid de César peut être autant - comme nous
l'avons vu - un exemple de force d'esprit que le résultat d'une *patientia naturalis* qui ne doit rien à l'esprit de charité. Un exemple similaire est donné en la
personne de Diogène qui se débarrasse de l'argent qu'il avait posé sur sa tête et
qu'un voleur voulait lui prendre pendant son sommeil, afin de dormir en toute
quiétude. L'anecdote sert dans la quatrième partie du recueil à dissuader de
l'avarice, puis dans la cinquième à montrer que certains n'ont pas le mérite de
la pauvreté car s'ils refusent les richesses c'est pour éviter les soucis et non
pour Dieu et le salut de leur âme.[45] Sous l'angle de la simple vertu Diogène est
un exemple, sous le feu des impératifs chrétiens il devient un modèle répulsif.
Et ce, pour une même attitude.

    Le contenu d'un récit est parfois même rigoureusement contrôlé, en dehors de
tout commentaire allégorique, quand il met en scène une pratique réprouvée par
le christianisme. C'est ainsi que dissuadent de l'adultère les *exempla gentilium*.
Le montrent les exemples de Pauline et de Lucrèce qui se tuent toutes deux
pour échapper à la honte et à l'adultère. Etienne de Bourbon précise bien que
ces deux femmes ne doivent pas être recommandées pour leur suicide mais
seulement pour leur désir de rester chastes et de ne pas commettre l'adultère.[46]

On ne saurait cependant donner trop d'importance à ces témoignages. Les vertus des païens sont présentées dans l'ensemble sur le même plan que celles des chrétiens, comme si la force du paganisme était en fin de compte largement désamorcée.[47]

A travers le succès des *exempla* tirés de l'Antiquité profane et qui prennent place, comme ceux mettant en scène Jules César, dans le recueil d'Etienne de Bourbon, est bien mis en valeur le lien fondamental qui existe au Moyen Age entre l'histoire et la morale. Pour le dominicain l'efficacité pastorale passe en bonne partie par la convocation des *exempla* historiques. Les personnages de l'Antiquité représentent, par leur caractère haut en couleurs et souvent spectaculaire, une matière de choix pour les prédicateurs et fournissent à profusion des figures exemplaires ou répulsives s'adaptant aux modèles de comportement exigés par l'Eglise. Il resterait bien entendu à étudier dans quelle mesure leur utilisation a été effective et, si cela est possible, quelle fut leur efficacité réelle sur le public.

## LES *EXEMPLA* DE L'ANTIQUITE PROFANE CHEZ ETIENNE DE BOURBON

| | THEMES | NOMBRE | POURCENTAGE |
|---|---|---|---|
| 1. | MONDE GREC | | |
| | Philosophes | 35 | |
| | Personnages divers | 5 | |
| | Total | 40 | 15,3% |
| 2. | MONDE ROMAIN | | |
| | Coutumes | 8 | |
| | Lieux | 11 | |
| | Personnages (sauf empereurs et César) | 20 | |
| | Empereurs | 46 | |
| | César | 16 | |
| | Peuples dans l'orbite romaine | 5 | |
| | Femmes romaines | 5 | |
| | Total | 111 | 42% |
| 3. | MYTHOLOGIE GRECQUE ET ROMAINE | 13 | 4,9% |
| 4. | ORIENT | 33 | 12,6% |
| 5. | ALEXANDRE LE GRAND | | |

| Seul | 26 | 10% |
| Avec les Brahmanes | 31 | 11,8% |
| Brahmanes | 7 | 2,6% |
| | | |
| TOTAL | 261 | |

| SOURCE OU CANAL D'INFORMATION | RESUME | Ms, PARIS, BIBL. NAT., LAT. 15970 |
|---|---|---|

## 1. AUTEURS CITES

**a. Lucain, *La Pharsale***

| - Item, sicut refert Lucanus quod cum... | César et Amyclas | 365c |
| - Item, refert Lucanus de Julio Cesare quod... | *Idem* | 647b |

**b. Orose, *Histoire contre les païens***

| - (...) Julius Cesar de quo dicit Horosius, libro .VI., et alia cronica. | Carrière et fin tragique de César | 363b |
| - Similiter legitur fuisse Julius Cesar (...) ut dicitur Horosii .V. libro | César fait couper la main de ses ennemis | 442b |

**c. Godefroi de Viterbe, *Panthéon***

| - Item, idem (Godefridus Parmensis) dicit in eisdem (cronicis) quod... | Sobriété des soldats de César | 436b |

## 2. LEGITUR

| - Item, similis sibi olle plene diris serpentibus, sicut de quibusdam legitur | César et les serpents (no 2) | 415c |
| - De Julio Cesare legitur quod... | César réformateur | 594c |
| - Sicut legitur fuisse in hiis Cesar qui ... | César refuse de s'emporter (no 2) | 657d |

## 3. FERTUR

| - (...) unde Julius Cesar (...) fertur dixisse ... | César refuse de s'emporter (no 1) | 655c |

## 4. DICITUR

| | | |
|---|---|---|
| - Item, de Julio Cesare dicitur quod ... | César précède ses soldats | 337d |
| - Item, similis (...) Julio Cesare qui (...) dicitur dixis-se... | *Idem* | 593c |

## 5. PAS DE MENTION DE SOURCE (PMS)

| | | |
|---|---|---|
| - PMS | César et les serpents (no 1) | 186c |
| - PMS | Ambition de César | 360c |
| - PMS | Les cendres de César | 437a-b |
| - PMS | César refuse de s'emporter (no 3) | 660d |
| - PMS | *Idem* (no 4) | 670d |

## NOTES

1.  Sur Etienne de Bourbon, voir Welter (1973: 215-23); notice biographique dans Lecoy de la Marche (1877: ii-xi); Quétif-Echard (1719: 184-94); Kaeppeli (1980: no 3633; pp. 354-5); Schenda (1983: 511-9); Berlioz (1981: 299-335); du même (1985: 83-92). L'édition intégrale du traité, placée sous la responsabilité de J. Berlioz, est préparée dans le cadre du Groupe d'anthropologie historique de l'Occident médiéval (Paris, Centre de recherches historiques, EHESS-CNRS), placé sous la direction de J. Le Goff. L'édition de la première partie du recueil, préparée par J.-C. Eichenlaub et J. Berlioz, est en voie d'achèvement. Voir Eichenlaub (1984: 37-40). L'édition de la troisième partie est achevée (Berlioz 1984).

2.  Sur la division du traité selon les dons du Saint Esprit, voir Berlioz (1983: 157-83).

3.  La constitution de ce *corpus* a été realisée sur le manuscrit de base de l'édition, Paris, Bibl.nat, lat. 15970 (XIIIe s.), abrégé ici en EdB.

4.  Sur cette question, voir Berlioz (1985: 65-120, surtout pp. 70-1).

5.  L'espace imparti ne me permet naturellement pas de citer et de dévelop-per toutes les références au traité. Je reprendrai la question dans son ensemble plus tard et de façon détaillée.

6.  J'ai écarté, peut-être à tort, un *exemplum* consacré à Hérode où inter-vient le jugement de César: *.VIII.* (*malum exemplum prostravit et occidit ...*) *Item, qui mala exempla in prelatione exhibent subditis suis similes sunt Herodi de quo fertur dixisse Cesar: Mallem esse Herodis porcus*

*quam filius, quia ipse occidit filios suos et nutrit porcos* (EdB 332b). Cette parole est attibuée plus loin (636d) à l'empereur Auguste. Il n'est donc pas certain qu'il s'agisse de Jules César.

7.    *XX. facit (peccatum) consciencie corrosionem (...) Item potest dicere peccator cum intrat conscientiam suam eam scrutando, quod dixit Julius Cesar Romanis, rediens de obsidione cujusdam civitatis rebellis: 'Inveni, ait, ollam plenam diris serpentibus'* (EdB 186b-c). Voir Tubach (1969: no 4276): seul renvoi au *Tractatus de diversis historiis Romanorum*, recueil compilé à Bologne en 1326, qui s'inspire manifestement d'Etienne de Bourbon. A l'instar de S. Herzstein (1893: 9, no. 19), J.-L. Eichenlaub et moi-même n'avons pu trouver pour l'instant la source de ce récit.

8.    Jeronimus: *'Sicut vipera filiis in utero positis lacerate perimitur et corroditur, ita nos cogitationes nostre intra nos nutrite'* (ibid).

9.    *Item (invidus) similis sibi olle plene diris serpentibus sicut de quibusdam legitur. Julius Cesar rediens a legatione sua dicensque ideo tamdiu tardaverat quia invenerat ollas plenas diris serpentibus, scilicet plenos omni invidia et malitia. Taliter potuit respondere Christus patri de Judeis rediens ad patrem qui omnia mala que potuerunt machinati sunt contra eum* (EdB 415c).

10.   *Quinta species (accidie) est insensibilitas (...) Similiter legitur fecisse Julius Cesar quibusdam hostibus suis qui diu ei rebellaverunt. Cum eos cepisset, manus ejus amputavit ut viventes in longa miseria punirentur, ut dicitur Horosii. V. libro. Similiter dyabolus manus accidiosis amputat dum eos reddit inutiles ad bonum* (EdB 442b).

11.   Eléphants de Pyrrhus, EdB 371c; les loups et les chiens (Tubach 5357), EdB 615c-d; Alexandre et les gryphons, EdB 535c-d; sculptures romaines, EdB 569c; femmes romaines libérant leur mari par le chant (Tubach 3893?), EdB 261a; soldats gelés (Orose, *Adv.pag.*, V, 18, 18-20, éd. citée, p.324-25), EdB 442b; révolte des esclaves (Orose, *Adv.pag.*, IV, 5, 3-5, éd. citée, p. 105-6); Hercule et Antée (Tubach 267), EdB 348a.

12.   L'*exemplum* illustre la règle générale par une analogie. Voir Bremond-Le Goff (1982: 116-7).

13.   *Item similis (avarus est) Julio Cesari qui interpretatur princeps possidens quasi totum mundum fecit sibi tributarium in auro et argento, ad ultimum possessus est ab hiis quia ejus cineres in urna aurea sunt sepulte et recondite Rome* (EdB 473a-b). Voir Gervais de Tilbury, *Otia imperialia*, II, 9 (Liebrecht 1856: 10).

14.   *Similes Alexandro de quo mortuo et in tumulo aureo et argento posito,*

*dixit quidam philosophus: 'Eri possidebat aurum et argentum, hodie possidebatur ab argento et auro a quo continetur'* (Edb 473a, Tubach 3751); Pour Cyrus confondu ici avec Darius, il s'agit du récit tiré d'Orose, *Adv.pag.*, III, 17, 6 (Zangemeister 1882: 176) montrant Darius conduit prisonnier à Alexandre, lié par des chaînes d'or.

15. *Secundo, debent prelatos movere ad obediendum suis superioribus, ut ipsi suos inferiores per exemplum suum ad obediendum Deo (...) Item similis debet esse prelatus Julio Cesari qui nunquam suis militibus dicitur dixisse: Ite sed Venite improbitatibus, precedens eos semper et ortans eos ad sequendum se, ut Christo qui dicebat discipulis suis: 'Venite post me'* (*Matth.* III: 4, 19) (EdB 593c).

16. EdB 588c (citation du *Pantheon* de Godefroi de Viterbe, XXI, 12).

17. *Item de Julio Cesare dicitur quod nunquam dixit militibus suis: Ite sed: Venite, eos precedens in strenue agendo* (EdB 337d).

18. (la *gula* détruit la force de l'esprit et toute la vigueur des vertus) *Item, idem (Godefridus Parmensis) dicit in eisdem (cronicis) quod avidius Cesar extraordinarius precepit militibus ut nullus portaret in expeditione aliquid victualium preter lardum et panem et accetum. Hoc fecit ut expeditiones essent et ne deliciis emolliti vim perderent* (EdB 536b). Voir Godefroi de Viterbe, *Pantheon*, XXI, 21 (Waitz 1872: 165).

19. *1. Secundus gradus fortitudinis est in grava ardua appetere et humilia et parva contempnere (...) Sic Alexander et Julius Cesar prelia magna virorum appetebant ut confligerent contra eos, quod patet ex eorum gestis, humilium personarum conflictus declinabunt. Unde Julius Cesar cuidam vili qui se opponebat fertur dixisse: Dignum te Cesaris ira nullus honor faciet* (EdB 665c; Tubach: 828). *2. IX (fortitudo) mala presentia equanimiter portoat (...) Sicut legitur fecisse in hiis Cesar qui ait cuidam se opponenti: Dignum te · Cesaris ira nullus honor faciet* (EdB 657d); *3. Septima (patientia demeritoria) est patientia naturalis ut illorum militum qui licet non sunt in caritate, naturali quadam animi probitate et (...) multa dura et aspera equanimiter tollerant (...) Sic Julius Cesar cuidam vili <qui> provocare nitebatur ad iram: Nullum te Cesaris ira dignus honor faciet* (EdB 660d); *4. Patientia nobilis facit (...) Julius Cesar attendens cuidam rustico qui sibi injuriam intulerat, respondit vincendo animum suum: Dignum te Cesaris ira nullus honor faciet* (EdB 670d).

20. *Legitur in gestis Alexandri quod cum quidam offendisset eum nec vellet ei parcere, probante sibi Aristotele magistro suo quod victor esset gloriosor vincendo cor suum quod vicerat et sibi subjecerat totum mundum, vicit cor suum quod fuit maxime fortitudinis et remisit injuriam* (EdB 657d).

21.    *Seneca loquitur de quodam Mucio qui patientia sua vicit duos reges in ignem in quo manum sustinuit comburi; et videns eam in foco distillantem non est animo dejectus. Ergo, inquit Seneca, ego non dubito magis laudabilem truncam illam manum salvam* (670d; voir Sénèque, *Lettres à Lucilius*, 66, 5, 1; Préchac-Noblot 1947: 134). *Talis fuit Socrates qui cum esset positus in carcere, cum essent qui eum abire permitterent, noluit exire sed remansit ut duarum rerum gravissimarum hominibus metum auferret, carceris et mortis* (EdB 670d-671a).

22.    *Sexto, quia ambitio est perpetratio et mater omnium fere scelerum et vitiorum (...) Ex eo (sic) fuerunt fere omnes guerre Assyriorum et Medorum, Grecorum et Romanorum et Britonum et maxime cum Arthuro...* (EdB 360c).

23.    *Julius Cesar Pompeium consobrinum suum et has cedes fecerunt fere totius mundi solo amore dominandi... (ibid.)*

24.    *Quarta monarchia fuit Romanorum. Primus eorum monarchus et imperator fuit Julius Cesar de quo dicit Honorius, libro . VI., et alia cronica. Cum jussus esset ad partes gallicanas et cisalpinas et per multos annos impugnasset Britones, Saxones et gentes circa Renum et Rodanum, et omnia subjugasset que erant circa Romam, tandem insequtus Pompeium usque in Egyptum agens bellum civile per quatuor annos in quo fere totum mundum involvit, quia in eo habebat omnes fere occidentales Pompeyus orientales, et cum utroque cives romani senatores maxime erant cum Pompeio socio suo, quem cum vicisset et fugasset in Egyptum ob favorem ipsius victoris Cesaris a Ptholomeo adolescente rege Egypti ad quem confugerat decapitatus est et caput missus est Cesari. Cum autem omnia sibi Cesar subjugasset, Roman venit rerum summam solus agens quam Greci monarchiam vocant, qui post .3. annos et .VI. menses post quos imperare ceperat et cum intraret Capitolium pro re publica tractanda auctoribus Bruto et Cassio .23. vulneribus confossus interiit. Ecce per quem longum et pericolosum laborem iste dominium adquisivit et cum quantis sceleribus et quam breve fuit! Mortuo Julio Cesare, ut dicit Orosius quod vere competit facta est Roma ut agit ille...* (EdB 363b; Orose, *Adv.pag.*, VI, 6-17, Zangemeister 1882: 367-407).

25.    *Ambitio facit hominem servum (...) Item refert Lucanus <quod> cum Julius Cesar pugnaret contra Pompeium omnibus in stipendiis providebat et omnes metuebat et cum solus in navicula venisset ad domum piscatoris pauperis de arundine cum junco contexta, in qua ille securus pauper quiescebat, cum cor Cesaris trepidaret, paupertatis ejus securitatem beatificabat et libertatem status suis Cesar (EdB 365c).* Voir Lucain, *La Guerre civile*, V, v. 510-531 (Bourgery 1926: 155-6).

26.    *Paupertas facit homines securos a ponderibus, latronibus, calompniatori-*

*bus (...) Item refert Lucanus de Julio Cesare qui cum timeret commotio-*
*nem exercitus proprii, pre timore etiam suorum, solus de nocte in navi-*
*culam parculam intrans et periculo fluctuum se committens, applicuit ad*
*litus ubi invenit tugurium cujusdam pauperis piscatoris quod erat factum*
*junco calamo in quo securus pauper, dictus Amiclas, quiescebat. Et*
*tangente imperatore manu domum et pulsante ad ostium domuncule dicte*
*domus debilis conterravit. Cessare etiam timore trepidante, ubi dicit*
*auctor quod per manus imperialis impulsum timebat pauper, ad cujus*
*accessum tremebant munitissime mundi urbes, une beatificans auctor et*
*pauper securitatem, quem timebat imperator potius quam eum, exclamat*
*pro hoc et pro paupertatis felicitate dicens:*

> *O vite tuta facultas*
> *paupertas angustique lares! o munera nondum*
> *intellecta deum! Quibus hoc contingere templis*
> *aut potuit muris in illo (nullo legend.) trepidare tumultu*
> *Cesarea pulsante manu? Hanc autem ille pauper non timebat*

(voir ci-dessus, n. 25).

27. EdB 647b-c. Le premier récit est emprunté à Lucain, *De bello civili*, VIII,
v. 238-43 (Bourgery 1926: 97).

28. *De Julio Cesare legitur quod infra (sic) benignus extitit ut quos artius*
*ceperarant (sic) vicerat superaret. Hic dum consuetudines Romanorum in*
*clementiorem statum reformaret, occisus est a Bruto et Cassio.* Pour la
source supposée, voir ci-dessous, note 35.

29. EdB 520d-521a. Voir également ci-dessous, note 46.

30. *(Collegi) de libris Orosii ad Augustinum tendentis et prosequentis hysto-*
*rias diversas usque ad sua tempora, de diversitate et situ et mirabilibus*
*diversorum locorum, de historiis gencium diversarum et maxime Romano-*
*rum, et de cladibus seculorum usque ad Christi tempora et sua* (Lecoy
de la Marche 1877: 5-6).

31. EdB 200c-d; 221c-d; 237b; 338b; 341b-c; 341c; 345a; 349d; 355d; 363a;
363a-b; 363b; 365a; 371c; 382d; 382d; 389d; 414d-415d; 416c; 426a; 442b;
453b; 453b; 453b-c; 458a; 467a; 467a-b; 467d; 471a; 473b; 475d; 496c; 500a-
b; 505c; 505d; 505d-506a; 507c; 513a; 513a; 519d; 535c; 550c; 551a; 575a;
636d; 637a; 658d.

32. Voir note 18. L'étude de la 'matière de Rome' dans le *Pantheon* de
Godefroi de Viterbe menée par L. Meyer (1933: 28-100) ne concerne
malheureusement qu'Enée, la légende de l'origine troyenne des Francs et
Alexandre.

33. *(Collegi) de libro qui Pantheon dicitur Godefridi Parmensis, imperialis*

*aule capellani, quem scripsit Gregorio VIII, de omnibus historiis gentium et regum et regnorum ab inicio mundi usque ad imperium Frederici primi, de gestis maxime Romanorum imperatorum atque pontificum, et de situ et conditionibus et descriptionibus urbis Romane, et de historiis et gestis Hebreorum, Grecorum et Latinorum (et) christianorum aliorum usque ad annum Domini MCXLXI* (Lecoy de la Marche 1877:6). Mentions dans notre *corpus*: 213d-214a; 221d; 221d-222a; 222a; 222a-b; 222b; 365c; 469b; 470d; 500a; 504a; 536b; 550d-551a; 551a; 569c; 588b-c; 589c; 639d; 668a. On aura remarqué que, comme pour l'emploi de l'ouvrage d'Orose, les références venaient généralement par vagues.

34.    Voir notes 7 et 9.

35.    Vincent de Beauvais, *Speculum historiale*, VI, 42 (éd. Douai, 1624, p. 187b): *Richardus. Denique Caesar dum Reipublicae statum juxta morem maiorum clementer instauraret, authoribus Bruto et Cassio, in curia viginti tribus vulneribus confossus, interiit.* Cette citation appartient à Richard de Saint-Victor, *Liber exceptionum*, V, 21. Voir Paulmier (1978: 83-4). Etienne de Bourbon a sans doute connu l'oeuvre de Vincent de Beauvais (ou une de ses ébauches) mais sans jamais la citer. Voir également note 24.

36.    *Vies des douze Césars*, I, 57 (Ailloud 1931: 41-42): *In agmine nonnunquam equo, saepius pedibus anteibat, capite detecto, seu sol seu imber esset.*

37.    EdB 177d (Hippocrate de retour chez lui); 189a (Alexandre et son maître Léonidas); 327c-d (Ulysse et les sirènes); 327d (Antigone reproche à Alexandre son goût pour la musique); 341a (Alexandre et son maître Léonidas); 341b (le paysan devenu philosophe); 348a (Hercule et Antée); 418c (Médée); 422b (Méduse); 535c (Alexandre et les gryphons); 568c-d (l'espor de vaincre fait avancer l'armée d'Alexandre).

38.    *(Collegi) de libro magistri Gervasii ad Othonem quartum imperatorem, de Solaciis imperialibus et mirabilibus terrarum diversarum* (Lecoy de la Marche 1877: 7).

39.    Ne serait-ce que sous la forme de florilèges. Voir Paulmier (1978: 71-90); Reynolds-Wilson (1984: 77).

40.    Valère Maxime ne semble s'imposer dans les recueils d'*exempla* qu'à partir du début du XIVe siècle. Dans la *Scala celi* de Jean Gobi par exemple, composée entre 1322 et 1330, 7,5% des oeuvres ou des auteurs cités appartiennent à l'Antiquité profane, dont 36% pour Valère Maxime. Voir Polo de Beaulieu (1984: 12).

41.    Tubach 1351 place sous le nom de Jules César une anecdote fournie par

le *Tractatus de diversis historiis Romanorum* (déjà cité à la note 7), et où l'on voit le signe de croix apparaître sans répit à César (*cap.* 32, p. 15). Or le texte donne en fait *Julianus Cesar* dans lequel on peut voir autant Julien l'Apostat que Jules César.

42. Pour J. Le Goff en effet: 'Le 'héros' de l'*exemplum* médiéval c'est n'importe qui, n'importe quel homme ou femme, n'importe quel chrétien, car l'exemple est fourni par l'histoire du héros, non par le héros lui-même. D'autre part la crédibilité de l'histoire du héros ne vient pas du héros de l'anecdote, mais de la qualité du narrateur et plus encore de son *informateur*' (Bremond-Le Goff 1982: 45). Disons simplement que dans le recueil d'Etienne de Bourbon coexistent des *exempla* proches des *exempla* 'héroïques' de l'Antiquité et les *exempla* tels qu'ils sont définis par J. Le Goff. Répétons que ce sont les éditeurs des recueils d'*exempla* qui sont au fondement d'une vision partielle de la littérature exemplaire médiévale.

43. J'en compte deux: voir notes 6 et 14 (César pour Auguste et Cyrus pour Darius).

44. Sur ce type de paradoxe, voir les remarques de Von Moos (1984: 223-36). Sur César et Alexandre,*idem*, bibliographie n. 77, p. 233.

45. EdB 465d et 640 d.

46. *In hoc autem non est commendanda Paulina supradicta vel Lucrecia quod se occidisset in hoc quod fraudes pudicitie illa doluit, alia violentiam sibi illatam et quod utraque forte exemplum reliquit de servanda castitate et adultero non consentiendo* (EdB 521a).

47. Sur ce sujet, voir Von Moos (1984: 247-8; 248, note 123).

# BIBLIOGRAPHIE

**AILLOUD 1931**
Ailloud, H. (ed.), *Suétone, Vies des douze Césars*. Paris 1931 (repr. 1967).

**BERLIOZ 1981**
Berlioz, J., Quand dire c'est faire dire, exempla et confession chez Etienne de Bourbon (m. v. 1261). In: *Faire croire. Modalités de la diffusion et de la réception des messages réligieux du XIIIe au XIVe siècle*. Rome 1981: 299-335.

**BERLIOZ 1983**
Berlioz, J., La Mémoire du prédicateur. Recherches sur la mémorisation des récits exemplaires (XIIIe-XVe siècles). In: *Temps, mémoire, tradition au Moyen Age (Actes du XIIIe congrès de la Société des historiens médiévistes de l'Enseignement supérieur public (Aix-en-Provence 4-5 juin 1982)*. Aix-en-Provence 1983: 157-83.

**BERLIOZ 1984**
Berlioz, J., *Édition critique du 'Tractatus de diversis materiis predicabilibus' du dominicain Etienne de Bourbon (M. v. 1261), troisième partie, 'de dono scientie'*. Paris 1984 (Thèse dactyl. de 3e cycle, Université de Paris I, Paris 1984.

**BERLIOZ 1985**
Berlioz, J., Etienne de Bourbon: de l'utilité de la confession. In: Schmitt, J.C. (ed.), *Prêcher d'exemples. Récits de prédicateurs du Moyen Age*. Paris 1985: 83-92.

**BERLIOZ 1985**
Berlioz, J., Virgile dans la littérature des exempla (XIIIe-XVe siècles). In: *Lectures médiévales de Virgile. Actes du Colloque organisé par l'Ecole française de Rome. Rome 25-28 octobre 1982)*. Rome 1985 65-120; 70-71.

**BOURGERY 1926**
Bourgery, A., (ed.), *Lucain, La Guerre civile*. Paris, 2 Vol., 1926-9.

**EICHENLAUB 1984**
Eichenlaub, J.L. Le Tractatus de diversis materiis predicabilibus d'Etienne de Bourbon. Première partie: de dono timoris. Édition et étude. In: *Positions des thèses ...* Paris 1984.

**HERZSTEIN 1893**
Herzstein, S. (ed.), *Tractatus de diversis historiis Romanorum*. Erlangen 1893.

**JENNINGS 1974**
Jennings, M., Lucans's medieval popularity: the exemplum tradition. In: *Rivista di cultura classica e medioevale* 16 (1974): 215-33.

**KAEPPELI 1980**
Kaeppeli, Th., *Scriptores Ordinis Praedicatorum Medii Aevi*. Romme 1980.

**LECOY DE LA MARCHE 1877**
Lecoy de la Marche, A. (ed.), *Anecdotes historiques, légendes et apologues d'Etienne de Bourbon*. Paris 1877.

**LIEBRECHT 1856**
Liebrecht, F., *Gervais de Tilbury, Otia imperialia*. Hannover 1856.

**MEYER 1933**

Meyer, L., *Les légendes des matières de Rome, de France et de Bretagne dans le Panthéon de Godefroi de Viterbe.* Paris 1933 (repr. Genève-Paris 1981).

PAULMIER 1968
Paulmier, M., Le portrait de César dans le Speculum Historiale. In: *Spicae Cahiers de l'atelier Vincent de Beauvais* 1 (1978): 71-90.

POLIO DE BEAULIEU 1984
Polio de Beaulieu, M.A., Étude et édition d'un recueil d'exempla du XIVe siècle, la Scala Celi de Jean Gobi (thèse de 3e cycle). In: *EHESS 1.* Paris 1984.

PRÉCHAC-NOBLOT 1947
Préchac, F., Noblot, H. (eds), *Sénèque, Lettres à Lucilius.* Paris 1947.

QUETIF-ECHARD 1719
Quetif, J., Echard, J., *Scriptores Ordinis Praedicatorum...* Paris 1719.

REYNOLDS-WILSON 1984
Reynolds, L.D., Wilson, G., *D'Homère à Erasme, la transmission des classiques grecs et latins.* Paris 1984.

SCHENDA 1983
Schenda, R., Etienne de Bourbon. In: *Enzyklopädie des Märchens ....* Berlin-New York IV, 1983: 213.

TUBACH 1969
Tubach, F.C., *Index Exemplorum. A Handbook of Medieval Religious Tales.* Helsinki 1969.

WAITZ 1872
Waitz, G. (ed.), *Godefroi de Viterbe. Pantheon.* MGH ss, XXII. 1872.

WELTER 1927
Welter, J.Th., *L'exemplum dans la littérature religieuse et didactique du Moyen Age.* Paris-Toulouse 1927 (repr. Genève 1973).

ZANGEMEISTER 1882
Zangemeister C. (ed.), *Orose, Historiarum adversum paganos Libri VII,VI,II,* 29-30. CSEL 5. Vienne 1882.

G.H.V. Bunt

# Exemplum and Tale in John Gower's 'Confessio Amantis'

John Gower was probably born in the 1330s; he is known to have died in 1408. He was a man of some wealth and a substantial landowner; he spent his last years, blind and in poor health, in his dwelling on the grounds of the priory of St Mary Overy near the Southern end of London Bridge, and it is in the church of this house, which in 1905 was made the cathedral of the new diocese of Southwark, that we find his tomb.[1] There he is depicted with his head resting on three voluminous books which represent his major poems. In a Latin colophon which stands, in a number of different versions, at the end of many of the forty or so manuscripts of his *Confessio Amantis*, Gower gives a conspectus of these three long poems, which, he says, were made *doctrine causa* (for the sake of instruction). The first, in French, deals with the vices and virtues, and is known as *Speculum Meditantis* or *Miroir de l'Homme*. The second poem, entitled *Vox Clamantis*, is in Latin and treats various contemporary misfortunes, notably the Peasants' Revolt of 1381, and the political and social evils of the time. The third long poem, in English verse, is the subject of this paper. Gower gave it the title *Confessio Amantis*, the confession of a lover.

In his prologue Gower announces that he intends to change his manner of writing; he will now *go the middel weie* (Prol. 17) and make a book which shall combine pleasure and instruction. In the early version we read that one day, while rowing in a boat on the river Thames, he met the royal barge; king Richard II invited Gower aboard and asked him to write a new poem for him. In the later version the commission by king Richard and the dedication to him are omitted, and a passage of the same length is substituted which dates the poem in the sixteenth year of king Richard (i.e., 1392-3) and dedicates it to his cousin and rival, the Earl of Derby, the later king Henry IV. The Prologue, we are told, belongs all to wisdom; but after the Prologue the book shall be about love. The remainder of the Prologue is then given to a survey of the failings of the three estates, leading to an account of Nebuchadnezzar's dream of the statue and a brief passage on the four monarchies. We are now in the last age, an age of division as symbolised by the feet of clay and iron of Nebuchadnezzar's statue.

In Book I the poet then declares that he will no longer attempt to set the world in order. He will henceforth write of love. He is himself of this school, although he has no success. Lest we should confuse fiction and reality, however, a Latin marginal note explains:

*Hic quasi in persona aliorum, quos amor alligat,*
*fingens se auctor esse Amantem, varias eorum passiones variis huius libri*
*distinccionibus per singula scribere proponit. (I 61-3 margin)*

(Here the author, as if in the person of others, who are bound by love, feigns himself to be a lover and sets out to write their various afflictions one by one in the various divisions of this book.)

In the English text the unhappy lover goes to the woods to lament his fate and to pray to Venus and Cupid. Cupid passes him by and pierces his heart with a fiery dart, but Venus lingers by him and demands to know what his malady is; she tells him to make a full confession to her priest Genius and then departs.

Most of the poem's 34,000 lines are thus taken up by a lengthy confession scene in which Genius examines his penitent on his behaviour as a lover. Many subjects pertaining to the ethics of love are discussed, and the lover's plight and his behaviour are treated with a mild humour. At the end of the poem Venus returns, makes the lover realise that he is too old for love, extracts the fiery dart and tells him to go 'where moral virtue dwells' and to pray for peace.

Genius begins his task as confessor by questioning the lover on his failings through the five senses, limiting himself to hearing and sight; after a few hundred lines he adopts the scheme of the seven deadly sins with their several branches. Each of the seven sins is given one book; in the first few books five branches of each sin are distinguished, but later in the poem this neat classification is abandoned. In Book VII Genius, at the request of Amans, expounds the instruction that Alexander the Great received from his tutor Aristotle. This long book has the character of a Mirror for Princes, and thus reintroduces the moral and political concerns of the Prologue. Throughout the poem, we must add, questions of individual as well as political ethics are brought up for discussion. Although love is the professed subject of the poem, and the lover is questioned on his behaviour as a lover, very frequently the ethics of love and the ethics of human society and of politics seem to coincide, and the good lover becomes indistinguishable from the good man and the good ruler.

Genius enlivens and reinforces his lessons by a large number of illustrative tales. In the Latin summaries which in many manuscripts stand in the margins, most of these tales are described as *exempla* against a vice or against those guilty of a vice. In the text itself, many are also announced as *ensamples*. Genius is generally careful to authenticate his stories, and he points out in advance what the tale is intended to be an example of and underlines the main points in retrospect. Many of the tales have the brevity and the straightforwardness of the classic exemplum as it is described by Bremond-LeGoff-Schmitt (1982), and indeed many are derived from exemplary traditions. For instance, in Book III, which deals with the sin of Wrath, the discussion turns to unjust wars, and Genius points out that whether soldier or lord, all those who engage in wrongful warfare are of the same kind (III 2351-62). The well-known anecdote of Alexander and the Pirate, which follows, is summarised in the Latin marginal note:

*Hic declarat per exemplum contra istos Principes seu alios quoscumque illicite guerre motores. Et narrat de quodam pirata ...*
*(III 2363 margin)*

(Here he speaks out through an exemplum against those rulers or others of whatever kind who wage an illicit war. And he relates about a pirate ...)

Alexander's soldiers take a notorious pirate prisoner and bring him before their king. The pirate tells Alexander that they are really engaged in the same kind of activity; but since he is poor and has only few men he is known as a robber, and Alexander, who is rich and powerful, bears the title of emperor. Alexander takes the pirate into his service and makes him a knight, thus confirming that they are indeed of the same condition. The whole story occupies 59 lines (III 2363-2421). Its structure is very simple: a situation is sketched in which a dialogue takes place which leads to a change in the initial situation. The lesson to be learned is administered as part of the dialogue: a wrongful conquest is mere robbery. There is nothing really that distracts our attention away from this lesson, although there might just be a faint suspicion that the story could also be used to illustrate Alexander's magnanimity.

Not all tales, however, are as brief and relatively straightforward as this. Some of them run to great length; the longest is also the last, the story of Apollonius of Tyre in Book VIII, which occupies 1737 lines. In many tales there are tensions between the complex meaning of the story and the explicit lesson of the exemplum, and these tensions have received a fair amount of critical attention. We shall return to this matter presently.

The material for a large number of stories is derived from Ovid's *Metamorphoses* and *Heroides*, but there are also tales from the Bible and from medieval sources, such as the *Roman de Troie* by Benoît de Sainte Maure and Godfrey of Viterbo's *Pantheon*. Gower often treats his sources with considerable freedom, changing emphases as he sees fit, and highlighting the lessons his tales are intended to inculcate. He takes care to motivate the events narrated carefully, and avoids leaving loose ends. The stories are told in a plain style with a minimum of rhetorical ornament, and the narrative generally moves rapidly and fluently. By no means all the stories which Genius tells to illustrate his teaching are about love. The tale of Alexander and the Pirate is only one of the many tales which are quite unconnected with love; instead it is an instance of Gower's persistent concern with moral and political questions.

As was hinted above, the relations between the tales and the lessons that they are intended to drive home are not always simple and straightforward. It has been argued that here and there Genius, who is after all a priest of Venus, not of God, should not always be taken as a reliable guide on matters of morality, and that sometimes Gower expects his readers to know better. A propos of the tale of Dido and Aeneas (IV 77-137), which is told against negligence and procrastination in love, and the immediately following account of the letter that Penelope wrote to Ulysses while he was away at the siege of Troy (IV 147-233), Burrow (1971:84-5 and again 1982:113) suggests that the reader is led to think that both Aeneas and Ulysses were justified in keeping their ladies waiting, since they had more urgent and more important business on their hands. This is certainly open to discussion, although it must be said that Gower does not give us very firm clues in this direction.[2]

Complications of this kind seem to arise chiefly when the discussion between Genius and Amans and the accompanying tales are explicitly about love. Possibly Gower used such sections to increase temporarily the element of delight in Genius' teaching, and we may be invited to take a correspondingly more detached view of the lessons that he offers us. On the other hand, we cannot be sure that Gower intends us to interpret the tale of Dido with the Vergilian background of Aeneas' high mission in mind; after all, his source was the more sentimental version of the story in Ovid's *Heroides*, which also gave him the material for Penelope's letter. Moreover, there is no evidence that Gower knew the *Aeneid*; he certainly makes no use of it in his *Confessio Amantis*.

The tales of Dido and Aeneas and of Ulysses and Penelope, as well as those of Grosseteste's head of brass (IV 234-43) and of the Foolish Virgins of the biblical parable (IV 254-60), which are also told against procrastination, are relatively brief, and select or highlight those points which are of immediate relevance to Genius' exposé. When, however, stories run to hundreds of lines, other complications arise. In such cases the complexity and the multiple layers of meaning which inevitably belong to such well-developed narratives may come into conflict with their explicit exemplary purpose. For instance, in Book IV, which deals with the sin of *Accidie* or Sloth, Genius, under the sub-heading of somnolence, comes to discourse on the subject of dreams and their possible validity. In order to illustrate his contention that dreams sometimes come true, he relates the story of Ceyx and Alcyone (IV/2927-3123) from Ovid's *Metamorphoses*. Ceyx and Alcyone are a happily married royal couple.

One day Ceyx goes on a long journey from which he does not return. Alcyone becomes worried and prays to Juno, who sends Iris to the gods of Sleep. Morpheus appears to Alcyone in the form of her husband lying dead upon the shore after a shipwreck. Alcyone goes down to the sea and is about to drown herself, when the gods take pity and change the couple into seabirds. The Confessor introduces the tale by pointing out that although some place little confidence in dreams, they do quite often come true:

*A man mai finde of time ago*
*that many a swevene hath be certein,*
*Al be it so, that some men sein*
*That swevenes ben of no credence.*
*But forto schewe in evidence*
*That thei fulofte sothe thinges*
*Betokne, I thenke in my wrytinges*
*To telle a tale therupon,*
*Which fell be olde daies gon.*　　　　　　*(IV 2918-26)*

(A man may find that in past times many dreams have been reliable, although some people say that dreams cannot be believed. But in order to show by an example that they very often signify true things, I intend in my writings to tell a tale on the subject which happened in times past.)

He returns to the subject of the possible validity of dreams after he has told the story:

*Lo thus, mi Sone, it mai thee stere*
*Of swevenes to take kepe,*
*For ofte time a man aslepe*
*Mai se what after schal betide.*　　　　　　*(IV 3124-7)*

(Lo thus, my son, it may persuade you to pay attention to dreams, for often a man may see in his sleep what is to happen later.)

This is Genius' characteristic practice, which firmly forces our understanding of the story in one single direction. But although, of course, dreams do play an important part in the story, to us the themes of grief over a lost beloved and of faithful conjugal love triumphing even over death may seem more essential and also thematically more important.[3] After all, marriage is to Gower the institution in which human love is to be regulated, as well as a symbol of stability which overcomes divisiveness and vice.

Similarly, at the conclusion of the last and longest tale in the poem, that of Apollonius of Tyre, Genius praises the hero for his faithful love within marriage and contrasts him with king Antiochus in his pride and misdirected passion (VIII 1993-2008). But in the Latin marginal note which accompanies the beginning of the story it is announced as an exemplum against incest:

*Hic loquitur adhuc contra incestuosos amantum coitus.*
*Et narrat mirabile exemplum de magno Rege Antiocho ... (VIII 271 margin)*

(Here he continues to speak (after telling briefly about the incest of Caligula, Ammon and Lot and his daughters] against the incestuous intercourse of lovers. And he tells a marvellous exemplum about the great king Antiochus ...)

Incest, one would be tempted to object, is only a minor theme in the Apollonius story, and king Antiochus is not its chief personage; faithful conjugal love and innate decency triumphing over a great deal of adversity and even over the supposed death of a spouse seem to be of much more central importance.[4]

A story in which incest *is* indeed of central importance is that of Canace and Macareus. Gower places it at the beginning of Book III, which deals with the sin of Wrath. Like his source, the eleventh epistle of Ovid's *Heroides*, Gower concentrates on the immoderate wrath of king Aeolus (he omits all suggestion of his being a god). Aeolus orders the death of his daughter Canace and of the baby she had by her brother and lover Macareus. Even more so than Ovid, Gower emphasises the innocence of the young brother and sister who are overcome by the irresistible force of love, and he seems to condone or gloss over their incestuous relationship.

What Gower appears to be doing here and elsewhere is, as Kelly (1975:131ff.) points out, to concentrate on one single lesson to be extracted from an exemplum, 'without much worry about whether it contradicts earlier or subsequent lessons'. If, he adds, Gower had really wanted to make his stories exemplary on all points, he could have made the necessary adjustments, but he evidently did not bother to do so. Nor did he, we might add, consider it essential that the lesson to be drawn from a tale should follow from its dominant theme. Kelly discusses what he terms cases of incongruity between Gower's stories and the moral lessons they are intended to teach under the heading 'Marriage Neglected, Adultery Overlooked, and Fornication Winked At', thus suggesting that there is something wrong with Gower's moral awareness. In an essay of 1979, Rosemary Woolf speaks of Gower's attempt to 'sympathize with characters for whom the plot forbids sympathy' and pronounces this attempt a failure; she compares Gower's moral consciousness unfavourably with that of his contemporary Geoffrey Chaucer.[5] It seems doubtful whether we can draw reliable conclusions about Gower's moral sensibility or his lack of it; the discrepancies that we have discussed seem to be inherent in his method of exemplification, in which potentially complex stories with a varied multiplicity of themes and moral meanings are used to illustrate a single exemplary lesson.

In the foregoing it has been hinted that Alexander the Great was of some importance in Gower's conception of the *Confessio Amantis*. He is referred to more often than any other famous hero, pagan, Jewish or Christian.[6] Towards the end of Book VI Genius recounts the story of Nectanabus' begetting of Alexander and of his sudden death at the hands of his son and pupil. The story is announced as a warning against the use of sorcery in furthering a love-suit, and the marginal note says:

*Hic narrat exemplum super eodem, qualiter Nectanabus ab Egipto in Macedoniam fugitiuus, Olimpiadem Philippi Regis - ibidem tunc absentis vxorem arte magica decipiens, cum ipsa concubuit ... Et sic sortilegus ex suo sortilegio infortunii sortem sortitus est.*                    *(VI 1789 margin)*

(Here he relates an exemplum on the same (i.e., sorcery in love), how Nectanabus, fleeing from Egypt to Macedonia, deceived Olympias, the wife of king
Philip, who was then absent, through his magical art, and slept with her ...
And thus the fortune-teller drew as a result of his fortune-telling the lot of
ill fortune.)

In the course of the tale Genius mentions Alexander's tutors Callisthenes and
Aristotle, who taught him philosophy, and Nectanabus, who instructed him in
astronomy and other subjects (VI 2272-9). This prompts Amans to request
Genius to tell him more about Aristotle's instruction of Alexander, and thus it
motivates the long digression on the duties of kings in Book VII. More implicitly, Aristotle as tutor of Alexander is contrasted with his earlier wicked mentor
Nectanabus.

At the beginning of Book VII Genius warns Amans that what he is going to
hear is not *in the registre / Of Venus* (VII 19-20); but yet he will tell him of
what Aristotle and Callisthenes wrote to Alexander. We are reminded at inter-
vals that Alexander's education by the philosopher is the basis of Genius'
exposé, which is in reality largely drawn from Brunetto Latini's *Livre dou
Tresor*. Philosophy is divided into three parts, *Theoric*, *Rhetoric* and *Practic*;
Practic has three divisions which are of importance to a king, Ethics, Econo-
mics and Policy. A discussion of the five points of Policy, which are Truth,
Largess, Justice, Pity and Chastity, takes up most of the book, and is again
illustrated by a number of brief tales. In three manuscripts one of the exempla
on Pity is the story of the knight who appealed from Alexander's wrath to his
pity. The section on Chastity ends with a praise of virtuous marriage, in which
the story of Tobias and Sara is used as an exemplum. A smooth transition is
thus effected to Book VIII, which deals with the sin of Lechery, and opens
with an exposition on the Laws of Marriage. Moreover, this conclusion to
Genius' excursus on the education of a king fits this book neatly into the
theme of love and of marriage as the institution for the regularisation and
legalisation of human love.

The tales of Alexander and Diogenes and of Alexander and the Pirate in
Book III are well-known anecdotes, which had been frequently used as exempla
and had a clear exemplary character. Gower was able to use them without much
need for adjustment. Matters were different with the story of Nectanabus. This
was not a self-contained narrative, but was part of the history of Alexander.
Stierle (1972) has rightly reminded us of the close ties between history and
exemplum, but it is another matter to adapt a piece of historical narrative for
use as an exemplum. For one thing, the Nectanabus story contains a number of
elements which might serve for moral-didactic purposes: a king who deserts his
people in time of war; the vanity of women or the nullity of pagan gods might
be easy targets; Olympias' adultery or Alexander's brutal murder of his father
might be highlighted, etc. Gower chose to use the story as a warning against
sorcery. He largely follows the account of Thomas of Kent in the Anglo-Norman

*Roman de toute Chevalerie* (Foster 1976-7); but he probably found Thomas' treatment of the murder of Nectanabus unsatisfactory. Thomas hardly motivates Alexander's sudden action against his father, but merely says that when the young prince had learnt the art of astronomy he decided to kill his master, and pushed him over the brink while he was asleep; Thomas adds as a final comment, *Dehé eit le clergon qui son mestre si veille* (1. 487: a curse on the pupil who looks after his master in such a way). Gower here used the more elaborate and better motivated account of the *Historia de Preliis*.

The tale of Nectanabus is immediately preceded by the story of Ulysses and Telegonus (VI 1391-1788), in which Ulysses overcomes the sorceress Circe through his superior magical skill and begets a son upon her. This son, Telegonus, later unwittingly kills his father. Both tales, which have marked similarities, are used as warnings against the use of sorcery in winning love. But in the Nectanabus story Gower lays a strong emphasis on the deceitfulness and deviousness of the sorcerer Nectanabus, while de-emphasising other elements. His flight from Egypt is dismissed in a few lines, but his use of his magical arts to seduce Olympias is given elaborate treatment. Olympias, on the other hand, is presented as a somewhat naïve but guiltless woman, who is tricked by Nectanabus into believing that a god wishes to sleep with her and beget a son upon her. If Thomas of Kent had made Olympias a vain woman, fond of being admired for her beauty, Gower reduces this element to only two lines in which he tells us in a neutral tone that she liked to be seen and to be praised by onlookers.[7] All blame is thus diverted away from Olympias and concentrated upon the trickster Nectanabus. Nectanabus' death at the hands of Alexander, like the death of Ulysses through the spear thrown by Telegonus, is presented as a just reward for the sorcery by which the child was begotten, and any guilt on the part of Alexander is ignored.

The tale of Nectanabus is another instance of Gower's habit of concentrating on a single lesson to be drawn from a tale, while smoothing over or ignoring other moral issues which the story might raise. Sorcery, which is here strongly condemned, is taken for granted in the tale of Jason and Medea (V 3247-4229), to which Gower devotes nearly a thousand lines, but which he uses as an exemplum against perjury in love.

We have seen that apparently Alexander was an important figure to Gower. In the Nectanabus story he plays a somewhat subordinate role, but yet Gower goes out of his way to assure us that, although Olympia was in part deceived,

*Yit for all that sche hath conceived*
*The worthieste of alle kiththe,*
*Which evere was tofore or siththe*
*Of conqueste and chivalerie;*
*So that thurgh guile and Sorcerie*
*Ther was that noble knyht begunne,*
*Which al the world hath after wunne.*     (V-2085-92)

(Yet in spite of all this she conceived the worthiest of all nations that ever lived before or since in conquest and knighthood; so that through deceit and sorcery that noble knight was begotten, who afterwards conquered the whole world.)

This would suggest that Gower had a high opinion of Alexander. This impression is strengthened by Book VII, in which Alexander appears as the pupil of Aristotle and the recipient of the wisdom of the greatest philosopher of antiquity. The minor references in Books II and V seem to point in a similar direction. Yet Gower also includes the tales of his meetings with Diogenes and with the Pirate, which are more critical of Alexander, as well as a synopsis of his wars and death which emphasises his refusal to be governed by reason, his covetousness and his pride. In his other English poem, *In Praise of Peace*, which he addressed to king Henry IV on his accession in 1399, Gower speaks of Alexander's conquests as a misfortune which could happen because the world was still pagan (ll. 36-49). It looks as if Gower was not concerned to give us a consistent view of Alexander, but merely to use certain well-known qualities of his and stories about him for exemplary purposes. My conclusions here strongly resemble those reached by Von Moos (1984:233) in his recent study of the exempla in John of Salisbury's *Policraticus*. Alexander's importance for Gower must have been that there was a great deal of material available on him, and that it could be readily used for exemplification. To him literature and history were storehouses of instructive and delightful tales; as Beryl Smalley wrote (1974:22) à propos of Valerius Maximus' collection of memorable deeds and sayings, 'you dip into the collection as though it were a chocolate box'.

In the foregoing I have attempted to show that some of Gower's source material was such that it could without much adjustment be fitted into his exemplary framework. But many of his tales give rise to complications; the explicit lesson they set out to teach fails to convince at least some modern readers, because the particulars of the story and the exemplary lesson seem to point in different directions. Gowers appears to make use of only one of the various exemplary opportunities offered by many of his tales, and to ignore or gloss over other implications. A number of his tales and one whole book have Alexander the Great as their subject, but Gower cannot be said to present a consistent view of this hero to us. He does not seem to have been much interested in Alexander as a historical figure, but primarily as the subject of a large number of well-known tales which he was able to use not only to please his readers but to present them with salutary and welcome lessons.

NOTES

1.     For what is known today of the life of Gower, see Fisher (1965). A convenient brief survey of his work is given in Pearsall (1969:5-22). The standard edition of his English poems is Macaulay (1900-1); all quotations are from this edition.

2.    Farnham (1974) proposes a much more radically comic-ironic reading of the *Confessio Amantis*, which I must regard as unconvincing. See Schmitz (1974) for what seems to me a balanced view of Gower's poetic methods.

3.    Cf. Esch (1968:224). By contrast, Chaucer, who uses the story of Ceyx and Alcyone in his *Book of the Duchess*, omits the final metamorphosis and emphasises the grief of Alcyone leading to her death.

4.    Runacres (1983:124), in an excellent discussion of Gower's use of exemplification, even goes so far as to speak of the tale as 'poorly chosen'.

5.    In his Introduction to the Man of Law's Tale, Chaucer has the speaker allude with disapproval to Gower's stories of incest (*Canterbury Tales* II(B) 77-89).

6.    The chief Alexander references are as follows:

1 Prologue 692-709: Alexander's empire of brass

2 II   1840-2:      *Wherof the Macedoyne lond,*
                    *Which thurgh king Alisandre honoured*
                    *Long time stod, was tho devoured.*

3 II 2413-5:        *..Bot if I sholde strengthe make;*
                    *And that I dar noght undertake,*
                    *Thogh I were as was Alisaundre ...*

4 III 1201-1330: Alexander and Diogenes

5 III 2363-2437: Alexander and the Pirate

6 III 2438-80: Wars and Death of Alexander

7 V 1453-96: Dindimus' epistle to Alexander on the Greek gods

8 V 1570-90: Alexander meets the god Serapis

9 V 2543-6:         *As was the riche qwen Candace,*
                    *Which to deserve love and grace*
                    *To Alisandre, that was king,*
                    *Yaf many a worthi riche thing.*

10 V 5532-5         *For I mi ladi love so,*
                    *That thogh I were as was Pompeie,*
                    *That al the world me wolde obeie,*

*Or elles such as Alisandre ...*

11 VI 1789-2366: Nectanabus

12 VII *passim*: Aristotle instructs Alexander

13 VII 3168-79 (3 mss. only): Alexander's knight appeals from his wrath to his pity

7.      VI 1828-9:      *And for hire list to be beholde*
                               *And preised of the poeple aboute ...*

# REFERENCES

BREMOND-LE GOFF 1982
Bremond, C., Le Goff, J. et J.-C. Schmitt, *L"Exemplum'*. Turnhout 1971.

BURROW 1971
Burrow, J.A., *Ricardian Poetry: Chaucer, Gower, Langland and the Gawain Poet*. London 1971.

BURROW 1982
Burrow, J.A., *Medieval Writers and their Work. Middle English Literature and its Background 1100-1500*. Oxford 1982.

ESCH 1968
Esch, A., 'John Gowers Erzählkunst' in: Arno Esch, hrsg., *Chaucer und seine Zeit. Symposium für Walter F. Schirmer*. Tübingen 1968: 207-239.

FARNHAM 1974
Farnham, A.E., 'The Art of High Prosaic Seriousness: John Gower as Didactic Raconteur' in: Larry D. Benson, ed., *The Learned and the Lewed. Studies in Chaucer and Medieval Literature*. (Harvard English Studies 5). Cambridge Mass. 1974: 161-73.

FISCHER 1965
Fisher, J.H., *John Gower, Moral Philosopher and Friend of Chaucer*. London 1965.

FOSTER 1976-7
Foster, B. (ed), *The Anglo-Norman* Alexander (*Le roman de toute chevalerie*) *by Thomas of Kent*. 2 vols. London 1976-7.

KELLY 1975
Kelly, H.A., *Love and Marriage in the Age of Chaucer*. Ithaca-London 1975

MACAULAY 1900-1
Macaulay, G.C. (ed), *The English Works of John Gower*. 2 vols. London 1969 (reprint).

MOSHER 1911
Mosher, J.A., *The Exemplum in the Early Religious and Didactic Literature of England*. New York 1911.

PEARSALL 1969
Pearsall, D., *Gower and Lydgate*. London 1969.

RUNACRES 1983
Runacres, Ch. 'Art and Ethics in the *Exempla of Confessio Amantis'* in: A.J. Minnis (ed), *Gower's* Confessio Amantis: *Responses and Reassessments*. Cambridge 1983: 106-34.

SCHMITZ 1974
Schmitz, G., *The middel weie. Stil- und Aufbauformen in John Gowers 'Confessio Amantis'*. Bonn 1974.

SMALLEY 1974
Smalley, B., *Historians in the Middle Ages*. London 1974.

STIERLE 1972
Stierle, K.H., 'L'Histoire comme Exemple, l'Exemple comme Histoire. Contribution à la pragmatique et à la poétique des textes narratifs'. *Poétique* 10

1972: 176-98.

VON MOOS 1984

Von Moos, P., 'The Use of *Exempla* in the *Policraticus* of John of Salisbury' in: Michael Wilks (ed), *The World of John of Salisbury*. Oxford 1984: 207-61.

WOOLF 1979

Woolf, R., 'Moral Chaucer and Kindly Gower' in: Mary Salu and Robert T. Farrell (eds), *J.R.R. Tolkien, Scholar and Storyteller. Essays in Memoriam*. Ithaca London 1979: 221-45.

M. Gosman

# Le discours référentiel du 'Quadrilogue Invectif' d'Alain Chartier

L'oeuvre littéraire a facilement, pour ne pas dire naturellement, recours à la référence extra-textuelle. En principe non gratuite celle-ci abrite l'idéologie (du moment), vise la consécration d'un ordre sociologique donné ou d'une pensée dominante. Ce mouvement confirmatif paraît revêtir deux aspects. D'abord l'oeuvre littéraire (ou historiographique) exprime de façon plus ou moins claire les pensées et les désirs de la société environnante et, ensuite, elle cherche à garantir son dire par l'introduction d'éléments puisés dans un corpus consacré par cette même société à travers le système scolaire hautement conditionné et conditionnant.

C'est ainsi que l'oeuvre reflète sans pour autant miroiter (car la mimésis n'est jamais l'objet d'une poursuite motivée)[1] une condition virtuelle. Il peut s'agir d'une condition sociologique, psycho-émotionnelle ou dogmatique. Peu importe. Virtuelle, cette condition l'est, parce qu'elle est censée produire l'effet compensateur indispensable à toutes les trois conditions-type. Si l'on ne peut donc pas s'attendre à la reproduction d'aventures ou d'idées reflétant fidèlement une condition donnée, toujours est-il que le Moyen Age 'mime' ce qui est considéré être conforme au rêve, au virtuel. On entrevoit à travers les différentes modulations de ce rêve une organisation sociologique, psycho-émotionnelle ou dogmatique réputée consacrée, érigée en modèle.[2] Et ce modèle sera fonctionnel, parce que les raisonnements qui se trouvent à sa base sont toujours conformes, ne nient jamais son 'Sitz im Leben' (Link 1976: 26).

Il n'y a au fond aucune différence entres les oeuvres dites 'de fiction' et les documents qualifiables de 'historiques', ou 'didactiques'. La comparaison de ces oeuvres ne montre que des déplacements d'accent, que des différences qualitatives. Toutes ont besoin d'un ancrage et d'une garantie. Mais le recours à des 'vérités' extra-textuelles est soumis à certaines exigences. Ce qui compte dans l'emploi de la référence-garantie, c'est la présence d'une double axiologie: interne, puisque la référence ne peut pas être fonctionnelle si la 'tonalité textuelle' de l'oeuvre réceptrice est perturbée; externe, parce que l'activité probante et illustrative de la référence n'emprunte son droit de cité qu'à la situation sociologique, etc. du moment, du *hic et nunc* auctoriel. Acceptée, voire recherchée pour sa 'vérité', elle joue le jeu de l'authenticité, contribue à l'établissement du/des sens poursuivi(s).[3] Et, comme on le verra dans la suite, la référence n'a pas besoin d'une exactitude indiscutable. Il suffit qu'elle en évoque la possibilité.[4] Les renvois à l'extra-textuel non contestable, non contesté font ainsi partie intégrante de la volonté auctorielle de l'époque.

L'auteur médiéval tourne volontiers son regard vers le passé, y puise des éléments qu'il utilisera, ou plutôt, exploitera à son gré afin de prouver que son message possède une valeur. Pratiquement jamais la référence ne sert dans un processus d'assimilation d'un savoir. Le fameux adage *historia magistra vitae* ne révèle qu'une volonté didactique, jamais scientifique au sens moderne (Von Moos 1984: 211). Comment en pourrait-il être autrement dans une société dominée par une religion qui se prétend supérieure et unique, qui ne recommande que l'utilisation de ce qui est (ou peut être rendu) conforme à la Doctrine? L'utilisation des pierres du Colisée pour la construction de la basilique Saint-Pierre à Rome n'est qu'un exemple de cette attitude générale du christianisme face aux valeurs païennes préfigurée déjà par la conduite des enfants d'Israël quittant la captivité égyptienne tout en prenant ce qui leur semblait utile.[5] Le savoir des païens sert. Mais il est aussi *modus scribendi*.

L'enseignement médiéval s'inspire volontiers d'une pratique scripturaire qu'il admire sans pour autant pousser l'imitation aussi loin que les auteurs des différentes 'renaissances'. Le Moyen Age prend son bien où il le trouve, s'en arrange, l'exploite. Une remarque comme celle d'Alain Chartier qui se veut *lointain immitateur des* orateurs (Droz 1950)[6] est probablement à prendre au pied de la lettre; Alain puise volontiers des renseignements dans des oeuvres 'classiques', mais vis-à-vis d'elles il gardera ses distances (l'adjectif *lointain* n'évoque pas uniquement un décalage temporel, mais aussi une certaine prudence).[7]

Si l'on pense également aux paroles de saint Paul que c'est l'esprit qui compte (vivifie) et non la lettre (2 *Cor.*, III: 6), il ne faut pas s'étonner de ce que la référence a toujours un statut secondaire, n'est jamais nécessairement conforme, puisque c'est sa teneur qui joue. En outre, l'homme médiéval s'accommode facilement d'un manque d'organisation (apparent ou non), s'assimile sans aucun problème un savoir non spécifié, puisqu'il se désintéresse des *realia*, ne prend en compte que ce à quoi elles servent, n'en vise que l'*intentio*.

Dans cette perspective il n'est point étonnant de constater que les références peuvent revêtir plusieurs formes, révéler plusieurs degrés de conformité au texte-source. Ce qui est de plus conforme, c'est la citation. Elle est cependant peu fréquente parce qu'en général son emploi impose une présence écrite, est lié, de par ce fait, à une habitude scripturaire basée sur la collation de différents textes.[8] Et si nous parlons ici de 'citation', nous pensons particulièrement à ces emprunts-là qui, de par leur envergure réduite, n'ont pas de statut (quasi) indépendant comme l'a, par exemple, le passage entier copié dans un autre texte ou l'oeuvre reprise dans sa presque totalité pour servir dans une encyclopédie.[9] Il ne s'agit ici donc pas de ces produits de scriptorium plus ou moins travaillés. D'ailleurs, en tant que mode référentiel la citation est peu favorisée par le système scolaire de l'époque qui délaisse volontiers - les possibilités fort réduites d'arriver à une multiplication convenable des livres a joué un rôle non négligeable - l'instruction écrite et cela au profit de la mémorisation orale.

Plus fonctionnelles dans le système persuasif sont les références modulées qui, parce que non-citation, s'emploient plutôt pour leur *teneur*[10] que pour leur éventuelle perfection formelle et/ou conformité intrinsèque. Elles sont puisées dans la mémoire collective censée être la gardienne d'une authenticité ou elles sont forgées pour le besoin de la cause tout en tenant compte de la plausibilité requise dans le processus de communication où s'intègrent émetteur et récepteur.[11] Quelle que soit d'ailleurs leur provenance, il faut que les références activées dans le jeu bénéficient du consensus du groupe auquel elles sont destinées (David 1980: 9-10).

En s'approchant du système référentiel on constate que les textes médiévaux utilisent les termes *exemple*, *exemplum* et *similitude* sans pour autant fournir de critères ou d'indices solides permettant de mettre ces trois termes à l'abri de toute contestation. Au fond, il ne s'agit aucunement de trois entités indépendantes, bien délimitables. Ce sont trois manifestations d'un même phénomène, à savoir le besoin de support que ressent toute logique textuelle.

Il faut faire remarquer qu'il y a une confusion terminologique considérable entre *exemple* et *exemplum*; le premier semble renvoyer à une ATTITUDE probante, le deuxième à une procédure de FORMALISATION de cette même activité.[12] Tandis que le premier ne saurait dépasser sa fonction primaire de 'prouver', le deuxième se parerait volontiers d'un statut ornemental. Pour ce qui concerne la similitude, il faut signaler que par rapport aux deux autres dénominations, il ne semble y avoir que des différences fonctionelles au niveau du discours. Nous y reviendrons.

La volonté persuasive qui a été l'objet de nombreux traités tant auprès des Anciens qu'auprès des auteurs du Moyen Age n'a visé que la mise en oeuvre d'une mentalité auctorielle centrée sur l'analogie indispensable à l'axiologie textuelle. Elle ne s'est guère souciée d'en circonscrire les aspects formels.

Ce n'est ici pas le lieu de faire l'inventaire des différentes approches ni d'en résoudre tous les problèmes (tentative fort hasardeuse si l'on pense à toutes les études des spécialistes).[13] Dans cette perspective nous laisserons de côté les problèmes spécifiques soulevés par les textes entiers qui se veulent *exemple/exemplum*.[14] Nous nous contenterons de signaler ici quelques aspects pragmatiques liés à la procédure d'insertion de la référence aux héros classiques et/ou médiévaux dans le *Quadrilogue Invectif* (= *QI*) d'Alain Chartier où se profile une procédure représentative de l'écriture didactique du XVe siècle.


Ce qui frappe dans l'emploi de la référence, c'est que la rencontre de deux aires idéologiques (chaque texte, texte pourvoyeur et texte récepteur, possède sa propre idéologie) implique en principe des procédures d'adaptation. On dépiste ici deux niveaux. Au premier niveau il y a le choix de l'élément intégrable:

*Solum quod facit ad rem est narrandum* avait stipulé Cicéron (Stierle 1972: 185). Ce choix est hautement conditionné par la culture de l'auteur. Au deuxième niveau se présentent des problèmes techniques: pour que la référence soit vraiment utile, réponde aux exigences de la pragmatique auctorielle, il faut sauvegarder certains principes argumentatifs garantissant la reconnaissance, par le destinataire, de la référence en tant que telle. Une fois reconnue, elle ne manquera pas d'évoquer une connaissance.

Quant au statut narratif de la référence, nous distinguons ici deux modalités d'expression.

En premier lieu, il y a la procédure directe où la référence 'indépendante' fait pratiquement figure à part dans le discours, ne se fonctionnalise qu'à travers les nuances de l'axiologie, puisque, formellement parlant, il n'y a aucun élément qui signale sa présence.[15] L'ensemble (qu'il s'agisse de références en principale ou en subordonnée) est visualisable de la façon suivante:

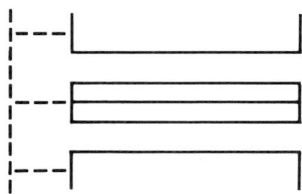

N.B.    Les blocs de discours marqués d'une barre horizontale supplémentaire indiquent les références (discours englobé). Là où il n'y a pas de barre supplémentaire, il est question du discours englobant. Les vides entre les différents blocs n'ont qu'une valeur optique. Il en est de même de la longueur des blocs. Les flèches en pointillé marquent l'influence réciproque exercée par les différents blocs de discours les uns sur les autres.

Il va de soi que l'interprétation d'une telle procédure de persuasion exige un effort considérable de la part du récepteur: il lui faut suffisamment d'expérience pour saisir le mécanisme axiologique à l'oeuvre dans englobant et englobé.[16]

En deuxième lieu, il y a la procédure indirecte avec comme objet la référence 'dépendante' dont l'insertion se fait en principe[17] à l'aide d'un enchaîneur initial et/ou final. Il est question ici de transitions marquant explicitement la présence d'une référence; elles peuvent la précéder (aiguille introductive) ou la suivre (formule concluante). Ce qui est cependant d'une importance capitale, c'est leur capacité conditionnante: les enchaîneurs peuvent abriter un commentaire auctoriel permettant, entre autres, la médiatisation immédiate ou non d'englobant et d'englobé, ce que la procédure directe ne permet guère. Graphiquement les possibilités se visualiseraient de la façon suivante:

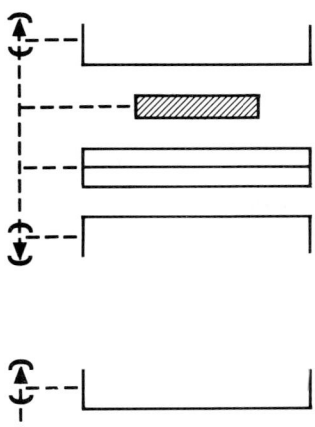

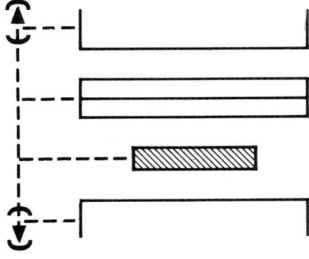

N.B.  Les flèches indiquent l'influence médiatisatrice exercée par l'enchaîneur (bloc hachuré). Les flèches entre parenthèses marquent sa possible influence. L'ordre des éléments constituants peut être inverti. Nous nous abstenons d'en reproduire toutes les possibilités.

Ces schémas (qui, il faut le dire tout de suite, n'épuisent pas toutes les possibilités organisatrices) nous invitent à faire les remarques suivantes. La procédure 'directe' ne permet guère de médiatisation. Le choix d'une conjonction influence, bien sûr, la réception de l'ensemble (englobant et englobé), mais en dehors d'une signalisation interne, c'est-à-dire, une organisation syntactique et sémantique d'englobant et d'englobé, il n'y a pas d'autres moyens pour conditionner l'interprétation. Il en est tout autrement des schémas qui représentent la procédure 'indirecte' (du moins, ses facettes les plus fréquentes). L'enchaîneur (aiguille introductive ou formule concluante) a plusieurs fonctions:

1)   marquer la rupture du discours: englobant versus englobé.
2)   annoncer ou reprendre la thématique-clé de la référence.
3)   abriter les éléments médiatisateurs (auctoriels/actoriels).
4)   assurer l'axiologie pertinente (au micro-niveau aussi bien qu'au macro-niveau).
5)   identifier la provenance.

Ces fonctions ne s'actualisent pas nécessairement toutes à la fois. La fonction 1 peut être camouflée par la procédure de médiatisation (fonction 3). Et la fonction 5 peut parfois être omise sans que la qualité de l'argumentation en souffre. Par contre, elle est d'importance primordiale lorsqu'il s'agit de fournir des preuves appuyées par l'*auctoritas* d'auteurs connus et respectés.

Comme nous l'avons déjà fait remarquer, il n'est pas indispensable que chaque référence soit pourvue d'enchaîneur. Dans le cas de références en série, 'en escalier' ou 'en étage' (voir *infra*), un seul enchaîneur peut régir plusieurs références. Une construction 'en escalier' avec des principales ou des subordonnées se visualiserait de la façon suivante:

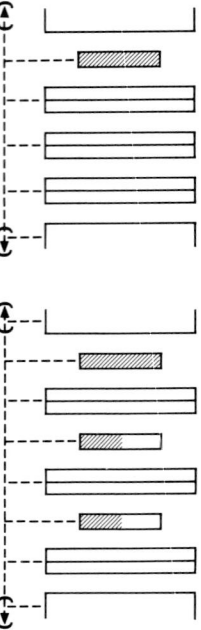

En cas de reprise (entière ou non) de l'aiguille entre les références, on aura:

Des structures inversées se présentent pour ce qui concerne les enchaîneurs récapitulateurs (formules concluantes). Nous ne les produirons pas ici: le système est identique.

Intéressant dans la perspective esquissée ici est le cas des références 'en étage'. A l'encontre des références 'en escalier', qui se trouvent en succession directe ou quelque peu retardée par la reprise (entièrement ou partiellement) des enchaîneurs, celles qui s'organisent 'en étage' se trouvent à quelque distance les unes des autres séparées par un morceau de discours primaire (l'englobant) avec lequel elles entretiennent des relations déterminées. Nonobstant leur isolement elles font bel et bien partie d'une argumentation homogène facilement délimitable dans le discours global. Cette structure particulière favorite auprès des auteurs prolixes (et nous présentons ici une structure compliquée comprenant des reprises d'enchaîneurs) se présenterait de la façon suivante:

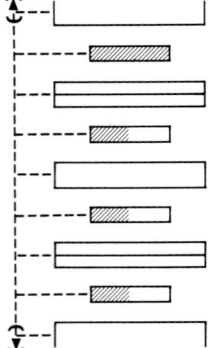

On s'imaginera facilement des structures intermédiaires. Afin de ne pas trop alourdir notre exposé, nous ne les présenterons pas.

Avant d'entamer l'analyse du discours référentiel dans le *QI* il faut faire quelques remarques préliminaires au sujet des effets dus à l'insertion de la référence dans un discours englobant. La procédure référentielle ne manque pas d'exercer une certaine influence et sur la structure logico-narrative du discours récepteur et sur le fragment extra-textuel appelé à renforcer l'argumentation ou à procurer l'illustration. Il semble (mais c'est encore à vérifier, puisque cet aspect n'a pas à nous retenir ici) que le discours référentiel de signature 'indirecte' se centre surtout sur *l'argumentatio*, tandis que celui qui s'appuie sur la référence en système 'direct' délaisse un peu *l'argumentatio* au profit de *l'ornatio*. C'est dans cette deuxième catégorie que s'insérerait la *similitude*, la référence la moins travaillée, bien que le système de liaison ('comme', 'comme si', etc.) semble suggérer une structure subordonnée, donc conditionnée. Nous ne nous occuperons pas ici des problèmes soulevés par les enchaîneurs des comparatives. Cela mériterait une étude séparée. Ce qu'il faut relever, c'est qu'il y a un besoin de correspondance entre la teneur de la référence, qui constitue le critère décidant de sa possible insertion, et la teneur macro-textuelle mentionnée parfois expressis verbis dans les oeuvres (les prologues et les épilogues sont ici des marqueurs importants). Cela vaut pour les références développées (citation, exemple, etc.) aussi bien que pour la référence au micro-niveau qu'est la similitude.

L'insertion de cette 'contraire chose' (Freeman-Regalado 1981: 63) qu'est la référence est intimement liée à l'intention de l'auteur d'atteindre, grâce à la combinaison de son propre dire et de l'emprunt *l'auctoritas* désirée. Celle-ci n'aura son effet maximum que si l'intégration de la référence que l'auteur a appelée à son secours (éventuellement à l'aide d'une formule médiatrisatrice) respecte l'axiologie macro-textuelle. Et tout cela demande un certain effort du destinataire, car celui-ci sera continuellement invité à neutraliser les dissonances inévitables entre englobant et englobé. La mesure dans laquelle cet effort lui pèsera dépend évidemment de la qualité des marqueurs. Plus le narrateur glose et conditionne ses références, plus la 'pureté initiale' ou 'exactitude textuelle' de la référence est obnubilée. Un auteur comme Rutebeuf respecte en principe l'altérité de la référence (Freeman-Regalado 1981: 71-4; Stierle 1972: 180), mais Philippe de Mézières, Froissart, Pierre Chastellain ou Cerveri de Gérone (pour ne nommer que ces auteurs-là) la travaillent à leur guise, la traitent pour elle-même ou l'introduisent en série (la privant ainsi de son indépendance).[18] Quelle que soit cependant la modalité épousée par l'écriture englobante, la référence à *l'auctoritas* extra-textuelle permet de s'approcher davantage d'une vérité qui, d'une autre façon, n'aurait pas pu se valoriser.

Il faut ajouter ici un autre détail, non négligeable. Nous avons déjà fait remarquer que la mémoire auctorielle constitue de par sa formation scolaire le véritable fonds où se puisent les références. Cette mémoire est sélective, chacun le sait. Elle ne conserve que ce à quoi elle tient, n'hésite pas à introduire au coeur même de la référence des changements ou à déplacer quelque accent. Mais ce n'est pas tout: la référence n'a qu'un statut de servante (à moins que l'amour de la référence ne tourne à la passion et subjugue le discours englobant) et elle se modifie volontiers, voire nécessairement, car le respect de l'axiologie macro-textuelle le demande. Cette nécessité ne dégénère cependant pas en contrainte absolue, car l'écriture médiévale, nous l'avons déjà fait remarquer, supporte fort bien la *discordia* textuelle. Qui plus est, elle s'y délecte même. Cela se voit, entre autres, dans la statuaire des églises où le sacré et le profane (quelle qu'en soit la nature) voisinent. Et dans la littérature le réel et le merveilleux se mélangent joyeusement. Philosophiquement parlant cette fusion d'éléments de statut disparate ne choque guère le public médiéval. On reconnaît (ou suppose) tout simplement l'existence d'une autre logique et on s'en accommode.[19]

Le statut auctoriel d'une oeuvre à référentialité poussée est donc équivoque. D'un côté, il est essentiel qu'on en arrive à une structure aussi homogène que possible; de l'autre côté, on n'y est pas à un dissonant de près. Auteur et lecteur/auditeur puisent (et ici nous acceptons provisoirement la prémisse que le texte atteint effectivement le public initialement visé, tout en faisant abstraction ici du rôle que jouerait ce public) dans le même système référentiel où, sur la base de techniques et d'attitudes appropriées et typiques de leur groupe, ils procèdent aux encodages et des décodages nécessaires.[20]

Ecrit en 1422, le *Quadrilogue Invectif (= QI)* manifeste ce qu'on pourrait appeler un 'patriotisme' à toute épreuve. Alain Chartier (1385-1433) s'y présente comme un partisan infatigable de la cause 'française'.[21] Il n'a de cesse de stigmatiser les fauteurs de trouble et les profiteurs (parmi lesquels il comprend les trois états dont il met en scène un représentant: Peuple, Chevalier et Clergé).[22] Ses conceptions politiques traduisent déjà l'intérêt de l'homme au service de l'Etat, construction socio-politique de signature abstraite qui se greffe sur la notion de Bien Public si soigneusement définie et délimitée par les auteurs romains auxquels il emprunte volontiers .ses (parfois trop) nombreuses références.[23] A côté des renvois à la culture romaine on relève aussi des emprunts à l'Ancien Testament et à l'histoire de 'France'.[24] Rares sont les renvois aux événements contemporains.[25]

Ce qui frappe dans ce songe allégorique où, abstraction faite de l'Acteur, figurent quatre personnages: Peuple, Chevalier et Clergé ainsi que France (de là: *Quadrilogue*), c'est que la plupart des attaques parfois fort violentes ne visent que les deux premiers acteurs. Clergé reste un peu à l'écart.[26] Les références de provenance extra-textuelle servent toutes à garantir l'effet des critiques exprimées par les trois acteurs principaux. Elles ne constituent aucunement, et la suite de notre exposé le prouvera, 'un fatras savant de citations empruntées aux auteurs de l'antiquité ...' (Droz 1950: vi). Bien au contraire. L'auteur du *QI* a recherché, et atteint, un degré d'insertion maximum en insistant a) sur la pertinence de la référence par rapport à l'axiologie dominante, et b) sur l'analogie situationnelle indispensable à toute référence qui se veut fonctionnelle.

Avant d'entamer l'analyse proprement dite de ce texte, il est nécessaire de signaler que toute approche de la technique démonstrative du *QI* devra tenir compte de la perspective didactique mentionnée *expressis verbis* dans le prologue: englobant et englobé ne font qu'un. Et Alain Chartier s'efforcera, comme nous le verrons, de ne laisser subsister aucun doute sur les critères ayant présidé au choix des références qui sont surtout d'origine livresque. Ce sont les enchaîneurs, initiaux ou finaux qui marquent les effets didactiques du discours englobé et du discours englobant.

La tactique persuasive du *QI* est basée, implicitement ou non, sur le principe de la *laudatio temporis acti*. Cette procédure référentielle (bien traditionelle à l'époque) exige une confrontation du présent, jugé négativement, avec un *perfectum*, un événement appartenant à un passé. On n'a donc pas à s'étonner de la rupture: le passé classique (*perfectum* amène 'parfait') prend souvent la relève du présent. Et ce passé, qui dans le *QI* est surtout de provenance classique ne pose pas de problème de conscience chez Alain Chartier. Avant lui, il y avait eu de nombreux auteurs, eux aussi, de statut clérical, qui avaient déprécié l'apport de la civilisation antique à cause des distractions fatales qu'il pourrait y avoir pour le salut de l'âme. Il n'en est plus rien chez Alain Chartier; celui-ci ne voit que vertus là où ses prédécesseurs ne dépistaient que des possibilités de damnation éternelle.[27]

Dans ce qui suit nous nous pencherons d'abord sur les différentes modalités référentielles dont nous venons de présenter schématiquement les principes organisateurs. On verra que l'auteur du *QI* les connaît pratiquement toutes. Ensuite (le discours d'Alain étant fort compliqué), nous insisterons surtout sur le maniement de la référence en contexte (c'est, et le truisme est évident, la quintessence même de son emploi) et sur son fonctionnement en série, pratique particulièrement chère à Alain.

Après avoir mis à jour la technique d'insertion de la référence dans le discours du *QI*, nous procéderons à l'analyse des enchaîneurs (et ce sur la base d'un inventaire) afin de pouvoir saisir le mécanisme médiatisateur de ce type d'intervention auctorielle. Cette analyse nous permettra de circonscrire le concept 'exemple' manié plusieurs fois par notre auteur.

Comme nous l'avons déjà fait remarquer, l'analyse de la technique démonstrative du *QI* devra tenir compte de sa macro-structure allégorisante. Dès le début il est clair que les discours prononcés par Acteur, France, Peuple, Chevalier et Clergé font partie d'un ensemble didactique dont l'enjeu est le sort de 'France'. Le destinataire n'a qu'à rattacher la totalité du *QI* (englobant et englobé) à la perspective indiquée par l'allégorie didactique. Alain Chartier s'efforce de ne laisser subsister aucun doute. Un passage qui illustre bien son approche est celui où France produit des références à l'histoire des Troyens, des Grecs et des Scythes (12-3). L'aiguille est formelle: *Retournons au fait des homes et jugons nous mesmes par autruy, et nous souviengne que ...* Le discours insiste ici sur le courage des Scythes qui, après avoir dû reculer devant les troupes de Darius de Perse, se battirent à mort sur les tombes de leurs ancêtres. La formule concluante qui lie le discours englobant subséquent à ce qui vient d'être dit au sujet des Scythes est évidente: *Dure chose est a moy que ainsi me convient plaindre, mais plus dure et de mains de reconfort que vous, qui me devez soustenir, defendre et relever* ... Le discours continue en soulignant les effets néfastes d'une non-solidarité vis-à-vis du bien commun incarné par 'France'. Nous n'y insisterons pas. Ce qui nous intéresse ici, c'est l'encadrement formel de la référence (en l'occurrence il y en a plusieurs, mais elles n'ont pas toutes la même importance). L'aiguille marque la séparation entre englobant et englobé et, fait capital, signifie l'utilité didactique; le destinataire ne saurait se tromper sur la fonction de ce qui va suivre: *jugons nous mesmes par autruy.* La formule concluante rattache le secondaire au primaire tout en spécifiant les rapports du passage entier avec le sort de 'France'. On constate que les enchaîneurs remplissent chacun les fonction 1, 2 et 4. La formule concluante se distingue ici de par le fait qu'elle abrite également un début de médiatisation actorielle (fonction 3).

La référence 'indépendante', (en procédure 'directe') c'est-à-dire, non pourvue d'enchaîneur(s), se découvre dans le prologue où Alain présente toute une série de questions (sous forme de principales interrogatives) qui, puisque renvoyant à un passé révolu possesseur d'éléments positifs disparus avec le temps, suggèrent a) le manque (sens proppien) à combler: il faut lutter contre la perdition du royaume (de 'France') et b) l'inévitabilité quasi certaine de la disparition de toute gloire humaine comme une punition imposée par Dieu. Voici le passage en question où Alain énumère les questions distillées des *anciennes escriptures* mentionnant les *mutacions, subversions et changemens des royaumes* (3-4): ...

> *Ou est Ninive, la grant cité qui duroit trois journees de chemin? Qu'est devenue Babillone, qui fut edifiee de matiere artificieuse pour plus durer aux hommes, et maintenant est habitee de serpens? Que dira l'en de Troye la renommee ...?*

Sont mentionnées *Thebes, Lacedemone, Athenes, Cartage* et *Romme*. La série se termine par:

> *Mais parlons de Romme qui fut derreniere en souveraine magesté et excellente en vertu, et notons bien la parolle de Lucan qui dit que d'elle mesmes, par sa pesanteur elle decheut, car les trop pesans fais font les griefves choistes.*

Grammaticalement, ces principales interrogatives, qui débouchent sur la discussion du sort de Rome, sont indépendantes: il n'y a pas d'enchaîneurs. Pourtant, elles ne sont pas des îlots indépendants, car il y a, à l'arrière-plan, un réel encadrement qui leur confère et une certaine homogénéite et une logique indéniable. L'histoire garantit leur succession, car le texte reprend immédiatement le thème de la mutabilité des choses en renvoyant à la succession des *regna*: ... *la monarchie du monde et la dignité du souverain empire fut jadiz translatee des Assiriens aux Persans et des Persans aux Grecs, ... es mains des François et des Germains* (4). La procédure est adroite. La sériation amène ce qui constitue l'essence même du discours. Il y a cependant plus. Le prologue fournit par le biais du discours primaire (l'englobant) une série de réflexions sur la mutabilité et la dégradation des affaires humaines. La série des principales interrogatives produit les preuves requises par l'argumentation; la succession des *regna* fournit l'ancrage souhaité; l'histoire et ses péripéties sert de leçon de morale. L'enseignement des Anciens ne saurait cependant suffire. Alain invite le récepteur à se rendre compte de ce que *les jugemens de Dieu, sans qui riens ne se fait, sont une abisme parfonde ou nul entendement humain ne sceit prendre fons* ... La hiérarchie se réaffirme: l'apport des Anciens ne peut que servir, ne produira jamais de solution totale, privilège du christianisme. En faisant aboutir le discours sur des renvois aux *Sainctes Escriptures*, qui font contrepoids aux *anciennes escriptures* païennes, notre auteur montre que les malheurs contemporains (actions désastreuses entreprises par le roi d'Angleterre sur le sol français) ne sont dus qu'à la colère de Dieu. Le recueillement s'impose. Surtout après la lecture du *tiers chapitre de Isaïe* (5) qui révèle que les *coups feruz ... sont signes de mort et donnent ensaignes de la divine indignacion, se nous n'y querons briefves medicines.* Le *Quadrilogue Invectif* proposera une *medicine,* mais *par maniere d'envaïssement de paroles et par forme de reprendre* (5).

Nous avons insisté sur ce passage parce qu'il révèle l'attitude d'Alain face à la référence de provenance 'classique' (h.l. romaine!). L'ancrage est évident. Le destinataire n'aura aucun problème avec l'identification des interrogatives ni avec leur insertion dans le discours englobant. Il faut cependant faire une remarque au sujet du renvoi à la chute de Rome. L'attaque de la phrase *Mais parlons de* maintient la référence au niveau de la principale, mais l'isole cependant, de par la présentation formelle, des questions posées au sujet des puissances antérieures. C'est que Rome jouera un rôle déterminant dans l'argumentation référentielle du *QI*.

Un dernier élément est encore à relever. La mention de la *parolle de Luçan* fonctionne comme une *auctoritas* en deuxième instance. Alain s'abstient ici de fournir une citation exacte. Il ne s'intéresse qu'au statut autoritaire de Lucain. C'est probablement (le problème ne présente, en l'occurrence, qu'un faible intérêt) une réminiscence de lectures antérieures qui jaillit de la mémoire auctorielle. On relève encore un autre exemple de cette technique dans le même passage: parlant du repentir qui vient toujours trop tard, Alain intercale *ainsi que dit Vallere* (4). Ce renvoi non spécifié renforce l'argumentation didactique greffée sur le christianisme sauveur. Il en est de même de la phrase *et ay curieusement encerchié par les discours des Sainctes Escriptures les faultes et les punicions de noz peres et des primerains* (5). L'autorité de la Bible est suffisamment à l'abri de toute contestation. Aussi un renvoi général comme celui-ci fonctionne-t-il dans le cadre persuasif. Ce qui compte surtout, c'est le renforcement axiologique: *faultes et punicions.* Que l'auteur en vienne à rappeler à la mémoire les prophéties et les lamentations d'Isaïe n'a donc rien de bien étonnant.

En résumé: le prologue dénote une architecture réfléchie, marque non seulement, de par le fait que la perspective chrétienne finit par prendre la relève, une supériorité (philosophiquement motivée par les docteurs de l'Eglise), mais suggère également une analogie possible: tout comme les règnes antérieurs, la 'France' pourrait tomber en proie au dépérissement inhérant à l'existence humaine (en filigrane: le thème de la *degradatio temporum*). Le fait cependant que le *Quadrilogue* a été écrit doit être placé et dans la perspective générale de l'optimisme foncier du christianisme (la voie de Dieu est salvatrice; de là peut-être l'adjectif *comicum* marquant le *Quadrilogue* dans la seule rubrique latine présente dans le texte) et dans celle de la pragmatique textuelle porteuse de *medicines*.

On le constate: la référence (quelle qu'en soit d'ailleurs la provenance ou la complexité) est fonctionnelle dans le discours *invectif* (simple modalité de 'persuasif'). Sans insister ici sur les enchaîneurs des mini-références (Lucain, Valère, Bible, etc.), nous pouvons conclure de tout ceci que la référence non enchaînée doit son effet à l'encadrement général. L'ensemble se représenterait de la façon suivante:[28]

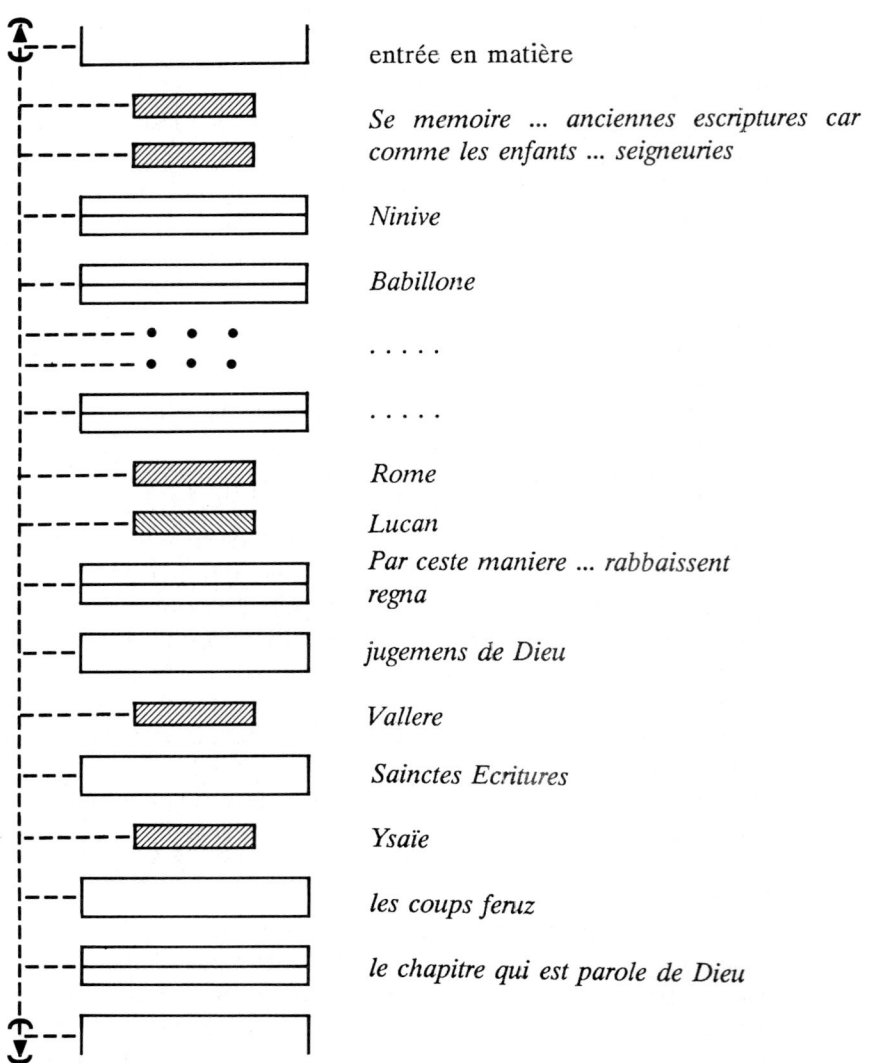

entrée en matière

*Se memoire ... anciennes escriptures car comme les enfants ... seigneuries*

*Ninive*

*Babillone*

. . . . .

. . . . .

*Rome*

*Lucan*

*Par ceste maniere ... rabbaissent regna*

*jugemens de Dieu*

*Vallere*

*Sainctes Ecritures*

*Ysaïe*

*les coups feruz*

*le chapitre qui est parole de Dieu*

Le dessin, qui ne fait que visualiser ce que nous venons de dire, montre bien que notre auteur fait de son mieux pour intégrer le discours secondaire (celui qui fournit les 'preuves') dans son discours primaire (celui qui doit être 'prouvé').[29] L'englobé se lie ici à son englobant sans l'intermédiaire d'enchaîneurs formels.[30] C'est le destinataire qui, en décortiquant le passage entier, saisira le sens global du primaire et ce sur la base de l'analyse du secondaire. Compteront ici le contenu 'analogique' des références, leur insertion dans l'ensemble et, surtout, leur efficacité dans la *narratio* (en d'autres termes: la référence fait-elle progresser ou changer l'argumentation?)[31]

Quant à la référence 'dépendante' (en 'procédure 'indirecte'), on peut renvoyer aux spécimens suivants: la principale conditionnée par un enchaîneur se rencontre à la page 17 où France mentionne le courage de deux frères saxons venus secourir le roi de Grande-Bretagne: *Et se bien en enquerez, c'est la lignee de Forgestus et de Hangestus, les Saxons, qui* ... L'enchaîneur (aiguille introductive) est purement formel, ne médiatise guère. Un spécimen plus intéressant (en l'occurrence il s'agit d'une formule concluante régissant plusieurs références) est le renvoi à Alexandre le Grand qui perdit la vie à cause du laxisme de ses troupes. La formule concluante de généraliser: *Puis doncques que les grans conquereurs ... quelle seurté ...* ? L'analyse du passage en question (il s'agit de références 'en escalier') nous occupera dans la suite (voir p. 180), mais il est déjà clair qu'Alain se sert des deux possibilités de médiatisation: anticipatrice et récapitulatrice. Pour ce qui concerne les subordonnées enchaînées, on peut se référer au sort du roi Roboam introduit de la façon suivante: *Assez le peut on noter et prendre exemple du roy Roboan, qui pour les oppressions de son peuple ...* (23). L'enchaîneur insiste sur le côté didactique du passage cité. Et la référence à la désastreuse bataille d'Azincourt (exemple réduit *ad nucem*!) donne lieu au commentaire suivant ... *Agincourt, dont nous avons chier comparé et encore plaignons ...* (35) On le constate. Ces quelques spécimens (il serait d'ailleurs fort aisé d'en fournir davantage) montrent la vitalité de la procédure conditionnante. Le contexte décide de sa charge éventuelle.

Ces quelques principes de base relevés dans le *QI* ne suffisent cependant pas à en expliquer le mécanisme persuasif. Loin de là. Alain Chartier ne se sert guère de la référence isolée; il préfère accumuler les renvois et cela non seulement aux passages qu'on pourrait qualifier de cruciaux. Le cumul des références est même un procédé cher aux auteurs de la fin du Moyen Age.[32] Aussi allons-nous nous pencher sur quelques passages dotés d'une solide charpente argumentative et illustrative pour essayer de mettre à jour le fonctionnement de la référence dans le discours de *QI*.

Dans ce qui précède nous avons déjà fait remarquer que notre auteur a une certaine prédilection pour la référence 'en escalier'. Nous produirons ici quelques passages où il est question de ce système référentiel. Dans le premier passage on constatera que les références dévoilent une gradation fonctionnelle dans le discours englobant et dans les autres on remarquera un effet particulièrement intéressant: les deux discours finissent par se confondre (voir infra).

Le premier passage (14-15) traite des dangers inhérents à la poursuite du luxe et du confort matériel, péché trop familier au Chevalier et aux nobles (d'après France). Dans son attaque virulente celle-ci renvoie à trois héros de l'Antiquité: Scipion (l'Africain), Hannibal et Alexandre le Grand. Ces trois chefs d'armée confrontés au laxisme de leurs hommes dû au fait que ceux-ci manifestaient un trop grand attachement aux *choses ... provocans a volupté* durent chacun en constater les conséquences: une combativité réduite ou même pire. Scipion ordonna que toutes ces choses *fussent tantost degeteez*. Hannibal, après la prise de Capoue, dut constater que les *cuers de ses chevaliers était changez et matiz de leur premiere vertu* (ils avaient été *haultement receu et delicativement traictié*). Et Alexandre, après la conquête de Babylon, *perdy sa seigneurie et vie*. L'ensemble (sur lequel nous reviendrons) montre une structure soignée: chaque référence est construite de la même façon: principale, subordonnée adverbiale (de temps) et principale. Ces trois phrases composées gardent leur indépendance grammaticale vis-à-vis du discours primaire, mais elles produisent une hiérarchie: le sort d'Alexandre est le résultat d'une négligence dont Scipion a su éviter les pièges, etc. Cette hiérarchie est également manifestée par la présence d'une aiguille introduisant la troisième référence: *Et pour exemple de hault prince adjouster, le pareil cas en avint a ...*[33] Axiologiquement, le luxe et le bien-être corrupteurs renvoient à ce que France reproche aux nobles et aux chevaliers.

L'enchaînement de cette triple référence dénotant un véritable mouvement de crescendo mérite quelques réflexions. L'aiguille n'est pas trop bien marquée. France, déchaînée dans sa diatribe contre les corrompus de la société, vante les effets positifs d'une réorientation morale: *delaisser longue acoustumance* (négative!) et embrasser les *honnourables fais ... dont l'onneur et la renommee naissent aux vertueux.* Les trois chefs d'armée sont de tels *vertueux.* L'enchaînement est implicite, ne revêt pas de caractère formel: l'aiguille elle-même se présente sous forme de principale; elle fournit cependant une perspective interprétative. Par contre, la formule concluante est claire: *Puis donques que les grans conquereurs en la grant gloire de leur victoire ont esté avillez et amendriz par acueil de voluptuz, quelle suerté peuent avoir ceux qui soubz les dangiers de tresperverse fortune s'endurcissent a delicieuse vie et corruption de leurs meurs?* D'apparence isolée (formellement il s'agit d'une formule concluante sous forme de principale), l'enchaîneur interprète les références et lie leur contenu au discours englobant. La procédure conditionnante est assumée par la formule concluante. La médiatisation (fonction 3)[34] est ici pertinente: l'auteur du *QI* (à travers le discours de France) élargit le cadre présenté par la thématique produite par les références en marquant bien une deuxième hiérarchie: le sort des trois héros était lié à des expéditions qu'ils avaient entreprises à leur propre instigation. Le sort de 'France' est différent: elle est assiégée, attaquée. Le résultat de la mollesse n'en sera que plus néfaste. La conclusion tirée des références amène de nouvelles diatribes de France adressées aux personnages impliqués. Ce procédé ne pourra pas nous occuper ici. Ce qui est clair, c'est que le recours à la référence est fonctionnel au niveau de la persuasion et que les renvois à l'extra-textuel amènent ici une hiérarchie qui ne trouve son effet maximum qu'en dehors du système référentiel proprement dit.

Le discours englobant ne saurait se passer de cette hiérarchie référentielle 'en escalier', puisqu'il y emprunte et son point de départ et le fondement même de l'argumentation totale.[35] L'ensemble se visualiserait ainsi:

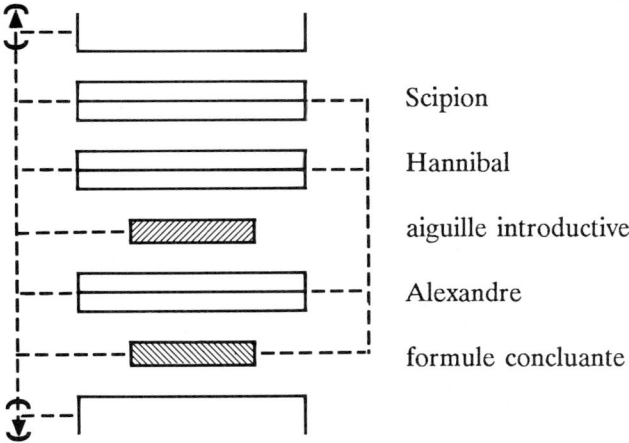

On le constate. La référence dans le *QI* fait partie intégrante du discours et le fait même avancer. Ce n'est pas bien étonnant. Mais, il y a plus. Comme nous l'avons déjà annoncé, il y a des passages où la référence assume la fonction du discours primaire. Un spécimen frappant de ce flottement se trouve dans le discours de Peuple (23). Celui-ci se plaint de ses malheurs et insiste sur la nécessité de respecter ses droits: *Si avient que, pacience faillie, toute obeissance, subjection et constance defaillent, et tourne l'ordre de vertu en desordonnee confusion.* Dans cette phrase Peuple évoque le dépérissement des structures socio-politiques sans pour autant pousser le raisonnement à sa fin. C'est la référence qui révèle, et cela sur la base d'un fait historique réel, les véritables conséquences du non-respect des intérêts populaires: *Assez le peut on noter en prendre exemple*[36] *du roy Roboan,*[37] *qui, pour les oppressions de son peuple qu'il ne voult amendrir ne cesser en delaissant le conseil des saiges anciens et ensuivant la sote oppinion des jounes et non saichans, perdy de sa seigneurie dix lignies et demie.* On note ici un phénomène intéressant. L'enchaîneur (*Si avient que, ... confusion*) pose une vérité générale.[38] La référence qui suit immédiatement est introduit par: *Assez le peut on noter et prendre exemple du ...* qui fonctionne comme un deuxiéme enchaîneur initial amenant la spécification (ainsi que la médiatisation: *prendre exemple*). Le premier enchaîneur ne contient pas d'éléments formels séparant les deux niveaux du discours. En fait, il ne fait que suggérer la possibilité d'une référence. Le deuxième, par contre, l'amène. Il en est de même de l'enchaîneur final qui ne s'associe que de façon axiologique au contenu de la référence: *Le peuple si est membre notable d'un royaume, sans lequel les nobles ne le clergé ne pevent suffire ...* Le discours primaire ne tire pas (ou n'ose pas tirer) la conclusion des 'preuves' alléguées. C'est la 'preuve' elle-même qui, possédant une certaine autonomie, prend la relève du discours primaire. Graphiquement, on se représenterait la structure de l'ensemble de la façon suivante:

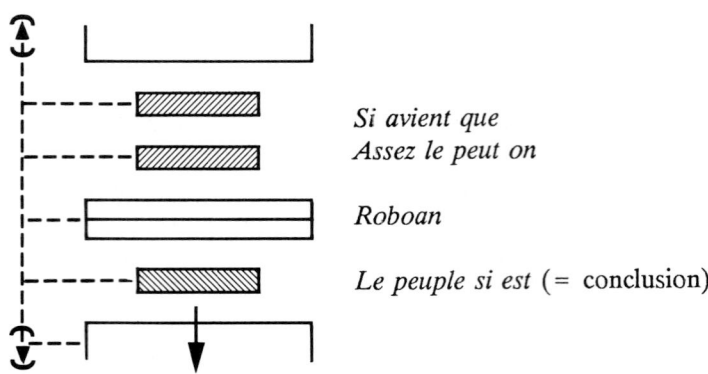

*Si avient que*
*Assez le peut on*

*Roboan*

*Le peuple si est* (= conclusion)

Le *Quadrilogue* a volontiers recours au procédé cumulatif parce qu'il permet un certain mélange des deux discours impliqués (l'englobant et l'englobé). L'argumentation s'en trouve fortifiée et l'*auctoritas* de l'ensemble se fait plus crédible (puisque les deux discours peuvent assumer les mêmes fonctions et/ou épouser la même structure).

On le repère également dans la description des guerres intestines dans l'Empire romain qui avaient entraîné la chute de cette grande puissance. La référence au sort des Romains (26) exprime sans ambages ce que le discours primaire n'avait fait que suggérer. Celui-ci parlait de *douloureux mesaie*, tandis que celui-là spécifie *decheue du tout et sans ressources* ... On le constate: la référence cherche son droit de cité dans une analogie, mais elle l'abandonne aussitôt pour amener le destinataire à réfléchir sur les véritables conséquences de la situation décrite dont elle seule fournit la clef. Il en est de même de la référence aux punitions imposées au peuple juif *es temps de Moyse et d'Aaron* ... (27). Là aussi, la spécification est fournie par la référence qui change de statut: d'illustration elle devient explication.[39]

Il est donc question ici d'une certaine émancipation de la part de la référence: elle se fait la compagne du discours englobant (et abandonne ainsi son statut de servante). Mais il y a plus. Il est curieux de constater que le discours englobé peut lui-même servir de point de départ à un raisonnement illustratif et/ou explicatif. Dans de pareils cas la référence assume une des fonctions typiques du discours primaire dans l'argumentation persuasive. Cela se remarque dans le passage qui souligne la nécessité des sacrifices personnels au profit du bien commun (31-2). L'enchaîneur séparant le discours primaire d'avec le secondaire donne: *Assez trouvons es histoires romaines* ... Suit alors un exposé au sujet de l'esprit de sacrifice des Romains en face de dangers de provenance extérieure. L'exposé sauvegarde cependant un caractère général, n'insiste que sur les habitudes du peuple romain. Cependant, Alain trouvant probablement son discours illustratif trop peu pertinent renchérit afin d'augmenter la valeur persuasive de son message. Il abandonne le discours secondaire, sans pour autant le terminer par un marqueur quelconque (ce qu'il n'avait d'ailleurs pas fait non plus à la fin du discours primaire générateur de la référence) et il passe à une spécification jugée sans doute plus efficace. Celle-ci débute par l'aiguille que voici: *Encor, afin de monstrer par exemple,* ... qui amène une espèce de climax: le premier renvoi avait fait allusion au sens civique général; le deuxième raconte comment les dames romaines se faisaient couper les cheveux pour qu'on en fît de solides cordes pour les engins de guerre. La référence n'a pas de formule concluante. On ne peut marquer sa fin que par la présence de l'attaque qui réintègre le discours primaire (l'englobant): *Maintenant, las, dolent, m'est advis que je voy le contraire; ...* Il n'y plus de doute: le marqueur temporel *Maintenant* combiné avec la réapparition de la première personne (auctorielle) *m(e)* dans *m'est* et *je* dans *je voy* termine de façon péremptoire le discours secondaire. La neutralisation, voire la disparition de quelques-uns des enchaîneurs, dénote, ici encore, de la part de la référence une certaine tendance à l'autonomie. Plus le discours secondaire est clair, plus son fonctionnement est manifeste, moins il semble avoir besoin de commentaire(s) explicatif(s). Les références (généralisantes et spécifiantes) assemblées 'en escalier' se soutiennent les unes les autres, peuvent se passer (de quelques-uns) des enchaîneurs.

On remarque cette même volonté d'autonomie dans le discours où Clergé vilipende le manque de discipline militaire, véritable fléau des armées médiévales. Par le biais de son porte-parole Clergé, Alain Chartier renvoie à la sévérité des Romains dans ce domaine et il insiste particulièrement sur la conduite de Manlius Torquatus qui fit décapiter son propre fils (couvert de gloire!) parce que celui-ci avait transgressé ses ordres. Le discours primaire interprète la référence: *et en ce cas la victoire que fist le vaillant jouvencel comme vaingueur ne peut effacer la desobéissance qu'il fist comme transgresseur, pour quoy la rigueur de la discipline chevalereuse vainqui la pitié naturelle du pere, car cellui que Nature admoneste d'estre pere misericors pour le devoir de sans acquiter se monstra juge rigoureux pour la loy d'armes* aigrement observer (54-5). Le discours primaire engendre la référence-illustration qui, à son tour, provoque un long commentaire auctoriel (au niveau du discours primaire). Il est question ici d'un renversement: l'englobé conditionne l'englobant.

Il serait aisé de fournir d'autres spécimens de cette technique particulière qui, au niveau du raisonnement, fait disparaître la différence entre discours englobant et discours englobé. Ce remplacement (car il s'agit bel et bien d'une prise en charge) n'entame guère la structure formelle de l'ensemble. Dans la plupart des cas les enchaîneurs sont toujours mis en évidence. C'est-à-dire, on peut pratiquement toujours déterminer le lieu où se termine le discours englobant et où commence l'englobé. Et cela vaut même pour les cas où la phrase du discours primaire s'ancre dans l'axiologie de la référence, en exploite les données et les amène au niveau du discours englobant. Une parfaite illustration de ce procédé se repère, entre autres, dans la référence à la bataille d'Azincourt que nous rencontrons maintenant.

Une variante de la procédure 'en escalier' qui marque de temps à autre un arrêt dans la démonstration argumentative créant ce qu'on pourrait appeler un 'palier' (espèce de pause permettant la reprise de certains éléments constituants du discours, primaire ou secondaire) est ce que nous désignerons, pour filer la métaphore, par procédure 'en étage'. Nous en présenterons ici deux spécimens. Le premier se trouve aux pages 34-6 où le discours primaire est assumé par Chevalier. Celui-ci procède à une longue incrimination de Peuple qu'il accuse de ne convoiter que ce qui appartient naturellement aux nobles et aux membres du clergé et de ne critiquer que fort injustement la conduite militaire des premiers. L'insistance de la part de Chevalier sur la nécessité de temporiser quelque peu les efforts militaires, c'est-à-dire, de ne pas se lancer dans des expéditions par trop impétueuses et, partant, catastrophiques, est articulée de la façon suivante: il y a d'abord une remarque générale faisant partie du discours primaire: *Et doit estre reputé a plus grant honneur et louenge au chief de bataille savoir saigement retraire et sauver son ost ...* (34). Suit alors un renvoi à la défaite d'Azincourt (le 25 octobre 1415) amené par l'aiguille généralisante que voici: *Il ne m'est besoing, pour ma raison confermer, de querir anciennes histoires du temps passé.* Elle cède la place à ce que l'on pourrait appeler une aiguille spécifiante: *mais nous vaille pour leçon ce que nous avons veu n'a gueres et de noz jours ...* (35). Abstraction faite de la procédure médiatisatrice (cf. *confermer, leçon*), il faut faire remarquer que la référence n'est aucunement narrativisée. Elle est tellement métonymique qu'elle frise la réticence. Il lui manque donc un statut indépendant et on constate que le discours primaire accapare l'exploitation de cette référence qui en reste au stade virtuel, c'est-à-dire, réduite *ad nucem*: ... *(Agincourt) dont nous avons chier comparé et encore plaignons la douloureux infortune et emportons sur nous toute celle malle mescheance, de laquelle ne pourrons saillir sinon par ...*[40] Le clivage entre le discours secondaire et le primaire se trouve entre *avons chier comparé* et *encore plaignons*. De par la structure même de cette phrase composée, deux principales reliées par la conjonction *et*, la transition entre passé et présent est neutralisée. Le discours primaire ne sert qu'à amener la référence 'supérieure' qui, elle, relate la tactique de Fabius Maximus Cunctator (le Temporisateur)[41] face à Hannibal trop victorieux. Et l'aiguille de fournir: *Telle oeuvre avons nous a mener en quoy plus chiet d'aguet et de sens que d'ouvraige de chaude colle. En pareil cas le monstra bien le saige Rommain Fabius Maximus ...* (35). La référence fournit une analogie frappante avec la conduite idéalisée, (par Chevalier, bien sûr), de la noblesse française à l'époque du *QI*: provocations par l'ennemi, prudence de la part du chef de guerre face à ces provocations, etc. Elle motive l'enchaîneur final: *Plaise a Dieu que ainsi nous en puisse avenir, et si fera il s'en nous* (= les Français) *ne tient* (36).

On remarque a) la séparation toujours bien marquée entre les deux discours: primaire versus secondaire, et b) la tendance d'Alain Chartier de ne pas permettre à la référence de mener une vie trop indépendante: le discours primaire reprend immédiatement ses droits en replaçant la leçon du passé dans le contexte du présent. Ce qui constitue cependant le point essentiel de ce passage référentiel construit 'en étage', c'est que le crescendo des références en série est temporairement stoppé (le discours englobant refait surface) pour que le discours secondaire puisse reprendre de plus belle. L'ensemble est organisé de la façon suivante: il y a d'abord le discours de Chevalier (*Et doit estre ...*). Ensuite l'aiguille généralisante fournit: *Il ne m'est ...* L'aiguille spécifiante donne: *mais nous vaille pour leçon ...* La référence à la bataille d'Azincourt prend la relève. Après cela, le discours primaire, repris en charge par le Chevalier, brode sur le thème du passage: *Moult a grant différence, ou doit avoir, en conseil et en oeuvre entre le prince eureux de prosperité, qui veult icelle garder et defendre, et cellui qui de perverse fortune se veult ressourdre et oster la victoire de la main du vainqueur.* L'autre aiguille produit: *Telle oeuvre ...* ouvrant ainsi la porte à la référence amenée par une spécification: *En pareil cas* ... Suit l'histoire de Fabius. La formule concluante donne, on l'a vu: *Plaise a Dieu* ... L'ensemble, qui contient des aiguilles 'en escalier',[42] se présente de la façon suivante:

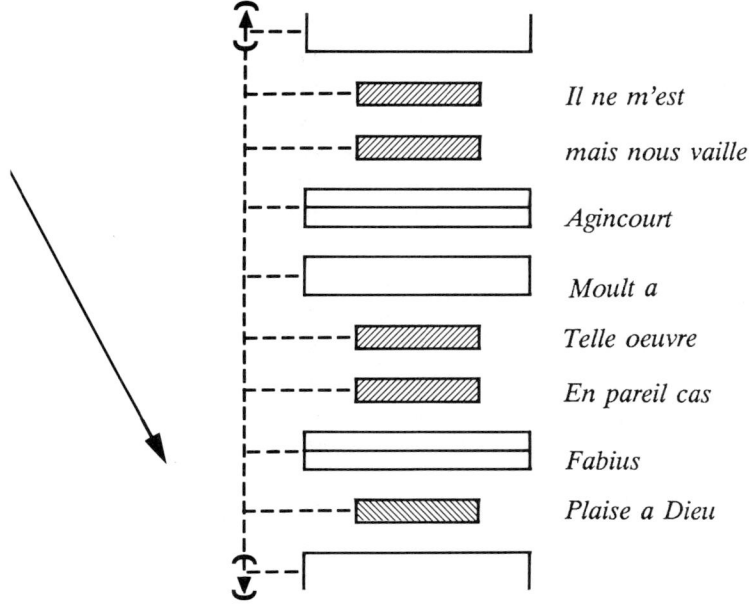

*Il ne m'est*

*mais nous vaille*

*Agincourt*

*Moult a*

*Telle oeuvre*

*En pareil cas*

*Fabius*

*Plaise a Dieu*

Nous ne pouvons pas analyser ici le discours entier de Chevalier qui dénote dans sa totalité un mouvement de crescendo allant de pair avec une procédure de plus en plus spécifiante. La référence à la conduite victorieuse de Fabius retiendra encore notre attention, puisque c'est une des rares références suffisement narrativisées pouvant mériter la dénomination *exemplum*.[43] L'analyse du système référentiel nous a montré combien le discours persuasif d'Alain Chartier profite de l'apport extratextuel, en fait l'essence même de la démonstration.

L'examen de la structure 'en étage' montre bien un certain souci de la part de notre auteur de ne superposer des références que si l'encadrement garantit l'axiologie indispensable à la compréhension globale. Les interventions (explications et/ou moralisations) qui, parfois, ont tendance à s'allonger considérablement, permettent d'aménager l'appareil référentiel en vue de l'effet visé. Cela est particulièrement clair dans le passage où Clergé traite de la *savance* ('sagesse') que devrait (entre autres) posséder *tout prince qui maine guerre et a puissance de gens* (45). Il y est question de quatre références; deux de teneur négative (ou presque) et deux de teneur positive. La référence I, amenée par une aiguille 'neutre': *Et se des oeuvres passees en ce temps de guerre se peut faire rapport sans vanterie et sans arrogance* met en scène les conséquences néfastes de l'absence de cette sagesse princière. Le renvoi, fort abstrait (pour des raisons psychologiques?), donne: ... *on a peu veoir, en pou de jours, ung prince en joune aage esloignié par fureur et sedicion de la maison royal dont il est filz et heritier ...* (47).[44] Une formule concluante amène les réflexions au niveau du discours primaire: *et qui bien a tout comparé ...* Elle se termine par: *Les plus simples l'ont peu jugier et les plus rudes clerement le cognoistre* (47-8). Le discours est immédiatement suivi de la deuxième référence introduite par une aiguille de signature identique à celle qui avait amené la référence I: *Et n'a pas encores trois ans que j'ay veu ...* Alain parle ici (sans mentionner de noms) des *hommes* qui avaient déserté leur seigneur. Cette référence (II) au début négative (*si enferme et petite foy; fuioyent l'adhesion de leur seigneur ... comme chose perdue, etc.*) se termine pourtant par une petite lueur d'espoir: ces hommes *ont reprins cuer et bonne fiance ...* L'englobant (= 'palier') brode sur la nécessité d'une solidarité collective afin de sauvegarder l'existence 'nationale'. Il engendre deux références (positives) tirées, (III) de la Bible et (IV) de l'histoire romaine. La référence III (introduite par: *Ceste maniere tint ...*) relate les exploits heureux de Mathathias et les Macchabées qui se sacrifièrent *pour remettre le royaume de Juda en sa franchise et haulte dignité* (48-9). La référence IV, immédiatement enchaînée (*Quel exemple avons nous en ce cas du vaillant magnanime Scipion ...*), peint la conduite de Scipion qui sut insuffler du courage aux Romains et cela par la menace: il tuerait celui qui parlerait d'abandon. Les Romains comprirent son avertissement, se reprirent et *se releverent en leur haulte autorité* (49).

Les quatre références s'équilibrent: les deux premières, tirées de l'histoire très récente (il n'y a qu'un décalage de 2 ans entre le traité de Troyes et le moment où Alain rédigea le *QI*) sont négatives, nécessitent une réplique. Celle-ci est amenée par un retournement opéré dans la référence II qui s'ouvre sur l'espoir, suggère un juste retour des choses. Toutes les deux sont cependant suivies d'un commentaire auctoriel (discours englobant) ralentissant la vitesse de la démonstration, le sujet étant jugé trop sérieux pour que le passage en question puisse être expédiée sur la base d'une série de références 'en escalier' non suffissamment encadrées. Les références III et IV, toutes les deux positives, se succèdent immédiatement (il n'y a pas de 'palier'). Elles procurent une analogie: celle de Mathathias et ses enfants peint les conséquences néfastes d'une attaque ennemie face à laquelle l'obstination seule peut apporter une solution positive (bref, le sens civique des héros est au premier plan); celle de Scipion présente un chef prêt à imposer l'autorité par le recours à la force même. On depiste ici une structure discursive en chiasme: les références I et II mentionnent respectivement le chef et les hommes, les références III et IV reprennent, grosso modo, les mêmes sujets, mais en sens inverse: hommes et chef. Pour les dirigeants Alain désiderait une autorité à poigne; pour les sujets un sens civique à toute épreuve. La combinaison des deux portera, d'après lui, une solution aux problèmes de 'France'. La formule concluante d'enchaîner: *De ce se peult ensuivre que savance et constance ont mestier a qui se veult tirer de perverse fortune, et nous, qui en tel estat sommes, en avons eu et avons bien besoing ...* (49). L'architecture de l'ensemble peut se représenter de la façon suivante:

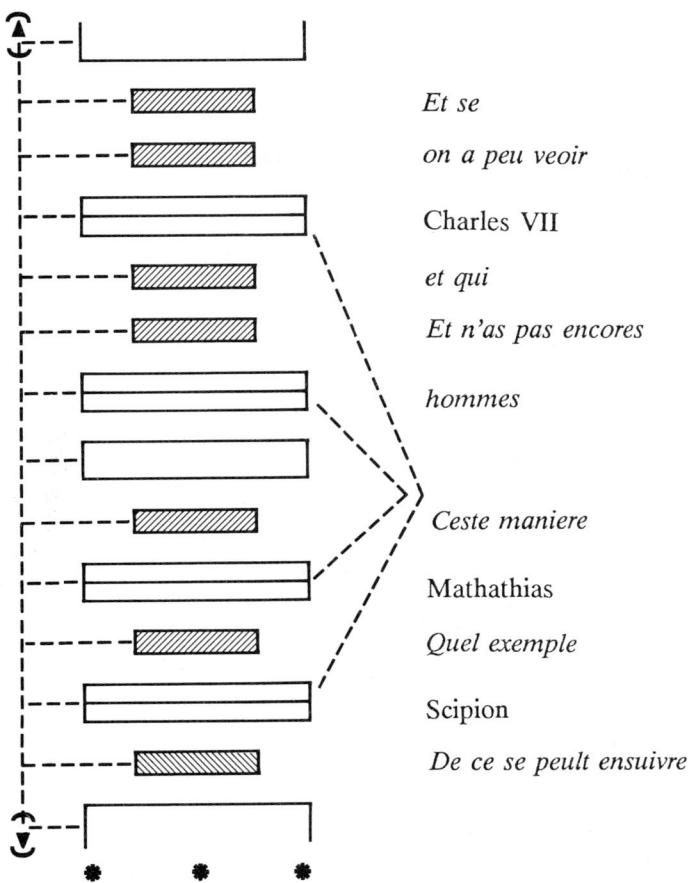

*Et se*

*on a peu veoir*

Charles VII

*et qui*

*Et n'as pas encores*

*hommes*

*Ceste maniere*

Mathathias

*Quel exemple*

Scipion

*De ce se peult ensuivre*

Dans ce qui précède nous nous sommes penché sur l'organisation du discours persuasif du *QI*, mais nous n'avons pas insisté sur la valeur intrinsèque de la référence. Cette valeur dépend, on l'a vu déjà, de la mise en évidence du discours secondaire (l'étude des enchaînements!), mais elle est également déterminée par le lexique employé. Dans cette perspective il est utile d'analyser le statut sémantique du mot *exemple* si souvent manié par notre auteur.

Ce mot a plusieurs acceptions. En premier lieu, il est utilisé dans le sens de 'preuve': accusant le Chevalier d'être la cause de la guerre, le Peuple dit: ' ... *je produiroye exemples en lieu de raisons ...*' (39).[45] En deuxième lieu, il peut signifier 'inspiration'. Cele s'avère, entre autres, dans l'aiguille introduisant le roy Roboam: *Assez le peut on noter et prendre exemple du roy R ...* L'ensemble *prendre exemple de* signifie approximativement: 'inspirez-vous de la conduite de ...' Une troisième acception, celle de 'spécification' se rencontre dans l'attaque *Encore, afin de monstrer par exemple ...* (31). Et, en dernier lieu, on rencontre *exemple* dans l'acception moderne: 'ce qui doit être imité' dans la phrase *Et s'aucun savoit de toutes ces choses moy monstrer une punicion dont l'exemple peust estre doctrine d'aucun amendement* (60).

Ces phrases montrent bien que le mot *exemple(s)* ne couvre pas de concept bien défini. Qui plus est, il semble y avoir confusion entre *exemple* et *histoire*.

L'énumération des hommes qui se sont sacrifiés pour le bien public (53-4) est amenée par l'aiguille que voici: *Des exemples peut on assez traire de pluseurs histoires* ... Cependant, la formule concluante donne: *D'autres histoires pourroit on assez amener* ..., où *histoires* se rapporte ou bien au même mot utilisé dans l'aiguille ou bien à *exemples* qui y figure également. Et à la page 55 on trouve dans la formule terminant le passage consacré à l'indiscipline à punir: *Diverses histoires se pourroient produire a ce propos d'autres punicions* ... Le mot *histoires* renvoie au même type de référence que celui introduit par le mot *exemples* (53). Il s'avère donc que le maniement du mot *exemple(s)* n'est aucunement inspiré par des critères solidement définis. Ce qui semble cependant se maintenir dans toutes les occurrences où se manifeste ce mot, c'est sa fonction de 'signal': il renvoie.

Avant d'entamer la discussion de quelques passages qualifiables d'*exemplum*, nous devons traiter ici un cas-limite où figure également le mot *exemple*. Ce passage, dont nous avons déja analysé la structure référentielle est celui des trois héros, Scipion, Hannibal et Alexandre (voir pp. 172). La troisième référence est introduite par l'enchaîneur *Et pour exemple de hault prince adjouster* (15). L'emploi du mot *exemple* suggère que les références précédentes sont également des *exemples*. Dans toutes ces références il y a une analogie avec la situation décrite dans le discours englobant, mais l'analogie est toujours partielle: la référence à Scipion ayant ordonné de faire disparaître de son armée tout ce qui pût inciter à la débauche suppose un état de désordre antérieur ayant nécessité cette action. Alain n'en dit mot. Il en est de même des deux autres références. Aucune ne présente un récit complet, composé d'un état initial, d'un transformateur, d'un état final (Patte 1976: 60-2); la référence à Hannibal produit la cause, mais non la conséquence (il n'est pas dit ce que fait Hannibal); celle qui amène Alexandre mentionne simplement la conséquence: la même chose arriva au Macédonien qui en mourut. En tableau, les différentes références montrent la structure suivante:

| état initial positif supposé | phase de transformation | état final positif | état final négatif |
|---|---|---|---|
| Sc | | (Sc)[46] | |
| H | H | | |
| A | | | A |

L'ensemble, repris par la formule concluante (*Puis doncques que les grans conquereurs en la grant gloire de leur victoire ont esté avillez et amendriz par acueil de voluptez, quelle sceurté* ... (15) atteint, nonobstant le manque d'analogie complète qu'on dépiste dans chacune des trois références, exactement le but visé: les trois héros antiques ont, eux aussi, été les victimes d'une relation de cause à effet. Ce que le discours englobant produit à propos de 'France', c'est la cause. L'analogie s'impose à travers la combinaison des renvois au passé, évoque les conséquences prévisibles. Voilà l'effet principal des références sériées (que ce soit 'en escalier' ou 'en étage', peu importe). Elles se tiennent, se complètent les unes les autres. De par leur statut particulier, elles exigent un certain effort du destinataire puisque, pour bien saisir le mécanisme argumentatif de l'ensemble, celui-ci est forcé d'impliquer l'apport des différentes références. Sans elle le raisonnement manquerait de quelques chaînons, risquerait même de se faire moins fonctionnel. Cet effet n'est pas l'apanage des références sériées. Une seule référence bien amenée (ou insérée, ce qui n'est pas tout à fait la même chose, parce qu'il n'est pas, on l'a vu, indispensable que toute référence soit enchaînée)[47] peut faire l'affaire.

Ce qui nous intéresse ici, c'est l'aménagement narratif des références. Celles que nous venons de rencontrer avaient toutes un 'défaut',[48] c'est-à-dire, il leur manquait un élément constituant de toute chaîne narrative (état, processus, état). Alain n'ignore cependant pas la référence dûment narrativisée, possédant tous les éléments qui permettraient de la qualifier d'*exemplum*. Il en fournit même plusieurs. La référence à la tactique de Fabius (cf. p. 176) produit les éléments indispensables à la narration: l'état initial désespéré, la conduite sage de Fabius faisant contraste avec celle, néfaste, de son concurrent Municius et la transformation du tout en victoire sur l'ennemi. La rupture formelle avec le discours environnant est évidente (on l'a déjà vu). Mais la démarcation se fait également par le biais du changement a) de temps:[49] le présent de l'englobant cède la place au passé simple de l'englobé,[50] b) de sujet: Fabius Maximus remplace le *prince* et le *nous* du discours primaire, et c) d'instance énonciatrice: Chevalier abandonne son propre discours pour introduire une narration centrée sur la sagesse du Romain. Techniquement parlant, c'est toujours lui qui assume le discours, mais le recours à la démonstration évoque, en filigrane, une autre instance énonciatrice, *in casu*, la source livresque, Valère Maxime, temporairement évincée par Chevalier qui ne reprend son (méta-)discours bien à lui qu'avec la formule concluante: *Plaise a Dieu ...*

La référence à l'histoire de Fabius face à Hannibal, qui peut être qualifié de 'récit', amène une solution, conditionne le discours primaire qui, grâce à elle, progresse. Il en est de même des références à Mathathias et à Scipion (48-9).

Il s'agit ici de ce que nous pourrions appeler '*exempla*', i.e., des récits complets comprenant les trois éléments-clé susmentionnés. L'architecture narrative de ces cas (il n'y en a pas trop dans le *QI*) correspond, grosso modo, à la définition de l'*exemplum* donné par Jacques le Goff: 'un récit bref donné pour véridique et destiné à être inséré dans un discours (en général un sermon) pour convaincre un auditoire par une leçon salutaire' (Bremond-Le Goff 1982: 37-8). Grosso modo, car Alain n'insiste pratiquement pas sur l'authenticité de ses références (il les accepte et les présente telles quelles) et il n'est pas tout à fait question ici d'un sermon proprement dit. La définition présentée par Le Goff ne manque pas d'utilité, mais elle ne tient pas compte de l'impact littéraire sur tout dire moralisateur: peut être qualifiée d'*exemplum* non seulement une suite de références sériées, 'défectueuses' ou non (pensons ici à la structure particulière des références à Scipion, Hannibal et Alexandre), mais également la référence réduite à une seule phrase et n'insistant que sur un seul des éléments-clé de la narration. Tout comme on l'a vu, l'effort du destinataire ainsi que l'aménagement du discours au moyen doit être impliqué dans l'interprétation des références.[51]

Résumons ce qui précède. Comme on l'a vu, Alain Chartier est bel et bien un enfant de son époque. C'est un auteur prolixe volontiers enclin à étayer son discours de références dont la plupart ont été ramassées pendant sa formation de clerc. Les nombreux renvois à la Bible et aux auteurs classiques (latins) qui auront figuré au programma en sont les indices. Mais il a également recours à des événements récents comme Azincourt ou le traité de Troyes dont le Dauphin fut la victime. Son *Quadrilogue*, présenté de façon traditionnelle comme un *Songe* (ce qu'avaient fait avant lui de nombreux autres auteurs: Guillaume de Lorris, Raoul de Houdenc, Dante Alighieri, Philippe de Mézières, etc.), se veut *invectif*.

Cet adjectif détermine une bonne part de l'axiologie macro-textuelle qui, à son tour, conditionnera l'effet des références dont nous avons analysé quelques spécimens. Bien qu'il n'ignore pas la référence en position isolée, Alain tend quand même à mettre ses renvois à l'extra-textuel en série: en ce que nous avons appelé 'en escalier' ou 'en étage'. Ceci pour en tirer un rendement maximum. Cette attitude n'est point typique. Ici encore, Alain fait ce que d'autres avaient fait. Il se sert de cette procédure pour tous les types de références. Qu'il s'agisse de principales ou de subordonnées peu importe. Tout est sériable.

Les références ne sont pas toujours exactes. Cela vaut évidemment pour celles qu'il puise dans sa mémoire et pour celle qu'il ne semble pas vouloir exploiter à fond. On rencontre ainsi des formules comme *ainsi que dit Vallere*, etc. Elles peuvent figurer aussi sous forme d'extrait, surtout au cas où il s'agit de morceaux puisés dans des sources livresques. L'aménagement des (bribes de) références en série montre presque toujours un effet de crescendo: la dernière référence, qui occupe, bien sûr, un lieu stratégique, est mise en évidence. Pensons-ici aux références sériées où Rome et Alexandre figurent à la fin du discours englobé. L'effet de cumul approfondit le contraste entre englobé et englobant, amène (et c'est vraiment la quintessence de ce système) une gradation dans la démonstration qui fait avancer le discours global. La gradation peut d'ailleurs aussi être assurée par l'introduction de 'paliers' a(u)ctoriels ralentissant et accentuant le sens de l'ensemble.

L'analyse a montré qu'il n'est aucunement nécessaire que la référence ait un statut narratif bien développé. Il se peut qu'elle ne présente que quelques-uns, ou même un seul, des éléments constituants d'un programme narratif. Dans des cas pareils l'axiologie contextuelle devra venir au secours du destinataire forcé d'amalgamer l'information partielle de l'englobé avec le métadiscours a(u)ctoriel. Ou bien (et c'était le cas des références à Scipion, Hannibal et Alexandre) chacune d'entre elles doit assumer un élément de ce qui constitue un programme narratif. La combinaison de tous les éléments produit ainsi une *narratio* complète. Ailleurs, on repère des structures si soigneusement organisées et délimitées qu'on peut parler de véritables *exempla*.

Mais, quel que soit l'effort d'intégrer le renvoi aux *realia* de provenance extérieure (et *realia* implique *concreta* aussi bien qu'*abstracta*), la séparation de l'englobant d'avec l'englobé restera toujours dépistable, même à l'intérieur des séries. Il est toujours possible de repérer la 'contraire' chose. Cependant 'contraire' ne suppose pas la présence de ce qu'on pourrait appeler un 'choc': il y a toujours, et il le faut sous peine d'illisibilité, recherche d'analogie et, surtout, de transition, même lorsqu'il s'agit de références 'défectueuses' ou réduites *ad nucem*. La transition responsable du maintien de l'axiologie s'abrite dans les enchaîneurs initiaux ou finaux. Signalée clairement, elle n'en impose pas trop au destinataire. Elle peut même le guider (cf. les 5 fonctions que nous avons distinguées) et le discours global passe. Non extériorisée, elle lui rend la vie difficile, car le destinataire sera forcé de fournir ce que le discours global lui refuse.

Alain cherche à intégrer les références. On ne peut cependant pas parler d'homogénéité dans sa façon de présenter l'ensemble: le *QI* se caractérise comme un discours axiologiquement bien mené (ce qui n'est pas bien difficile, car la morale a bon dos), mais la répartition des références dans l'ensemble évoque quand même un certain opportunisme référentiel au macro-niveau, tenant sans aucun doute de la verbosité proverbiale du Moyen Age finissant. Au micro-niveau on constate cependant une volonté et une capacité d'organiser le discours pour en tirer l'effet maximum. L'équilibre entre l'apport extra-textuel assuré par la référence et le dire auctoriel reste cependant fort fragile.

C'est dans cette perspective qu'il faut voir les références aux héros (classiques ou non). La réduction de leur fonction 'exemplaire' (on a vu que la mention seule d'un nom fameux produit l'effet voulu) neutralise quelque peu leur statut. Alain ne les introduit pas pour ce qu'ils sont, mais pour ce qu'ils censés être à un certain moment, ce qui, nous le répétons, n'est pas la même chose. La vie d'Alexandre par exemple est pleine d'éléments pouvant être valorisés dans une démonstration, mais Alain ne prend que ce qui l'intéresse, omet tout ce qui, à un certain stade de son raisonnement, lui semble être dénué d'utilité.

Notre analyse a insisté sur l'importance des enchaîneurs (initiaux ou finaux) qui conditionnent la réception de la référence. Dans la pratique il n'y aura pas de différence entre la référence de provenance 'classique' et celle puisée dans d'autres sources. Ne compte que l'effet global. On rejoint ici quelque peu l'opinion de Fritz Peter Knapp qui dans sa description de l'exemple (= *exemplum*?) préfère placer les deux contenus (celui du comparé et du comparant) l'un en face de l'autre (1975: 181). Au macro-niveau il n'est plus nécessaire que le héros, sujet/objet de la référence, soit le protagoniste d'un *programma narratif* complet. L'ellipse ne constitue pas un obstacle pour la compréhension de l'ensemble. L'apport de l'enchaîneur (qui peut se trouver à quelque distance) permet la revalorisation du héros de la référence: isolé de son contexte original, il lui incombe une nouvelle vie, celle de comparse dans une oeuvre qui a d'autres héros.

1. La littérature, médiévale ou non, n'atteindra d'ailleurs jamais le stade de l'*imitatio* complète. Cf. Zumthor (1972: 112-3).

2. La 'perfection' idéalisée des romans d'un Chrétien de Troyes renvoie à des procédures psycho-émotionnelles particulièrement fonctionnelles dans une société inhibée (de trop) de contraintes. C'est ce qui explique, entre autres, le succès des 'fées' celtiques ou des rêves 'indiens'.

3. Au fond, le texte médiéval est perméable au rêve à cause de la quasi-impossibilité de vérifier les faits allégués. C'est ainsi que le compte rendu de Marco Polo doit s'assimiler une bonne part de la légende que Rusticien de Pise semble avoir jugée indispensable à la 'vérité' textuelle.

4. Pour ceci, voir Gosman (1986).

5. *Exode*, XII: 35-6: *Fecerunt filii Israel sicut praeceperat Moyses: et petierunt ab Aegyptiis vasa argentea et aurea, vestemque plurimam; dominus autem dedit gratiam populo coram Aegyptiis ut commodarent eis, et spoliaverunt Aegyptios.* Cf. également saint Paul (*Rom.* 15:4): tout ce qui a été écrit avant nous, sert.

6. Les chiffres entre parenthèses que l'on rencontrera dans la partie qui analyse la technique référentielle du *Quadrilogue Invectif* renvoient aux pages de cette édition.

7. On constate une ambiguïté constante auprès des auteurs médiévaux: d'un côté, il y a des auteurs comme Eginhard qui exploite un modèle latin (in casu *Les Vies des douze Césars de Suétone* pour sa *Vie de Charlemagne*; de l'autre côté, on voit que l'utilisation de la culture 'classique', véritable mine de sagesse, ne peut trouver grâce aux yeux d'auteurs fort peureux de s'engager dans des voies pouvant mener à la damnation. Les exemples de cette attitude sont légion (Wolff 1971: 25; Berlioz 1985: 76-9).

8. A en croire Francis A. Yates (1984: 70), saint Thomas d'Aquin aurait eu une mémoire si étonnamment entraînée qu'il retenait tout ce qu'il avait lu. Vu la possibilité que cette capacité ait été l'apanage d'autres auteurs, on doit observer une certaine prudence face à la citation. Il se peut qu'elle soit conforme sans qu'il y ait eu consultation effective de textes écrits.

9. Qu'on pense ici par exemple au récit de voyage de Simon de Saint-Quentin inséré dans le *Speculum* de Vincent de Beauvais.

10. C'est la perspective dominante dans les sermons par définition moralisateurs où les auteurs soumettent tout à la mise en valeur du but final (Schmitt 1985: 15).

11. Signifiant et signifié sont ainsi soumis à des procédures d'authentification destinées à rappeler un 'déjà-existant'. C'est la formule-clé des nombreuses mystifications médiévales.

12. Nous parlons ici d'*une* procédure de formalisation. L'emploi de l'article indéfini implique l'existence de nombreuses autres expressions et/ou formalisations. Voir également Schmitt (1985: 10).

13. Peter von Moos a raison de souligner l'impossibilité de décrire l'*exemplum*. Ce phénomène 'should be understood in the widest possible sense, as both event and as account of an event, as both a model and a warning, as both an exemplary moral figure and as evidence of a thought (1984: 211).

14. C'est ainsi que le *Couronnement de Louis* se veut *essemple* (Langlois 1966: vers 10). Ailleurs (dans le '*Roman d'Alexandre*' d'Alexandre de Paris), le mot renvoie tout simplement à une procédure de réception: ... *Pour prendre bon exemple de prouece acueillir* (Armstrong-Buffum 1937: vers 2). Dans la plupart des cas ce 'signal' est même supprimé dans le discours. Une intervention de l'auteur de *Reynardus Vulpes* à propos de la conduite trompeuse de Reynardus envers les autres animaux érige le particulier en universel: *Sic quoque sunt multi qui coram dulce loquuntur, / sed tamen est nequam post et iniqua fides* (Huyghens 1968: vers 473-4. Le même effet (en sens inverse, parce que l'universel sert de point de départ au particulier) se repère chez, par exemple, Philippe de Mézières qui utilise la parabole de l'homme riche qui, lors de son départ pour une terre lointaine, confie des talents à ses serviteurs. Le reste du *Songe du Vieil Pèlerin* exploite la thématique signalée par la référence au texte de saint Matthieu (Coopland 1969). Philippe connaît fort bien la valeur persuasive de la référence, car il dit explicitement vouloir recourir aux *exemples*, *hystoires* et *figures* pour mieux instruire son destinataire. Voir pour ceci, Gosman (1986).

15. Abstraction faite de la ponctuation. Mais comme celle-ci fait pratiquement défaut dans les manuscrits médiévaux, nous n'en tiendrons pas compte ici.

16. Dans ce qui suit nous donnerons des exemples de cette technique. On peut également penser à la structure référentielle ouverte de la *Lettre du Prêtre Jean*: l'auteur n'y fait pratiquement aucun effort pour guider son destinataire. (Gosman, *Le royaume* ...)

17. En principe, car au cas des références sériées, l'enchaîneur peut régir plusieurs références et, par là, se trouver à distance. Voir *infra*.

18. Cf. Mühletahler (1983: 168-9). Pour Cerveri, voir Gosman 1987.

19. Cf. Taviani (1976: 9-23); Mâle (1958: passim). Même Alexandre le Grand peut occuper le tympan d'une église (Settis-Frugoni 1973: 298, planche 105; Schmidt, Alexander ...). Abélard réunit de nombreuses citations qui se contredisent parfois joyeusement. Il n'en fait pas de problème: le destinataire n'a qu'à faire des efforts pour chercher la vérité (Wolff 1971: 218).

20. La référentialité permet la construction d'une plausibilité, la non-référentialité n'aboutit, en principe, qu'à des structures non relatées (Todorov 1978: 86-7).

21. Pour les renseignements biographiques, consulter Laidlaw (1974: 1-26).

22. Comme il s'agit ici d'un songe allégorique nous écrirons, avec majuscule: Peuple, etc. Ce sont pratiquement des *personae* abstraites.

23. Parmi les auteurs pourvoyeurs de références pertinentes figurent Lucain, Valère Maxime, Tite-Live et Végèce.

24. Il faut signaler ici le rôle que joue Bertrand DuGuesclin.

25. On doit penser ici au sort du dauphin, le futur Charles VII, renié par son père.

26. Cela pourrait s'expliquer par le fait qu'Alain appartenait lui-même au clergé. Pour une étude pertinente du discours d'Alain, voir Blanchard (1986).

27. Bien sûr, Alain ne choisit que ce qui lui semble utile. C'est pourquoi il n'a pas recours au merveilleux 'classique' sans aucun doute non fonctionnel à ses yeux.

28. L'amplitude des blocs englobants ou englobés n'a, nous le répétons, aucune valeur hiérarchique; elle ne vise qu'à mettre à jour le mécanisme argumentatif. Ce passage retiendra encore une fois notre attention lorsque nous analyserons quelques effets de la référence sériée. Voir p. 168 sqq.

29. Il y a dans ce passage un élément structurel intéressant: entre les références 'classiques' et celles 'tirées de la Bible', il y a un commentaire auctoriel qui interrompt et ralentit le mouvement référentiel. Ce sont des préfigurations des 'paliers' que nous analyserons plus loin.

30. Cette remarque ne vaut, on l'a vu, que pour les principales interrogatives mentionnées ici.

31. Cette question sera d'importance capitale lors de l'analyse du fonctionnement de l'exemple et de la similitude. Disons-le dès maintenant: la dernière a une capacité d'appel beaucoup plus réduite, tend davantage à immobiliser le discours.

32. Philippe de Commynes et Philippe de Mézières, pour ne nommer que ces deux-là, aiment, eux assi, l'accumulation des références (Demers 1975: passim; Gosman 1986).

33. Alain semble prédilectionner cette technique où l'une des références, de préférence la dernière, est mise en relief. Rappelons-nous la série des principales où le sort de Rome mentionné en dernière instance (parce que plus importante dans le *QI* que celui des autres) était également mis en évidence par une aiguille.

34. Afin de ne pas trop alourdir notre exposé, nous n'insisterons pas sur toutes les fonctions des enchaîneurs. En l'occurrence les fonctions 1 et 2 sont également actualisées.

35. La même procédure se repère à la page 16 où les références à *Semiramis de Babilone*, les *dames de Romme* et la *prise du roy Jehan* (1356) produisent également une hiérarchie argumentative reprise par le discours primaire sous forme de question.

36. Nous reviendrons sur les formule où figure le mot *exemple*.

37. Roboam, fils (et successeur) de Salomon. A cause de sa tyrannie la Judée se divisa en deux royaumes.

38. Il s'agit bel et bien d'une aiguille introductive, car la phrase qui précède commence par: *Et quant patience fault,* ... Suit la discussion des misères qui en sont la conséquence. Notre enchaîneur, attaqué par *Si avient que, pacience* (sic) *faillie* ... ne reprend non seulement le thème du discours englobant, mais, par la formule *avient que* et par la reprise de *patience fault* sous forme de *pacience faillie* (où le participe passé se fait épithète), il provoque également la référence. Ce jeu des reprises formelles et thématiques devrait faire l'objet d'une analyse poussée, car c'est un élément important du discours argumentatif de notre auteur. Afin de ne pas trop compliquer notre exposé, nous n'y insisterons pas maintenant.

39. Il serait intéressant d'étudier les structures internes des références. On relève dans ces deux références (celle qui concerne les Romaines aussi bien que celle qui se rapporte aux Juifs) un schéma identique: présenta-

tion d'un cadre général, suivi d'une délimitation temporelle: *es temps de*, etc.

40. Il nous est impossible d'étudier ici le lexique axiologique. Alain prend soin d'établir des liens clairs entre englobé et englobant. En l'occurrence on relève une forte actualisation du registre de la complainte: *maleureuse (bataille), chier comparé, plaignons, douloureux infortune, malle mescheance*, etc.

41. 275-204 avant J.C.

42. Ici encore, on relève cette habitude curieuse d'Alain de débuter par une aiguille généralisante et de n'attaquer la référence que par le biais d'une aiguille spécifiante.

43. Voir p. 181.

44. Il s'agit du Dauphin, le futur Charles VII, renié par son père Charles VI lors du traité de Troyes (le 17 janvier 1420).

45. On dénote ici a) un clivage, implicite, entre englobé et englobant et b) une certaine idée argumentative incarnée par le mot *exemple* puisqu'il semble pouvoir prendre en charge ce qui est l'affaire de *raison* ('raisonnement').

46. Nous embrassons ici la perspective du destinataire. Le texte d'Alain ne fournit pas de spécifications au sujet de la fin de la deuxième guerre punique dont Scipion l'Africain sortit vainqueur (bataille de Zama en 202 avant J.-C.). Le *QI* ne fait que suggérer une issue positive.

47. On n'a qu'à se référer aux principales étudiées plus haut.

48. Nous ne produirons pas toutes les références 'défectueuses' (ou plutôt 'réduites'). Qu'on pense ici à la référence aux punitions infligées au peuple d'Israël par Dieu (27): l'agent de la narration, Dieu, est mentionné par le discours englobant; les punitions figurent dans l'englobé, etc.

49. Bien souvent amené par un enchaîneur comme *audivi, memini*, etc. Voir Gosman (1986).

50. L'inverse se produit aussi. Et il est même possible que le temps de la référence soit la même que celui du discours englobant.

51. Dans notre analyse nous n'avons pas pris en compte le rôle des similitudes. Tout comme la référence à l'extratextuel elle amène un discours juxtaposable. A l'encontre de la référence que nous avons prise comme

discours englobant, puisque son rôle premier est de procurer une analogie complète, mais vraiment complète, avec un détail du discours englobant. En d'autres termes: elle ne fait que reformuler en langage autre ce que le discours primaire avait présenté. Elle peut être de signature simple: en parlant de la *duree des seigneuries et des citez* ... (2), Alain dit qu'elles *ont leurs maladies et leur mort comme les hommes en leur endroit*. Elle ne fait que récapituler ce qu'avait amené le discours englobant et elle reste au même niveau, ne cause aucun progrès. Elle peut cependant épouser des structures complexes. A la même page on trouve la comparaison du *potier* qui *a tour de sa roe* produit plusieurs pots dont il casse parfois ceux qui ne lui plaisent pas. Cette comparaison renvoie à Dieu (cf. *potier*) et au *mouvement des cieulz* (cf. *roe*). La similitude peut également se combiner avec des références qui, elles, font bel et bien progresser l'argumentation. Aux pages 22-3 on compare d'abord (*Par droicte comparaison*) la *police françoise* à un *ostel d'ung mauvais mesnagier* qui mange son blé en herbe, de sorte que pendant l'hiver il lui manque tout ce qu'il faut. Suit alors une référence à la conduite de la fourmi travailleuse qui pense à l'hiver. L'ensemble est suivi d'un commentaire actoriel où Peuple vilipende la conduite des *hommes françois* qui font exactement le contraire. En fait, le commentaire englobant reprend exactement le contenu de la comparaison (*mesnagier*) et s'oppose, à des fins didactiques bien sûr, au contenu de la référence mentionnant la fourmi. La conduite de la fourmi ne peut pas être considérée comme une similitude, puisqu'elle suggère autre chose que la *droicte comparaison* du *mesnagier*. Ces quelques spécimens suffisent pour montrer que l'effet de la similitude diffère considérablement de celui des références étudiées ici. Le clivage n'est pas toujours bien net, il faut le dire tout de suite, mais tant que les différences entre *exemple* et *exemplum* m'ont pas bien été formulées, il sera difficile d'y opposer la similitude.

# BIBLIOGRAPHIE

ARMSTRONG-BUFFUM 1937
Armstrong, E.C., Buffum, D.C., Bateman Edwards, Lowe, L.F.H. (eds), *The Medieval French Roman d'Alexandre, vol. II. Version of Alexandre de Paris. Text*. Princeton 1937.

BERLIOZ 1985
Berlioz, J., Virgile dans la littérature des exempla (XIIIe-XVe siècles). In: *Lectures médiévales de Virgile. Actes du Colloque organisé par l'Ecole française de Rome (Rome 25-28 octobre 1982)*. Rome 1985 65-120; 70-71.

BLANCHARD 1986
Blanchard, J., L'entrée du poète dans le champ politique du XVe siècle. In: *Annales* 41 (1986): 43-61.

BREMOND-LE GOFF 1982
Bremond, Cl., Le Goff, J., Schmitt, J.Cl., *L'exemplum*. Turnhout 1982.

COOPLAND
Coopland, G.W. (ed.), *Philippe de Mézières, chancellor of Cyprus. Le Songe du Veil Pèlerin*. 2 Vols. Cambridge 1969.

DAVID 1980
David, J.M., Rhétorique et Histoire. L'exemplum et le modèle de comportement dans le discours antique et médiéval. In: *Table Ronde organisée par l'École française de Rome (le 18 mai 1975)*. Rome 1980: 9-15.

DEMERS 1975
Demers, J., *Commynes méMORiALISTE*. Montréal 1975.

DROZ 1950
Droz, E., *Alain Chartier, Le Quadrilogue Invectif*. Paris 1950.

FREEMAN-REGALADO 1981
Freeman-Regalado, M., 'Des contraires choses': la fonction poétique de la citation et des exemples dans le 'Roman de la Rose' de Jean de Meun. In: *Littérature* 41 (1981): 62-81.

GOSMAN 1985
Gosman, M., Le royaume du Prêtre Jean: l'interprétation d'un bonheur'. A paraître dans les *Actes du Colloque L'Idee du Bonheur au Moyen Age (Amiens, 1985)*.

GOSMAN 1986
Gosman, M., La réception de la matière 'classique' chez Philippe de Mézières: la référence persuasive dans le 'Songe du Veil Pèlerin'. In: *Actes du Ve Colloque international sur le Moyen Français (Milan, mai 1985)*. Milan 1986: 27-38.

GOSMAN 1987
Gosman, M., Cerveri de Gérone et la Lettre du Prêtre Jean. In: *Actes du Ier Congrès international de l'Association d'Études Occitanes (Southampton 1984)*, Londres 1987: 219-27.

HUYGHENS 1968
Huyghens, R.B.C. (ed.), *Reynardus Vulpes. De latijnse Reinaertvertaling van Balduinus iuvenis*, Zwolle 1968.

KNAPP 1975

Knapp, F.P., *Similitudo. Stil- und Erzählfunktion von Vergleich und Exempel in dem lateinischen, französischen und deutschen Grossepik des Hochmittelalters*. Vienne 1975.

LAIDLAW 1974

Laidlaw, J.C., *The Poetical Works of Alain Chartier*. Cambridge 1974.

LANGLOIS 1966

Langlois, E. (ed.), *Le couronnement de Louis. Chanson de geste du XIIe siècle*. Paris 1966.

LINK 1976

Link, H., *Rezeptionsforschung. Eine Einführung in Methoden und Probleme*. Stuttgart 1976.

MALE 1958

Mâle, E., *L'Art religieux du XIIIe siècle en France*. Paris 1958.

MÜHLETAHLER 1983

Mühletahler, J.Cl., Introduction à la pratique de Pierre Chastellain: lecture du Temps Perdu. In: *Vox Romanica* 43 (1983): 157-69.

PATTE 1976

Patte, D. et A., *Pour une exégèse structurale*. Paris 1976.

SCHMIDT

Schmidt, V., *De luchtvaart van Alexander in de verbeelding der Middeleeuwen*. Groningen 1988.

SCHMITT 1985

Schmit, J.C. (ed.), *Prêcher d'Exemples. Récits de prédicateurs du Moyen Age*. Paris 1985.

SETTIS-FRUGONI 1973

Settis-Frugoni, Ch., *Historia Alexandri elevati per griphos ad aerem. Origine, iconografia e fortuna di un tema*. Rome 1973.

STIERLE 1972

Stierle, K., L'Histoire comme Exemple, l'Exemple comme Histoire. Contribution à la pragmatique et à la poétique des textes narratifs. In: *Poétique* 10 (1972): 176-98.

TAVIANI 1976

Taviani, H., Les voyageurs et la Rome légendaire au Moyen Age. In: *Voyage, Quête, Pèlerinage dans la littérature et la civilisation médiévale. (Senefiance II)*. Aix-en-Provence 1976: 9-23.

TODOROV 1978

Todorov, Tz., *Les genres du discours*. Paris 1978.

VON MOOS 1984

Von Moos, P., The Use of Exempla in the Policraticus of John of Salisbury. In: Wilks, M. (ed.), *The World of John of Salisbury*. Oxford 1984: 207-61.

WOLFF 1971

Wolff, Ph., *L'Éveil intellectuel de l'Europe*. Paris 1971.

YATES 1984

Yates, Francis C., *The Art of Memory*. Londres 1984.

ZUMTHOR 1972

Zumthor, P., *Essai de Poétique médiévale*. Paris 1972.